Dare To Stand Alone

The Story of Charles Bradlaugh

PLATE 1

Portrait by Walter Sickert of Bradlaugh standing alone at the
Bar of the House of Commons. (Painted 1891.)

DARE TO STAND ALONE

THE STORY OF CHARLES BRADLAUGH

Bryan Niblett

kramedart press

British Library Cataloguing in Publication Data
A catalogue record for this book is available from the British Library.

ISBN 978-0-9564743-0-8

Typeset by Amolibros, Milverton, Somerset
Consultant on book design: Jane Tatam
www.amolibros.com

Printed and bound by T J International Ltd, Padstow, Cornwall, UK

1 3 5 7 9 10 8
6 4 2

First edition

'Dare to be a Bradlaugh!

Dare to stand alone!

Dare to have a purpose firm!

Dare to make it known!'

(*The Secular Song and Hymn Book*,

edited by Annie Besant,

C. Watts, 17 Johnson's Court, Fleet Street,
London, 1876)

Preface

AS A YOUNG BOY I TOOK delight in stories of heroism. My first fledgling enthusiasm was for cowboys, such as Tom Mix and Buck Rogers, and their thrilling fights with outlaws in the American West. The weekly comics for boys, *Adventure* and *Hotspur*, kept me spellbound with their yarns of heroic daring and enterprise. I followed these with the novels of G. A. Henty, the epic narratives that recounted the heroic deeds of fictional characters participating in the campaigns of historical figures such as Clive of India, Wolfe in Canada and Kitchener in the Sudan. All these stories were linked by the common thread of courage and endurance in the exercise of physical prowess.

Then at the age of fourteen I came across Charles Bradlaugh. Reading the story of his parliamentary struggles, I realised that here was a type of real life hero that I had not met before. Though Bradlaugh was a strong man, who faced occasional bodily danger, it was not physical prowess that distinguished him. He displayed a moral quality, an uncompromising rationality, a commitment to justice, and he surmounted on a daily basis personal antagonisms of the most unremitting kind whilst remaining faithful to his purpose. The battles that Bradlaugh fought were battles of the mind, played out on public platforms, in courts of law, and in political debating chambers. This supplied a new dimension to my understanding of heroes, the recognition that the virtue of thinking for oneself, of engaging in action founded on reason as the guiding principle, was the essence of real heroism. And even as a boy I was deeply touched by the profound poignancy which permeated the circumstances of his death.

Many years later, after a lifetime of reading everything I could find about Bradlaugh, it has been an immense pleasure to write his biography. It is a story that has been written several times before but I tell it in a distinctive way emphasising what I judge to be the essential features of his life. Because my aim is to tell a story rather than produce a scholarly work, I have chosen not to include footnotes. My narrative is told nonetheless with assiduous adherence to the facts of Bradlaugh's life and the footnotes exist in the forty-one foolscap notebooks which record my extensive research.

I have recounted Bradlaugh's legal battles in greater detail than previous biographers. Bradlaugh was a natural lawyer, his approach to atheism, republicanism and all his other radical ideas was that of a legal mind. He believed passionately in individual rights and did not hesitate to assert his own or to defend himself vigorously against an attack on them by others. To a considerable extent the life of the mature Bradlaugh resides in the history of his legal encounters. He never became a solicitor or a barrister, professions which in Victorian England were the preserve of the upper middle classes, but representing himself, as he usually did, he proved more than a match for the most distinguished lawyer of his day and won the respect of the superior judges.

A literary work, whether it be fiction or non-fiction, a brief essay or a lengthy treatise, should be composed with constant attention to the underlying theme of the work, summarised if possible in one sentence. I have borne this precept in mind. The message that integrates the text of this biography is that one man, relying on reason, and daring to stand alone, can make a difference in the world.

Chapter One

ON 27 JANUARY 1891 CHARLES BRADLAUGH, Member of Parliament for Northampton, lay dying in his apartments at 20 Circus Road, St John's Wood, London. He was suffering from Bright's disease, severe inflammation of the liver, to which his family was vulnerable. Confined to bed and hovering in and out of consciousness, he was tended by his only surviving child, his beloved daughter Hypatia.

His life had consisted of a series of struggles, and the greatest struggle had been from 1880 to 1886 when, elected successively by his loyal Northampton constituency, he had endeavoured to take his seat in the House of Commons despite being a notorious atheist. Asserting in 1880 his right to affirm his allegiance to the Crown, he was prevented from doing so by a vote of the House. Choosing then to swear the oath of allegiance, he was again prevented by the opposition of a majority of Members.

Following these decisions, on 22 June 1880 Bradlaugh had been expelled from the House on a motion proposed by the leading lawyer of the day, Sir Hardinge Giffard, QC, which provided as follows: 'That, having regard to the Reports and Proceedings of two Select Committees appointed by this House, Mr Bradlaugh be not permitted to take the Oath or make the affirmation mentioned in the Parliamentary Oaths Act 1866 and the Promissory Oaths Act 1868.' This resolution, passed by a majority of 275 to 230, kept Bradlaugh from taking his seat.

There followed during the next five and a half years Bradlaugh's struggle in Parliament and in the Law Courts to take his seat as the Honourable Member for Northampton. It was not until 13 January 1886, at the beginning of a new Parliament, that Bradlaugh was at last permitted to take the oath. From then until his death he was a most effective and diligent member of the House. He had many legislative triumphs to his credit, most notably the Oaths Act 1888, which solved the affirmation problem for all time.

During Bradlaugh's five years as a successful sitting member, one matter was always at the forefront of his mind: his intention to secure the expunction from the Records of the House of Commons of that Resolution of 22 June 1880. He made an unsuccessful attempt to expunge the resolution in 1889. At the end of 1890 he again set down a motion to expunge, which was to be debated by the House on 27 January 1891. As he lay dying, his major concern was that he would not be able to attend the House to move that motion. By good fortune, and on the initiative of Hypatia, the motion was moved by a trusted colleague of Bradlaugh's, Dr W. A. Hunter, Liberal Member for Aberdeen North.

William Ewart Gladstone, the Grand Old Man, Leader of the Liberal Opposition, spoke in favour of the motion. Referring to the Resolution of 22 June 1880, he said: 'We believe that the proceeding in question is one that cannot be defended and that it was fraught with one of the most dangerous of all principles – namely, excess of jurisdiction. And to leave on our records, with a presumptive authority, a case of manifest excess of jurisdiction is to leave the seeds of future mischief to be appealed to and turned to account in evil times.'

The House was by no means unanimous in support of the motion and some members spoke against it. But the Leader of the House, Mr W. H. Smith, son of the founder of the great newsagents, said on behalf of the Conservative Government that he would offer no opposition. Accordingly, the Resolution to expunge the Record was accepted without a division. Immediately Dr Hunter sent a telegram to Hypatia to inform her of the result.

Bradlaugh was by then in a coma and could not be woken. He died three days later on 30 January. It was Solon, the Greek lawgiver, who said, 'Call no man happy until he dies.' Bradlaugh died in circumstances that would make him supremely happy. But he never knew it.

Chapter Two

THE SURNAME 'BRADLAUGH' IS A RARE one. It can be traced to a limited area of Suffolk based on Wickham Market and the neighbouring tiny village of Brandeston. Records show that a Bradilhaughe lived in Wickham Market in 1475 and the shortened form 'Bradlaugh' undoubtedly derives from this. Charles Bradlaugh's paternal grandparents were James Bradlaugh who lived from 1780 to 1811 and Mary (née Wood) who lived from 1780 to 1852. They were an impoverished couple and the *Ipswich Journal* tells us that James, late of Brandeston, was at one time insolvent and released from debtor's gaol only upon examination of his assets. James and Mary were married in 1803, had four children and later moved to London. Their youngest son Charles was born in 1811, a few months before his father died, and in 1832 married Elizabeth Trimble, a nursemaid who was two years older than him. Charles and Elizabeth had seven children, two of them dying in early childhood. Charles, the eldest, was born on 26 September 1833 at 31 Bacchus Walk, Hoxton, in the most simple of four-roomed terraced houses. Hoxton is part of Hackney and is today a lively district of East London populated largely by immigrants. In 1833 it was a depressing, meagre part of London in which to raise a family. Bacchus Walk no longer exists having been converted into part of a council estate, but there is in the neighbourhood a short Bradlaugh Street that commemorates the birth place.

Charles Bradlaugh senior served an apprenticeship as a law stationer and thereafter became confidential clerk to a firm of solicitors in Cloak Lane, just off Cannon Street in the City. His accomplished penmanship and conscientious work ensured that he remained with that firm for the rest of his life. He supplemented his small salary by writing occasional law articles. As the family grew, so they moved from Bacchus Walk, first to what is now Columbia Road, then to Mansford Street, and finally to Warner Place, Bethnal Green. These moves were within a tightly limited area of the East End. Warner Place still exists but the various Bradlaugh residences have long been converted to other uses.

Charles Bradlaugh junior was educated, if that be the right expression, first at a Boys British School, then at a nearby private establishment and finally at a school in the Hackney Road. This formal instruction was completed when he left school at the age of eleven. Formal education, however, was not the means of Bradlaugh's real education. He was of all men an autodidact. No doubt the reading, writing and arithmetic he acquired by the age of eleven supplied a foundation. But it was his omnivorous reading thereafter that provided his real learning.

Though the Bradlaughs, parents and children, perforce lived closely together, they were not a close family. But one great gift that Charles senior gave to his eldest son was a love of fishing. At every opportunity father and son rose early to take the long walk to Temple Hill on the river Lea for a day with the fishing rod. This splendid river, the favourite of Izaak Walton, flows from Hertfordshire to its outlet at the tidal Thames near Canning Town traversing the East End through the Hackney marshes. It supplied ample bream and pike and carp. Here with his father, young Bradlaugh developed that skill with the rod that was his only sporting pleasure. Throughout his busy life he turned to fishing for such relaxation as he allowed himself.

At twelve years old Bradlaugh joined his father's law firm as errand boy. His errands familiarised him with the streets of London and accustomed him to the dogsbody disciplines of the law. After two years of this he became wharf clerk and cashier to a firm of coal merchants. He spent his scanty leisure time at Bonner's Fields, now part of Victoria Park, Hackney, listening to the speakers on religious and political themes. He absorbed by attentive observation the art of open-air speaking, the art of badgering and heckling, and the art of effective response.

As an errand boy and clerk, Bradlaugh's work took him right

across London. He saved money by walking and running rather than taking the horse buses, using these savings to buy books. His first purchase, for a halfpenny, was a copy of *The Peoples Charter* and this formed the foundation for what became his large personal library. Books were expensive and in his early days were an indulgence he could rarely afford. So he haunted second-hand bookshops and educated himself standing up reading from the shelves. A book that had an immense appeal for him was a volume of *Emerson's Essays*. Too poor to buy it, he copied out by hand the essay on 'Self Reliance'. The precepts of Emerson, expressed in that essay in spare and sonorous tones, stayed with Bradlaugh all his life. 'Nothing is at last sacred,' wrote Emerson, 'but the integrity of your own mind.' The integrity of young Bradlaugh's mind was soon to be put to the test.

Chapter Three

SAINT PETER'S, OFF WARNER PLACE, HACKNEY Road, was the Bradlaugh family's parish church. Consecrated in 1841, it was the first of ten new churches created by Charles Blomfield, Bishop of London, who wanted to make an impact in the most overcrowded areas of the City. The first incumbent was the Reverend John Graham Packer, appointed in 1842, who remained vicar until he died in 1887 and was buried on the north side of the churchyard.

The young Charles Bradlaugh attended this place of worship every Sunday and being one of the brightest youngsters in the congregation he was made a Sunday school teacher. When it was announced that Bishop Blomfield was to visit Bethnal Green in order to administer confirmation to the more worthy youngsters of the parish, the Reverend Packer, wishing to make a good impression, put forward Bradlaugh as one of those upon whom the Bishop would lay his hands. This required preparation by the candidates so that they could respond intelligently to the catechism.

Accordingly, Bradlaugh studied the Church's 39 Articles and extended his enquiry to the four gospels. Employing that thorough textual analysis which became his hallmark, he discovered many discordances and wrote respectfully to Packer to seek advice and explanation. Packer's unfriendly response was wholly unexpected. He condemned Bradlaugh to his parents and suspended him for three months from his post as Sunday school teacher. It is ironic that Bradlaugh, who was to become the leading English atheist, was accused of want of faith at the very time he was endeavouring to be a Christian.

As a consequence of this suspension, Bradlaugh spent his

Sundays at Bonner's Field participating in the meetings and discussions but still as a Christian. It was during these three months that he renounced his beliefs. Invited to an indoor debate with James Savage, a scholarly heretic, on 'The Inspiration of the Bible', Bradlaugh put the Christian view as persuasively as he could, but was soundly beaten. This is one of the few debates that Bradlaugh ever lost and it converted him to atheism.

At the end of his three months' suspension, Bradlaugh irritated Packer further by sending him for comment a copy of that remarkable work, *The Diegesis*, by Robert Taylor, a clergyman well known for his heterodox sermons. It did not help that Bradlaugh had pledged himself as a teetotaller: those were the days when abstinence was associated with freethinkers. So the Reverend Packer persuaded Charles Bradlaugh senior to give his son three days to change his mind or lose his home and his employment. Faced with this bluster, because bluster it almost certainly was, Bradlaugh did not hesitate and did not compromise. He left his home and he left his job. At sixteen years old, Charles Bradlaugh dared to stand alone.

A freethinking friend gave him lodging for a week and then Bradlaugh found a home with Eliza Sharples and her three children. For work he decided to attempt to earn his keep as a coal merchant. This was a poor living because he could not offer credit and there were few customers able to pay in advance. By this means he earned some money but hardly enough to supply him with minimum subsistence.

Eliza Sharples had been the mistress and co-worker of Richard Carlile, the radical journalist. Carlile, born in 1790, was a champion of press freedom and had supported most of the radical causes of his day, especially republicanism and the emancipation of women. He wrote *Every Woman's Book*, published in 1826, which was the first in England to recommend methods of birth control. He had published Thomas Paine's *Rights of Man* which had brought him heavy fines and rather more than nine years imprisonment. Carlile separated amicably from his wife Jane in 1830 and in 1832 began to live with Eliza, a feisty young supporter from a prosperous family in Lancashire. He had three children with Eliza: Julian, Hypatia and Theophila.

By living with Eliza, whose house was known as 'the very hearth of infidelity', Bradlaugh aligned himself with a great radical tradition. After Carlile's death in 1847, Eliza was a defeated woman in dire financial straits. With the assistance of freethinking friends, she lived in a small house in Warner Street adjacent to a Temperance Hall that she managed. In 1849 when Bradlaugh moved in with her family he shared a bed with Julian. The elder daughter Hypatia was the one for whom he had an innocent juvenile affection. He loved not just the girl but her name, which symbolised pagan beauty, learning and science, and was derived from Hypatia the fourth-century Alexandrian who taught astronomy and philosophy. She was said to be the last librarian of the Alexander library, the greatest repository of knowledge in the ancient world. She was deeply opposed to the rise of Christianity and defended with vigour the traditional rationality of classical Greece. A fanatical Christian sect was responsible for her death by dragging her through the streets of Alexandria and mutilating her body with pottery shards. It was perhaps inevitable that the young Bradlaugh became enamoured of a girl whose name represented the vulnerability of reason and truth.

Bradlaugh spent his free time at the Carliles in fruitful study. He taught himself the elements of French and Hebrew and a smattering of Greek and Latin. On Sundays he engaged in debate, often on teetotalism, at the small Warner Place Hall in Philpot Street as well as Bonner's Field. His youthful precociousness as a speaker drew the crowds. At Bonner's Field he became friendly with Austin Holyoake, the younger brother of George Jacob Holyoake who had famously spent six months in Cheltenham prison for blasphemy and edited the weekly *Reasoner*, the foremost infidel publication of the day. Austin Holyoake was a printer publishing *The Reasoner* amongst other journals.

It was Austin Holyoake who brought about Bradlaugh's first success as a speaker. He arranged for George Jacob to take the chair at the Hall in Philpot Street when Bradlaugh spoke on 'Past, Present and Future of Theology' on 16 October 1850. The notice of the meeting announced that: 'A Collection will be made after the lecture for the benefit of C. Bradlaugh, victim of the Rev. J.

G. Packer of St Peter's, Hackney.' This was a remarkable occasion for a boy of seventeen who looked even younger. Chaired by the celebrated George Jacob Holyoake, it was Bradlaugh's debut as an infidel lecturer.

A group of freethinkers, impressed by Bradlaugh's abilities, and aware of his penury, organised a collection for him. This generous act brought home to Bradlaugh his dependence upon others. He had borrowed money on which to live and these humiliating debts amounted to £4 15s. Something had to be done. He noticed an advertisement for the army of the East India Company that would give him an enlistment bounty of £6 10s. So on 17 December 1850, Bradlaugh went to Trafalgar Square to take the Queen's shilling.

Chapter Four

BRADLAUGH HAD INTENDED TO ENLIST IN the army of the East India Company because a passage to India and experience of that exotic location attracted him. When he arrived at the recruiting office he discovered that Sergeant Kite of the East India Company had done a deal with Sergeant Hook of the South Foot, which meant that he would be serving in the British Army at home. Bradlaugh resisted this: it was not the bargain he had made. He complained to the medical officer examining him and was met with sympathy. The doctor asked Bradlaugh to look out of the window onto the parade ground where various soldiers were marching and asked him to pick one. Bradlaugh chose a smart, tall soldier dressed in a scarlet uniform. So with the help of the doctor, Bradlaugh came to be enrolled in a distinguished cavalry regiment, the 7th Dragoon Guards.

Bradlaugh informed his grandmother of his new circumstances and she informed his aunt Mary who in turn told his father. Bradlaugh senior, disturbed by the news, went immediately to see his son, learned of his determination to stay in the service, and then obtained permission for him to spend Christmas with his family. So Christmas Day 1850 saw an uneasy reconciliation at 13 Warner Place. That evening the father escorted his son back to his army quarters. That was the last time Bradlaugh saw his father alive.

In the New Year Bradlaugh had orders to sail to Ireland where his regiment was stationed. This was his first opportunity to meet his fellow recruits who proved to be a tough bunch. Although from a poor family himself, Bradlaugh discovered he was comparatively better educated and was cast with ribald and rowdy hooligans as companions. These shipmates immediately fell on Bradlaugh's luggage, revealing a Greek lexicon and an Arabic vocabulary that they used as footballs. Bradlaugh recovered the Arabic volume and kept it on his shelves for the rest of his life as a memento of this journey. The recruits were in civilian clothes and Bradlaugh was distinguished by wearing what had been his Sunday best, a shabby tattered black suit, far too small for him, and a black silk hat. The hat joined the Greek lexicon as a plaything for his companions. Bradlaugh did not present an attractive picture. He was tall beyond his years, pale, gangling and under-nourished.

The voyage to Dublin was eventful. Midway across the Irish Channel, the ship met exceptionally heavy seas and was in danger of sinking. The shifting and sliding cargo had to be moved and tied down to afford stability. The captain, concerned for safety of the ship, promised the recruits five pounds between them for the arduous work of rearranging the freight. Once stability had been assured, the storm blew itself out and the captain regretted what he now considered an unnecessarily extravagant offer. Instead he decided to give five shillings to each of four men selected as the strongest and most troublesome, so saving himself four pounds.

The captain had not anticipated Bradlaugh's reaction. His sense of justice was aggrieved by this breach of an agreement and he delivered an impromptu passionate speech, denouncing in the strongest terms the captain's outrageous attempt to evade his promise. The captain was startled by the transformation. A mild-looking, spindly youth had become a formidable and effective sea lawyer. The captain capitulated, the bargain was kept, and the recruits saw their comrade in a new and favourable light.

On arrival at Dublin the troops travelled to join their regiment at Newbridge Barracks, Kildare. Here Bradlaugh exchanged his shabby black suit for the regimental scarlet and spent many hours on the parade ground being taught a soldier's drill and learning to ride a horse. He was not a natural soldier, nor a natural horseman. The monotony of the parade ground, the irrationality of the drill, bored his individualist temperament. And his attempts to ride were hampered by his awkward and clumsy movements. Slowly Bradlaugh mastered these skills and eventually became a competent cavalry private. He was teased by his comrades for his clumsiness and called 'leaves' because he was so often seen turning the pages of a book and preferred tea to alcohol. He learned to hold his own and to give as good as he got in fights in which he became embroiled.

From Kildare the regiment moved to the Portobello Barracks in Dublin. Here Bradlaugh became an orderly room clerk and so was released from drill. He learnt the art of regimental book-keeping. Dublin gave him the opportunity to speak at meetings in the city. His chosen subject was teetotalism and these expeditions to the halls of Dublin, in his scarlet uniform, introduced him to circles not usually frequented by private soldiers. After a year in Dublin the regiment moved to the Barracks at Ballincollig, five miles from Cork. This is a delightful part of South West Ireland and the valley of the river Lee which goes through Ballincollig and where he occasionally fished must have often reminded him of expeditions with his father

One incident at Ballincollig illustrates the mettle of this young soldier. A newly arrived junior officer entered the orderly room where Bradlaugh was quietly working and gave him an order in discourteous tones. He was ignored. The order came once more. this time embedded in the most foul language. Bradlaugh stood up, went over to the officer, looked him in the eye, and asked him to leave, otherwise he would be thrown out. The officer did leave but only to return with the Colonel and intent on disciplining this recalcitrant private. The officer stated his case and Bradlaugh was asked to respond. He simply asked the officer to state the precise words in which he had given the order, and to his credit the officer repeated his insulting words to the letter. Bradlaugh showed remarkable sense. He turned to the Colonel: 'There must be some mistake. The officer's memory must be at fault, as he surely would not have used language so unbecoming to an officer and a gentlemen.' The Colonel said, 'Clearly there is an error.' That was the end of the matter.

A deep friendship sprang up between Bradlaugh and James Thomson, a Scotsman, who was based in the Barracks and training as an army schoolmaster. These two men loved words, Bradlaugh as a prelude to action, and Thomson for their poetic effect.

Thomson, a year younger than Bradlaugh, was already a poet with a particular feeling for the poetry of Shelley. When Bradlaugh was on night sentry duty, the two young men conversed for hours, confiding their hopes and aspirations. When they were free in the daytime they went for long walks in the Lee valley. Here was a friendship that would last for twenty-five years.

During Bradlaugh's posting to Ballincollig he witnessed an incident that he never forgot and that he recalled in a speech he gave on the Irish question in New York in 1873. The episode took place on a cold wet day in November at Iniscarra. Bradlaugh was one of a troop sent to protect Law Officers who had come from Dublin with a land agent to evict tenants from forty miserable squalid dwellings that were to be demolished. Out of one came a woman who prostrated herself before the captain of the troop to ask that her dwelling be spared for a little while. Her husband was desperately ill, would not live long, and she asked that he be allowed to die in peace in the dwelling in which he had been born. The agent from Dublin could not wait, and the captain had no power to delay. So the dying man was carried out of the house, in the sleet, on a wretched bed and died there before the soldiers. Three nights later, whilst Bradlaugh was on sentry duty, he found the poor woman outside the Barracks, raving like a maniac, with a dead baby on one arm and another clinging to the cold nipple of her breast. In his New York speech, Bradlaugh used his passionate rhetoric to reflect his horror at the incident: 'And if you had been brothers to such a woman, fathers to such a woman, would not rebellion have seemed the highest gospel you could hear preached?'

In August 1852 Bradlaugh's father, who had never recovered fully from the disaffection with his son, collapsed at his office in Cloak Street and was taken home unconscious. After eight days of delirium he died of inflammation of the brain. Bradlaugh was granted furlough to attend the funeral. By this time he saw no future for himself in the army and was anxious to come home to support his mother. At this family meeting his great aunt Elizabeth Trimble promised to purchase his release and Bradlaugh returned to Ireland in great relief.

Elizabeth Trimble died within a year. The money she left, about
£70, came to the Bradlaugh family and £30 was put by to pay the
cost of army release. Bradlaugh's mother was in two minds about
losing this money. She wanted her son home with the consolation
he would bring her and she wanted his contribution to the family
income. But his leaving home in defiance of his parents still
rankled. After some delay Mary Bradlaugh agreed that Elizabeth's
promise be kept and Bradlaugh was discharged from the army
in October 1853. He left with an honourable reference from his
Colonel.

Bradlaugh had many benefits to show from his three army years.
He entered it as an awkward, under-nourished youth, and he left
it as a man, strong and confident. He had learnt to fence, handle
guns, ride a horse – all useful accomplishments. He had developed
a love of Ireland and a sensitive concern for the Irish peasantry.
He remained all his life a Home Ruler. He had made a friend who
would touch his life in many ways in the years to come. He had
acquired respect for the British armed services and would work
to improve the condition of enlisted men.

He joined the army as a private soldier and he left as a private
soldier. Rank never favoured Bradlaugh.

Chapter Five

WHEN BRADLAUGH ARRIVED BACK IN WARNER Street he found many changes since his departure three years before. His father, his grandfather and his great aunt had died. Eliza Sharples, who had been his refuge had also died and Julian, Theophila and Hypatia, his first crush, had left for the United States. The Warner Street Temperance Hall, where he had spoken many times, was being used for other purposes. Bradlaugh too had to find a new purpose in his life.

His immediate task was to secure employment so that he could support himself, his mother and his sister Elizabeth. Bradlaugh's relationship with his mother was cool though he eventually paid back every penny of the family money that had secured his army discharge. His aim was to become a solicitor's clerk but three years as an army private was not an impressive qualification. A job was not easy to find. After two months of searching he walked into the offices of a solicitor, Thomas Rogers of 70 Fenchurch Street, and asked if he had a vacancy for a clerk. Rogers said he had no such vacancy, but added that he was looking for a lad to run errands and do minor office tasks. 'What are the wages?' asked Bradlaugh. 'Ten shillings a week,' replied Rogers without hesitation. 'I will take it.' So Bradlaugh began, just before Christmas 1853, a new job in a lawyer's office, on the bottom rung of the ladder.

He did not stay on that bottom rung for long. Rogers soon realised that he had recruited a remarkably effective employee. Bradlaugh already had some legal knowledge and he showed a natural appreciation of the law. He absorbed it like a sponge and had a gift for discerning the essence of a legal question. After three months with Rogers his weekly wage went to fifteen shillings, and after a further six months Rogers put him in charge of the firm's Common Law Department.

This was a good time to begin a career as a lawyer's clerk. The middle of the nineteenth century saw fundamental reforms in legal procedure. The Small Debts Act 1846 had created 500 county courts dealing with small claims. The law of evidence was reformed by Lord Brougham's Act of 1851, and the Common Law Procedure Acts of 1852 and 1854 transformed civil procedure. Bradlaugh took advantage of these developments to acquire an expert understanding of civil and criminal procedure. The nature of English law is that procedure is vitally important and Bradlaugh became a master of it. Rogers found the clients and then left the day-to-day practice to his clerk. Bradlaugh was capable of doing all that a managing clerk could do, and a great deal more. He appeared before masters and judges in chambers and proved to be a skilful advocate.

His advice was always practical. Shortly after joining Rogers, Bradlaugh was consulted by a group of artisans who had clubbed together to build a working men's hall in Goldsmith's Row, Hackney Road. They had erected the building on freehold land but without any lease or conveyance. Once the building was completed the freeholder asserted his right to the building as being a fixture. Bradlaugh immediately appreciated the weak position of the working men. He advised them to offer a rent of £20 per year. This was refused. He then organised a hundred or so of the men to demolish the building brick by brick and divide the materials between them. He said of the landowner, 'He had been too clever; he had relied on the letter of the law, and I beat him with a version of common law justice.'

In the evenings and weekends Bradlaugh began again to lecture on freethought subjects. Twice a week he spoke at the Philpot Street Hall or the John Street Institute in Fitzroy Square. On Sundays he chose to lecture at the London Hall of Science. Robert Owen the social reformer, known as the father of socialism, was an active secularist and had founded Halls of Science in major cities in England. These were intended as adult secular Sunday schools for the working class and attracted large audiences. The

Hall of Science in City Road came to be closely associated with Bradlaugh's Sunday lectures. This active lecturing gained him notoriety and gained Rogers some anonymous letters complaining about his infidel clerk. Roger was too sensible to fetter his valuable assistant but Bradlaugh arranged to give his lectures under the name of 'Iconoclast'.

This nom-de-guerre was used by Bradlaugh for his freethinking activities during the next fourteen years. Iconoclast was exactly the right name to use. Bradlaugh was an image breaker, he assailed cherished beliefs and shattered them. He attacked venerated institutions, which he regarded as erroneous or pernicious. For Bradlaugh, iconoclasm was positive. As he said in his lectures: 'Tell the backwoodsman who, with axe in hand, hews at the trunks of sturdy trees, that his is destructive work, and he will answer, "I clear the ground, that plough and reaping hook may be used by and by."'

By the end of 1854 Bradlaugh was earning £65 pounds a year from Rogers, £35 a year from work for a building society and smaller amounts from his lectures. From this he was supporting his mother and sister. He now had sufficient income to contemplate marriage.

Chapter Six

A CONSISTENT ADMIRER OF YOUNG CHARLES Bradlaugh was Abraham Hooper, a plasterer by trade who also kept a coffee-house in Leadenhall Market. Hooper, a big man over six feet tall, was a freethinker, a radical and a teetotaller. Before Bradlaugh went to Ireland, Hooper had heard him speak many times at Bonner's Field and attended his meetings again when he returned. He was a rough man but friendly withal and had a strong affection for this precocious, vigorous speaker with views so similar to his own.

Hooper's eldest daughter Susannah was tall and well built like her father, with fine black hair. She worked as a servant girl and was known as the prettiest nursemaid in Canonbury Square. Bradlaugh set out to win Susannah's affection and succeeded. He wooed her with letters and verses. He was an occasional poet who relished the rhythm of words. He also invoked the poetic power of James Thomson who supplied verses that enchanted Susannah. When Bradlaugh put the question of marriage to Hooper, an essential formality of those days, Abraham was at first doubtful and, with his usual bluntness and sound intuition, admonished Bradlaugh as a man who would never save money. However Bradlaugh was persuasive with this man who so much admired him, and consent was finally given.

The marriage took place on 5 June 1855 at St Philip's Church in Stepney. The bridegroom was twenty-two and his bride two years older. Here was Bradlaugh, a proclaimed infidel with an infidel bride and infidel father-in-law, marrying in a Christian church. The explanation lies with Mrs Hooper who did not share her husband's atheist views. When planning the marriage Bradlaugh suggested, and Susannah agreed, that they begin married life in his mother's house at Warner Place. Bradlaugh was providing for his mother, an arrangement which spared him expense. There were in that small dwelling two separate and distinct households, and his mother promised not to interfere in their lives. This arrangement between mother and daughter-in-law did not last long and the married couple soon moved to a four-roomed house at 4 West Street, Bethnal Green, a street which has not survived. Here their first child, Alice, was born on 30 April 1856. There was a further move to 3 Hedger's Terrace (now Hedger's Grove) between Wick and Cassland Roads, Hackney, and not far from Bonner's Field. In this house on 3 March 1858, Susannah gave birth to their second daughter Hypatia. Bradlaugh chose to have this daughter named after the child of Eliza Sharples.

Marriage did not restrict but rather intensified Bradlaugh's activities as a radical campaigner. Within a month of marrying, he participated in the Hyde Park demonstration of 1 July 1855. The source of this protest was a Bill, introduced in the House of Commons by Lord Robert Grosvenor, whose purpose was to prohibit Sunday trading. It did not much affect the rich who could send out their servants to buy during the week, but it distressed the poor who lived from hand to mouth, received their wages on Saturday and needed to buy their provisions the following day. Sir Richard Mayne, the Commissioner of Police for London, issued a proclamation giving notice that any attempt at a disturbance would be suppressed. When Bradlaugh read that notice he sensed that it was unlawful: the Commissioner was exceeding his powers. His further enquiries confirmed him in that view. So he determined to attend the meeting to resist the police in what he saw as an unlawful interference with the liberty to demonstrate.

In the event Bradlaugh played an active part in the meeting being more than a match for the police who attempted to restrain him. His army training came to his aid. When he was asked to move on by three policeman he skilfully caught hold of the truncheons of two of them and said to the third, 'If you attempt to touch me, I will take one of these truncheons and knock you down with it.' He then rapidly wrested the truncheons out of the hands of the two policemen, disarming them by surprise. This

successful manoeuvre so delighted the crowd behind him that a
few of them lifted him, heavy as he was, onto their shoulders and
carried him off in triumph. What especially pleased Bradlaugh
was that a Royal Commission was appointed to inquire into this
demonstration and, being called to give evidence, he was thanked
by the Commissioners. Despite spending much of his time away,
Bradlaugh was a family man who appreciated his home life. They
had little money but he and Susannah gave their friends generous
hospitality. He preferred to relax with friends at his home rather
than at theirs. Susannah was a lavish hostess and the house was
constantly filled with congenial company. However, for him
relaxation was infrequent. He was an earnest young man with an
incessant devotion to his intellectual improvement. He read
constantly, texts of all kinds: theology, philosophy, biography,
politics. Just as he saw the essence of a legal matter in a flash, so
he could gut a book in double-quick time. Buying books when
he could afford them, he was beginning to build a substantial
library. This was his preparation for making an impact on the world.

Chapter Seven

FOLLOWING HIS MARRIAGE, BRADLAUGH CONCENTRATED ON two objectives: to make a success of his legal work with Rogers; and to establish himself as the leading freethought lecturer. Rogers was pleased with his energetic clerk who was proving a great success in the practice. He was given a free hand and did not hesitate to take advantage of it. Judges frequently treated him as though he were a qualified lawyer, and he regularly appeared for clients in the magistrates' courts.

As a foundation for establishing himself as a freethought advocate, he embarked on a thorough study of the Bible which he came to know as well as any clergyman. He began by making a detailed analysis of the first five chapters of the Old Testament, the Mosaic chapters known as the Pentateuch. This scrutiny formed the basis of many of his early lectures in which he emphasised every error, contradiction and inconsistency in the text. He made himself a master of scriptural exegesis. His commentaries on these chapters were published at intermittent intervals and eventually compiled in his first major work, *The Bible: What Is It?*

In 1856 he began writing with two other authors a series entitled *Half Hours with the Freethinkers*. The authors were Iconoclast, John Watts and 'Anthony Collins', this latter a pseudonym for William Johnson, a journalist with strong infidel inclinations. The fortnightly series was published as a book. One of Iconoclast's contributions was a chapter on the seventeenth-century Jewish-Dutch philosopher Spinoza. This authoritative review of Spinoza's philosophy written by a man of twenty-four who had left school at twelve served to establish Bradlaugh's intellectual credentials. He was especially attracted to Spinoza's philosophy. It was his rationality that appealed, his creation of a complete philosophical system with an axiomatic foundation. Spinoza wrote in his Ethics: 'There is nothing more profitable to man than to live by the guidance of reason.' Bradlaugh heartily agreed and his speeches and writings constantly reveal the influence of this philosophy. Spinoza based his work on definition and Bradlaugh likewise understood the vital importance of definition in all that he spoke and wrote.

Until the end of 1857 most of Iconoclast's lectures were given in London on Sundays. He spoke frequently at the Hall of Science, often lecturing in the morning, afternoon and evening. Susannah regularly attended these occasions. He also developed his associations with other freethinkers. He came to know Austin Holyoake particularly well and through him often met George Jacob Holyoake. John Watts who collaborated with Bradlaugh as author was from Bristol and also a printer. He had a brother Charles Watts, three years younger than Bradlaugh, who was beginning to play a part in the freethought movement and moved in Bradlaugh's circle. Another association was with Robert Cooper, originally from the north of England and founder in 1855 of *The London Investigator*. Cooper was fourteen years older than Bradlaugh and taught him much about the art of freethought journalism.

In 1858 Bradlaugh extended his efforts to the provinces; the whole of England and Scotland becoming his oratorical terrain. The burgeoning railway network gave him access to the whole country, a facility that had not been available twenty years before. Money was tight so Bradlaugh travelled third class and on slow trains. He invested prodigious energy in these travels. He was particularly welcome in the north and early in 1858 he visited Manchester, Newcastle, Doncaster and Bolton. Sheffield was the centre of an especially strong freethought movement and he was often lecturing there. These journeys were by no means plain sailing. The welcome he received from freethinkers was matched by vigorous opposition from the churches and chapels and their supporters. Halls were often denied to him and he frequently had to find alternative accommodation for his lectures at the last moment. His advertisements were torn down and defaced. Hecklers habitually appeared at his lectures. He became practised at dealing with violent opposition for he was a strong man, toughened by army service, and not averse to physically removing the unruly and disorderly.

Lectures were important forms of education and entertainment in the middle of the nineteenth century and audiences were generally willing to pay a modest sum to attend. The audiences that Iconoclast attracted were sometimes small, for he was willing to talk to a few, but were mostly large, often well over a thousand. In those lectures he made many converts. To listen to him for an hour was to be persuaded, as much by his rational argument as by his oratorical passion.

The constant travelling was hard. He would leave Roger's offices at lunch-time on Saturday and return to London late Sunday evening or early Monday morning ready to resume work. It was unremitting endeavour. In an autobiographical fragment that he later published, he described graphically a lecturing expedition to Edinburgh in the middle of winter when the audience was minute and the profits miniscule. When he had paid his hotel bill he had hardly enough money to pay his railway fare to Bolton where he was next to lecture. He left his Temperance Hotel before the staff were up and went without breakfast. With difficulty he carried his box of books and a black bag to the station where he discovered that his train was delayed by a snow-storm. He took a faster and more expensive train but could only pay the fare to Preston, leaving him with a few pence for hot tea and a meat pie. On arrival at Bolton he deposited his bag at the station as security for the unpaid ticket and had only a few minutes to wash and change before, cold and hungry, he delivered the lecture in a gloomy candle-lit hall. The unkindest cut was at the close of the lecture when an opponent upbraided him for the prosperous life he was leading. Such were the hardships of a peripatetic infidel lecturer in the 1850s.

In addition to his lectures, Iconoclast was active as a debater. His first major debate was in June 1858 in Sheffield against the Reverend Brewin Grant, a polemical Congregationalist from that city,. Grant was known as a formidable speaker and a notable opponent. The debate lasted for four nights, two in the first week and two in the second, and the audience numbered 1,500. The terms of the debate were set out in an agreement between the opposing speakers. Iconoclast was to lead on the first night and Brewin Grant on the following nights. Each evening debate was for two and a half hours and equal time was allowed for each speaker. Iconoclast was to propose that the God of the Bible was revengeful, inconstant, unmerciful and unjust, whereas Brewin Grant was to sustain his own affirmations that the Bible was consistent with itself and with science.

In this first significant test of his debating skills Iconoclast succeeded with colours flying. He had the audience with him and he kept them there. Brewin Grant spent much of his allotted time in *ad hominem* arguments whereas Iconoclast remained calm and cool under this provocation. Iconoclast employed irony, Grant descended to sarcasm. Grant was not always serious whilst Iconoclast impressed by his composed refusal to be deflected from his essential points. Here was a young man, not yet twenty-five, proving himself the equal of an experienced debater twelve years his senior. Sheffield was an important centre of freethought and Iconoclast had won his laurels there.

Chapter Eight

TRAVELLING UP AND DOWN THE COUNTRY in those early years, lecturing at meetings large and small, constituted Iconoclast's apprenticeship in public speaking. He was determined to be the best platform orator in England. He was careful to dress the part for, poor as he was, he made sure that his clothes were never a source of censure. He wore a dark suit, usually a black frock coat with matching waistcoat and trousers. His white linen was impeccable. His tie was a black silk ribbon formed into a bow in the French fashion. On special occasions he added a black silk top hat.

His lectures always began on time. Whether or not the chairman was ready, and whether or not the audience had completely assembled, he began speaking at the time announced in the programme. Though he was no supporter of royalty, he observed that punctuality which is said to be the politeness of princes. Timeliness was part of his attention to detail.

His invariable practice was to charge for his lectures. He was a trader in the sense that he believed services should be paid for. What usually happened was that the total of the entrance fees was spent first on the expenses of the meeting, the printing of notices and the hiring of the hall, and Iconoclast would then take what was left over. Sometimes he got nothing, indeed may have had to subsidise the meeting from his own resources, but from a well-attended meeting he would garner a substantial sum.

He was a tall man, about six feet two inches, with broad shoulders and a thick chest. This gave him a big voice that could easily fill with resonant tones a hall of a thousand people. His voice tended to have a metallic edge and was sometimes likened to a trumpet. His accent was more akin to the East End than the West End of London but his words were articulated clearly and precisely. He began his speeches quietly and increased the volume as he progressed, ending with a passionate penetrating peroration that usually brought his audience to their feet. He understood the art of rhetoric and liked to speak in a carefully chosen unbroken order, using a succession of reasoned statements to supply accumulative power. His experiences at Bonner's Field had taught him the art of repartee and how to deal effectively with hecklers. His service in the army had given him strength and confidence: he could act as his own bouncer. There are reports of him ejecting three interrupters at once from one of his meetings, two under one arm and one under the other.

Rhetoric by itself is not enough, it must be matched with logic. Socrates declared that the secret of eloquence resides in a detailed understanding of the subject. Iconoclast brought to his lectures unremitting preparatory labour. He also brought a pile of books, with the pages marked with references that he might be called upon to give. He left nothing to chance. These books he laid out in order on the table in front of him before he began.

Bradlaugh believed in the vital importance of definition and carefully defined the terms he was using. He spoke like a lawyer in that he was always conscious of where the burden of proof lay. As an atheist the essence of his argument was to place the obligation to prove the existence of God clearly on his opponents. Typical of the passages he used in his theological debates is the statement: 'The atheist does not say "There is no God", but he says, "I know not what you mean by God; the word God is a sound conveying no clear or distinct affirmation. I cannot war with a nonentity." '

One of those who frequently attended Bradlaugh's lectures in the late 1850s was Thomas Allsop, a silk mercer and stockbroker who had early prospered from dealing in railway constructions. He had broad interests and was the favoured disciple of Samuel Taylor Coleridge whose letters he published on the poet's death. Allsop was an ardent atheist with a strong distaste for Christianity. When he wished to purchase a country house one of his requirements was that it be at least five miles from any church. He was over sixty when he first met Bradlaugh and acted as the young man's mentor, giving advice and counsel from time to time. He admired Bradlaugh's diligence and industry and his scorn for any form of propitiation. The greatest compliment that Allsop could pay a man was to describe him as 'thorough' and this was the appellation he gave Bradlaugh who thereafter was proud to have earned this designation from such a master.

Chapter Nine

AT BRADLAUGH'S FIRST PUBLIC LECTURE GIVEN at Warner Place Hall in 1850 he had been honoured to have George Jacob Holyoake, then acknowledged to be the leader of the freethought movement, as his chairman. Holyoake certainly had the necessary background to be the leader. During a public meeting in Cheltenham in August 1842, he had inadvertently, in reply to a questioner, condemned Christianity. He was consequently convicted of the common law offence of blasphemy and served six months in Gloucester gaol. His nine-hour speech in his own defence had made his reputation amongst freethinkers. In 1845 he had founded a journal, *The Reasoner*, which survived for sixteen years, had a circulation of 5,000 and proved an important means of campaigning for theological and political issues. But eight years after that first lecture Bradlaugh's growing significance as a vigorous advocate for atheism made him a strong contender to replace Holyoake as freethought leader.

Holyoake was a complicated character and less than single-minded in his opposition to Christianity. In 1851 he originated the term 'secularism' as an alternative to atheism and defined it as 'the province of the real, the known, the useful and the affirmative'. No doubt this imprecise formulation suited Holyoake who by nature willingly embraced ambiguity. He subsequently founded a number of local secular societies throughout the country and was President of the London Secular Society.

The fundamentally different approach of Bradlaugh and of Holyoake to freethought gave rise to a strong element of competition between them. Though Holyoake was without much formal schooling, he took a scholarly, pedantic approach to life.

In contrast, Bradlaugh was down to earth, forceful and driven by action. Holyoake lacked personal charisma. His voice was high-pitched, he was not a natural orator, and unlike Bradlaugh he could not set an audience alight with passion. He sought the company of the better off, rather than the working man, and tended to match his opinions to their interests. Strangely in these circumstances his views were tinged with socialism and he was a supporter of Owenite co-operatives. Whilst Bradlaugh admired Robert Owen he rejected his socialism. Notwithstanding his commercial success, Owen was a collectivist whereas Bradlaugh was, above all else, an exponent of individualism. This individualism contributed to an underlying unexpressed difference with Holyoake who, despite his middle-class aspirations, was a socialist in the Owen mould.

By 1858 freethinkers and secularists alike had become disenchanted with Holyoake's timid leadership and preferred the direct, uncompromising, militant advocacy of outright atheism supplied by Bradlaugh. Holyoake, a sensitive man, was fully aware of this growing disillusion and at a meeting of the London Secular Society in April 1858 he announced his resignation as President. He was succeeded by Bradlaugh who thereupon, at the age of twenty-four, became the effective leader of English freethought.

Chapter Ten

IN 1858 BRADLAUGH THOUGHT IT TIME to advance his position in the legal practice of Thomas Rogers. He wanted to become an articled clerk, which meant that within five years he could qualify as a solicitor. To obtain articles a stamp duty of £80 had to be paid, a requirement that effectively confined the legal profession to the middle class. Certainly, Bradlaugh had no possibility of finding this sum himself. So he wrote to Rogers seeking to discover whether there was a prospect of obtaining articles from the firm in the near future. The way he expressed this reveals his mode of thought: 'You must not be offended with me for this, because we are in the position of two traders. I have my brains for sale, you buy them.' The letter was written formally and courteously but it is clear from its final paragraph that Bradlaugh intended to leave Rogers's employ if articles were not forthcoming. The letter was evidently unsuccessful, for later in 1858 Bradlaugh joined Thomas Harvey, a solicitor at 36 Moorgate, from whom he thought he might have better expectations. Despite his practical experience of the law, he did not have a wide range of choice because of his controversial parallel career as Iconoclast. It emerged that prospects with Harvey were not good. Harvey's practice was unusual since he acted as a company promoter rather than as a lawyer and Bradlaugh became plunged into a doubtful side of commercial life. Harvey soon ran into financial difficulties from which Bradlaugh managed to extricate himself. The employment did not last long.

Despite this problem, Bradlaugh's income in 1859, coming largely from lectures and debates, was sufficient to allow him to move house in September from Hackney to Tottenham. This was a time when East End families intent on improving themselves moved those few miles north. The Bradlaughs' new address was Elysium Villa, Tottenham Park, conveniently near the railway into Liverpool Street. It also had the advantage of being near an attractive stretch of the river Lea. A few days after this move, on 11 September 1859, Susannah gave birth to their third child, Charles. Funds were sufficient to employ a young maid, Kate, who was devoted to the family and stayed with them for eleven years. These improved circumstances gave Susannah an opportunity to use her talents as hostess which she loved to do and the house was regularly full of family and friends.

In November 1858 Robert Cooper invited Bradlaugh to become the editor of the *London Investigator* renaming it simply as *The Investigator*. Cooper taught Bradlaugh how to be an editor and how to manage a journal, though Bradlaugh was by no means short of ideas. *The Investigator* had a small circulation, about 1200, and was hardly viable. In his first issue Bradlaugh set out his editorial aims in robust terms: 'We believe all the religions of the world are founded on error, in the ignorance of natural causes and material conditions, and we deem it our duty to expose their falsity. Our policy is therefore aggressive.' No half measures here.

Bradlaugh wanted to extend the ambit of *The Investigator* beyond theology, so in his third issue he invited James Thomson to supply an article on Emerson. Thomson wrote this under the pen-name 'B.V.', an affected pseudonym that he used regularly thereafter. The letters B.V. stood for Bysshe and Vanolis. Bysshe represented Shelley, Thomson's favourite English poet, and Vanolis was an anagram of Novalis, the name under which Friedrich von Hardenburg, his favourite German poet, wrote. This article was the first in a long co-operation between Bradlaugh as editor and Thomson as contributor.

The Investigator survived only until August 1859. It failed to attract a circulation that covered its costs and Bradlaugh had no means to subsidise it. He acknowledged this frankly in the final issue: 'My reason for this discontinuance of *The Investigator* is very simple, i.e. I am poor. *The Investigator*, supported only by a small section of the Secular party, never met its expenses and I am unable to meet the deficiencies.' Despite this failure, Robert Cooper had taught Bradlaugh how to edit a journal. Bradlaugh's next attempt would be successful.

Chapter Eleven

ICONOCLAST MADE FREQUENT VISITS TO SHEFFIELD in order to lecture and debate. He appreciated the significant numbers of freethinkers in Yorkshire, and they admired his vigorous, eloquent advocacy of atheism. So it was to his supporters in Sheffield that he appealed to propose the establishment of a new freethought journal. He realised that it was not enough to be a speaker and debater. He had to have his own periodical if he were to propagate his views effectively. His brief apprenticeship with *The Investigator* had made him realise that what was required was a journal with broad scope and a sound financial base.

The proposal he put to Sheffield freethinkers was to form a company limited by shares. The prospectus was published in Holyoake's *Reasoner* of 12 February 1860. The capital was £1,000 consisting of 2,000 shares of ten shillings each. The journal was to be a weekly priced at 2d and to consist of eight pages. Its purpose was to advance liberal opinions on social, political, scientific as well as theological questions. It would permit free discussion on every statement made and opinion advanced in its columns. The atheistic orientation of the journal was clearly identified: 'The platform of theological advocacy will be that of antagonism to every known religious system, and especially to the various phases of Christianity taught and practised in Britain; but everyone – Churchman, Dissenter, or anti-theologian – shall have full space to illustrate his views.'

The company would be controlled by a committee of management and Iconoclast would be editor for the first six months and continue as editor thereafter if he gave satisfaction. The journal's name was carefully chosen as *National Reformer*. These two words encapsulated its essence: it was to be a national periodical with sales throughout the country; and it would take radical reform as its purpose. It was about to begin publication when a new character arrived on the scene. Joseph Barker was a Yorkshireman just returned from America, who was known as an infidel, though before journeying overseas he had been a Unitarian minister so his atheistic testimonials were not convincing. He was fifty-four years old and was an experienced and knowledgeable writer. It was at Iconoclast's suggestion that Barker joined him as co-editor of *The National Reformer*.

The journal was launched on 14 April 1860, expressing clearly its aims: 'Our motto shall be: needful truth, however unpopular; but no falsehood or obscurity, however fashionable. Expect our paper to have more of the character of a literary, moral, religious, political and scientific periodical, than of a flashy, flippant newspaper.' From the third issue on 2 June it appeared regularly every Sunday. The co-editors agreed that each should have responsibility for half the paper and, in deference to his experience, Barker was allotted the first half. The quality of the writing was high. Barker had a fluent pen, was able to discourse in an interesting way on many subjects, and wrote all of the first half himself. Iconoclast wrote a substantial part of the second half but invited others to contribute. Among these were William Edwin Adams, writing under the name 'Caractacus', John Watts, and George Drysdale who used the pseudonym 'G.R.'. Drysdale was a Scotsman and a medical doctor and like Iconoclast a keen fisherman. He had been given the nickname George Rex by his fellow students at Edinburgh because of his intellectual brilliance.

As might have been expected a manifest friction developed between the two co-editors who were incompatibly yoked together. Whilst Iconoclast was an unequivocal atheist it was by no means clear where Barker's theological opinions were directed. Whereas Iconoclast kept silent as to the content of the first section, Barker constantly criticised the second half. Soon Barker placed a notice at the end of his pages disclaiming responsibility for anything that appeared in the remainder. This notice became a regular provocative feature.

When the journal had been published for just over a year, Iconoclast contributed an extended essay on 'Jesus, Shelley and Malthus' which appeared in the issues of 8 and 15 of June 1861 and was subsequently published as a booklet. In this essay he wrote:

> Jesus, Shelley and Malthus represent three conditions of thought. The first that of thought fettered. The second, Freethought:- learning, but not yet learned; honest but sometimes erring. The third, the special application of educated thought to the relief of the human family from at least some of the many evils under which its members suffer.

Here Iconoclast acknowledged for the first time his support for birth control. It is also in this essay that he commented on the foremost of the Christian beatitudes, 'Blessed are the poor in spirit', which always aroused his contempt. 'Poverty of spirit is no virtue,' he wrote. 'Honesty of spirit, manliness of spirit, bold, uncompromising, determined resistance of wrong, and assertion of right, should be taught in lieu of that poverty of spirit which allows the proud and haughty in spirit to trample upon and oppress the highest human rights.'

Later in that essay Iconoclast recommended for close study a book called *The Elements of Social Science*. It had been published in 1854 and written by George Drysdale but his authorship was not disclosed until many years later and meanwhile the book was described simply as having been written by a 'Graduate of Medicine'. *The Elements* dealt openly with sexual matters, advocated birth control, and was generally regarded as scandalous. The Victorian public considered it outrageous as connecting sexual abstinence, prostitution and poverty. Iconoclast not only recommended the book but advertised it in his pages.

For Barker this advocacy of *The Elements* was the last straw. On 3 August he wrote: 'Had I known that Mr Bradlaugh and his brother lecturers held and taught the views they do on sexual matters, I should sooner have sought a grave in the depths of the Atlantic Ocean, or have spent the remnant of my days among the red men of Nebraska, than have allowed myself to be identified with them for one moment, either on the platform or through the press.'

It is not easy to see why Bradlaugh exposed himself to the criticism that inevitably accompanied his support of *The Elements*. His sense of caution should have told him that his robust advocacy of atheism would bring him enough infamy and overflowing obloquy without handing this additional weapon to his many detractors. Perhaps his support of *The Elements* was in his mind a memorial to Richard Carlile, the author of *Every Woman's Book* which also encouraged birth control and may have been shown to him by Eliza Sharples. Bradlaugh's support for sexual freedom was inconsistent with his temperament, for in these matters he was something of a prude and a firm believer in life-long marriage. At the same time he was tolerant of the behaviour of others. He trusted passionately in liberty, as long as it did not degenerate into licence. Freethought for him extended to every aspect of man's life, not simply to the religious. To think freely on any subject, including sexual mores, was to exercise that individual freedom which he championed.

Bradlaugh realised that he had to deal successfully with the mounting hostility between himself and Barker. *The Investigator* had failed because of lack of funds, and Holyoake's *Reasoner* had also ceased. It was vital to ensure that *The National Reformer* did not go the same way. Accordingly, Iconoclast wrote to the shareholders to tell them that the experience of the last twelve months had taught him that the journal could be conducted effectively by one editor only. He suggested that both editors resign and that one of them be selected to have sole editorial responsibility.

An Extraordinary General Meeting was held in the Hall of Science, Sheffield, on 26 August. Iconoclast was the largest single shareholder and made sure he held a significant number of proxies. Despite the fervent arguments of Barker, Iconoclast emerged triumphant. The shareholders agreed, by 113 votes to 65, to continue publication of the journal, and by 41 to 18 to confirm Iconoclast as sole editor at a salary of £5 per week. This was a vital victory for Bradlaugh. He now had sole control of a freethought journal that could capture a substantial circulation.

The National Reformer would be a vehicle for his writings, a medium for his ideas, and a record of his working life. He had shown he could be decisive and if necessary ruthless. He had fought and beaten an experienced man twice his age. He emerged not just as a lecturer and debater but as an effective organiser and administrator.

Chapter Twelve

THE EDITORSHIP OF THE NATIONAL REFORMER did not take up all of the time that Iconoclast devoted to the freethought movement. If anything the journal encouraged him to increase his programme of lectures throughout the country. The north of England continued as his most popular destination and he held a second lengthy debate with the Reverend Brewin Grant, this time in Bradford. Visits to some towns he made on a regular basis. The audiences would first come to hear him out of curiosity and thereafter out of conviction. One town that especially welcomed him was Northampton. It was a noteworthy centre of radical thought and he first appeared there in 1859 to speak at the Woolpack Inn at the invitation of Joseph Gurney, a justice of the peace and a prominent local business man. Gurney had heard Bradlaugh speak at the John Street Institute and was so impressed he became a loyal supporter.

The West Country was also fertile ground for planting the seed of freethought and one of the most notable of Iconoclast's visits was to Plymouth and Devonport. He first lectured in Plymouth in December 1860 and intended to lengthen his stay in order to address large numbers at an open-air meeting in Devonport Park. But he was warned off the park on that occasion by Mr Edwards, Superintendent of Police, and so decided to delay an open-air campaign until later. It was in March 1861 that he made his next expedition to Devonport accompanied by Susannah and the children. He had laid careful plans by arranging with a local secularist to rent a field adjacent to the park. Accordingly, there was an agreement with the owner of the field, at a cost of ten shillings, duly receipted, that Iconoclast hold his meeting there on the following Sunday.

On hearing of this, Superintendent Edwards attempted to persuade the local secular society to cancel the agreement, and failing to achieve this he turned up at the meeting with his deputy and six sturdy constables. The Superintendent forbade Iconoclast to give the lecture but was told that possession of the field was lawful and the police had no right to interfere. Iconoclast then began his lecture with the words. 'Friends, I am about to address you on the Bible…' At this premature point the lecture was brought to an abrupt close by the six constables who, with excessive violence, strongly resisted, dragged Iconoclast from the field. When Iconoclast asserted that if released he would continue to lecture, he was marched off to the police station to spend an uncomfortable night in a police cell.

The next morning he was brought before the magistrates while Susannah and a group of secularists clapped and cheered him. It was not apparent what offence was alleged to have been committed. Iconoclast had not reached the stage of emitting blasphemous words and he was undoubtedly entitled to occupy the field. Eventually he was charged with 'exciting a breach of the peace and assaulting a constable in the course of his duty'. Iconoclast chose to represent himself and conducted a brilliant cross-examination of the prosecution witnesses. This took up the whole of Monday when the trial was adjourned to the following Friday. Iconoclast was hampered in the presentation of his case because evidence from secularists was refused as they were unable to take the oath. Non-conformists and Unitarians were not so handicapped and a number were pleased to testify in Iconoclast's favour. The result was inevitable and a reluctant bench acquitted him. He then announced in open court that he would on Sunday be delivering the lecture that had been so abruptly interrupted.

He had done his research thoroughly and discovered that the jurisdiction of the Plymouth and Devonport authorities extended only up to the bank of the river Tamar. The water itself was under the jurisdiction of Saltash, a neighbouring town. Accordingly the following notice was issued by the secularists: 'In consequence of advice received, "Iconoclast" will deliver an open-air address on Sunday morning, and will be present near Devonport Park

Lodge at about half past ten in order to vindicate the right of free speech.' That notice excited much local attention and, despite heavy rain, a large crowd assembled in the park on Sunday morning. The notice also caused consternation among the authorities and they prepared for a major encounter. Superintendent Edwards was there with twenty police officers. Devonport was a garrison town and soldiers were held in readiness to quell any disturbance. The mayor was ready to read the riot act.

Iconoclast, instead of remaining in the park, went to Stonehouse Creek, a branch of the Tamar, and boarded a skiff which took him to a larger boat equipped with a temporary speaker's platform which was moored three yards from the bank. He was distant enough to be beyond the jurisdiction of Devonport but near enough for his powerful voice to carry to the waiting crowd. He announced he was there to assert the freedom of speech of an Englishman and gave a brief address, brief because of the heavy downpour.

The matter did not rest there. Iconoclast decided to bring an action against Superintendent Edwards for assault and false imprisonment. He engaged a London solicitor, Montague Leverson, who had acted for freethinkers before, to conduct the trial which came on at the Assizes in Exeter before a special jury in July. Here Iconoclast made a mistake. He briefed Robert Collier, QC, MP to appear on his behalf. Collier's submissions amounted to a form of apology; his speech on behalf of his client was ambiguous in its support. It clearly suited Collier to show his own orthodoxy but it hardly helped his client. The special jury had no choice but to find for Iconoclast but they awarded damages of a farthing. A less penitent approach by counsel would have been more likely to produce realistic compensation for the substantial expenses that Iconoclast had incurred. Worse was to come. The judge declined to award the plaintiff his costs. Iconoclast learned from this expensive exercise that in future he had better represent himself; he was by far the best advocate on his own behalf.

Iconoclast was not yet finished. Never short of tenacity, he decided to pursue the matter further. Against the advice of friends he appealed to the Court of Common Pleas in Westminster. This time he did plead his own case before Lord Chief Justice Erle and three fellow judges. Despite his thorough arguments he gained nothing. The Court was against him, the damages remained at one farthing, and he was burdened with yet more costs. What Iconoclast did achieve, however, was perhaps more important. The case was widely reported in local and national newspapers, which revealed that there was much support for his lectures. Iconoclast had shown that freethinkers were not to be treated contemptuously and his persistence increased the respect that secularists held for him.

Chapter Thirteen

WHEN BRADLAUGH TOOK OVER SOLE EDITORIAL responsibility for the *National Reformer* his intention was to widen its scope and content whilst maintaining the focus on atheism, republicanism and malthusianism. He was determined that it become the foremost freethought publication. George Jacob Holyoake's *Reasoner* had closed in 1861 so out of misplaced generosity Bradlaugh decided to join forces with him. He entered into an agreement that from 1 January 1862 Holyoake become 'chief contributor' and provide himself or through others the first three pages. At the same time John Watts became sub-editor. From the £5 per week that Bradlaugh received, he paid £2 to Holyoake, leaving only £3 for himself, John Watts and other contributors.

It soon became clear that Holyoake and Bradlaugh could not work together and for the same reasons that had divided Barker and Bradlaugh. Holyoake was concerned at the continuing references to the *Elements of Social Science* (that 'Bible of the brothel') which he, like Barker, detested. He also disapproved of Bradlaugh's description of the journal as 'the advocate of atheism'. The word 'atheism' was too unqualified for the equivocal style of Holyoake. Furthermore Holyoake agreed with the Directors of the National Reformer Company, and against the wishes of the editor, that the format of the journal be changed to make it look more like a newspaper. The disagreement came to a head in March 1862 and Bradlaugh acted decisively, using much the same tactics as in the dispute with Barker. He resigned as editor, and then put himself up for re-election. A special general meeting of the company was held in Sheffield on 23 March. Whilst the Directors favoured Holyoake, the shareholders were for Bradlaugh who had as before armed himself with proxy votes. When all votes were counted there were 85 for Holyoake and 106 for Bradlaugh.

The newly confirmed editor then wrote to Holyoake to inform him that he was no longer chief contributor but a contributor only and with less space in the journal. Thus began a dispute with Holyoake over the terms of the original agreement that could be resolved only by resort to arbitration. The dispute process was a lengthy one largely because Bradlaugh was so busy with other matters. The co-arbitrators could not agree and an umpire was appointed who in August made an award in favour of Holyoake. Bradlaugh had lost this battle but he won the war in conclusive fashion. He was once more sole editor with full responsibility for the journal and in September the Directors decided that the company be wound up and that Bradlaugh be the liquidator. From that time onwards Bradlaugh was the proprietor of the *National Reformer* and owner of the copyright.

Not all troubles with the journal were yet over. Whilst it had a healthy circulation and was popular with freethinkers, it was reviled by the general public as a journal supporting not only atheism and republicanism but birth control as well. As an example of the hostility it engendered, W. H. Smith the fast-growing and highly conservative newsagent decided not to let its agents stock it on its railway newspaper stands. However, Bradlaugh had support from John Watts and Austin Holyoake who transferred his loyalty from his brother to Bradlaugh and continued as printer.

In 1863 Bradlaugh was overstretched. In addition to his editing, he was lecturing many times a week, requiring constant travel, and was attempting to create a successful business. In February he fell ill which meant limiting his activities. It was his editorship that had to go. In the issue of the journal for 28 February 1863 he wrote: 'Ill health in severe form has enforced upon me the necessity of partial cessation of my toil...John Watts will undertake the functions relinquished by me. I will be an occasional if not frequent contributor to its columns.' Bradlaugh did continue to write regularly for the journal but John Watts became editor and assumed editorial responsibility.

Chapter Fourteen

Bradlaugh still aspired to qualify as a solicitor. In January 1862 Montague Leverson, who had been associated with Bradlaugh in various freethought matters and had a high regard for his legal abilities, recruited him as managing clerk. In June Bradlaugh began to serve his articles. The agreement between the two was that Leverson would pay the cost of the stamp and other costs of the articles and that Bradlaugh would be paid £150 a year for three years, £200 a year for the following two years and then on qualification would become a partner. Encouraged by that agreement, the Bradlaughs moved from Elysium Villa to live above Leverson's office at 12 St Helen's Place just off Bishopsgate. Like most of Bradlaugh's residences, No. 12 no longer exists and is now the site of the Leathersellers' Hall.

At the end of October James Thomson was discharged from the army 'with disgrace'. He liked the bottle too much and had several times been found guilty of drinking offences. His association with the leading atheist of the day will not have helped. On his arrival in London he went to live with the Bradlaughs and also worked for Leverson as a clerk.

The legal practice was far from conventional. Leverson, like Bradlaugh's previous principal, was active as company secretary and company promoter. Major company legislation of 1856 and 1862 gave rise to a flurry of registrations of limited liability companies and Leverson was one of many taking advantage of this. Amongst others he was secretary to the Italian Coal and Iron Company Ltd, which had the benefit of mining concessions based on Naples, and Bradlaugh had to travel there regularly to conduct financial negotiations on Leverson's behalf. It did not take

Bradlaugh long to realise that Leverson's activities were not of the highest integrity. In September 1863 he had the good sense to leave Leverson who two years later was suspected of fraud and hastily left the jurisdiction. By leaving Leverson Bradlaugh also left behind any hope that he might become a solicitor. He was never to reach that middle-class status. He was thirty years old and his notoriety as an atheist made a successful legal career unlikely.

The Bradlaugh family left St Helen's Place that September and moved back to Tottenham to Sunderland Villa, next door to their previous house. At the same time Bradlaugh took an office at Windsor Chambers, 23 Great St Helens. He became a businessman, commuting to the City every day, exploiting his experience with Leverson to specialise in company promotion and financial negotiations generally. Once his family was installed in Sunderland Villa they remained there until 1870 and James Thomson again moved in with them.

There are few records of the sort of business Bradlaugh did though it certainly meant regular overseas travel. In 1864 he promoted the St Nazaire mining company which engaged in extractive operations in France. This company was wound up in 1867. In 1865 he founded the Caerhun Slate Company which quarried and sold slate in Caernarvonshire. That was wound up in 1870. Most important was the remarkable Naples Color Company, which Bradlaugh promoted in 1866. Its purpose was to exploit steel manufactured with the aid of black sand from beaches near Naples. It also marketed paint from this sand which helped to prevent rusting of ships. There were factories in Naples and near London. This venture also ultimately failed but for a while was a significant enterprise.

For a few years Bradlaugh prospered but he was not fully committed to the business life. His real purpose was the propagation of freethought, the advocacy of social reforms and the advance of radical policies. Meanwhile he had a young family to maintain. No doubt he hoped to create a sound and secure base for his future work. He had already formed the ambition to become a Member of Parliament and well knew that an MP received no salary. Like many prospective politicians, then and now, he was aiming at financial independence before devoting his time to Parliament.

At Sunderland Villa the Bradlaughs enjoyed a comfortable family life. They could afford an additional maid to work with Kate. They had the means to furnish the house well. Bradlaugh could indulge his friends and Susannah could entertain as much as she liked. Bradlaugh's sister Elizabeth (his favourite) and his brother William (far from being his favourite) often stayed with them. They all enjoyed a pleasant domesticity. Bradlaugh was frequently away from home because his business took him to the continent and there was also a constant stream of lecturing. His lecture programme was published each week in the *National Reformer* and any reader could see that he set himself a gruelling schedule.

There were occasional days off spent fishing on the river Lea. Bradlaugh's favourite spot was upstream at Broxbourne where there was a comfortable inn for dining after a long day's fishing. In summer he took his children there to play by the river while he fished. James Thomson was treated as one of the family and Bradlaugh helped him in any way he could, by inviting him to write for the *National Reformer*, articles as well as poetry, and by finding him clerical employment. Thomson was an unreliable employee, often disappearing for several days and returning only when emerging from an alcoholic binge. Despite this weakness Thomson was a favourite with the children. In 1864 Alice was eight, Hypatia six, and young Charlie five and they delighted to sit at Thomson's feet listening to the stories that flowed from him. He had a poet's vivid imagination and wove fascinating tales that captivated. When Bradlaugh was away, Thomson would take the children to Tottenham marshes or over the nearby countryside. Susannah enjoyed a close rapport with Thomson. These two were alike in many ways, had a natural sympathy and especially enjoyed drinking together in the evenings.

The year 1866 brought trouble, foreshadowing a less prosperous time. John Watts had made a valiant attempt to keep the *National Reformer* going but under his editorship it had lost the sparkle, the politically provocative character it had before. This was reflected in diminishing circulation and the necessity for Bradlaugh to subsidise it from his own resources. Early in the year John Watts became seriously ill and unable to continue as editor. So in April Bradlaugh (still writing under the name Iconoclast) resumed the position of editor whilst Charles Watts, younger brother of John, shared the post of sub-editor with Austin Holyoake who continued as printer. Bradlaugh was now in full control again, applied his energy to the journal and its sales slowly improved.

In 1866 Bradlaugh's business success also faltered. Friday 11 May came to be known in the City as Black Friday. There was a financial crash, interest rates rose sharply and some banks were in distress. Bradlaugh was in danger of going under. His operations were risky for he dealt in large sums on small margin and consequent high leverage. He survived without going bankrupt, but only just. As he told his friends, 'I have great facilities for making money and great facilities for losing it.' Savings had to be made including at Sunderland Villa. The second maid had to go and Thomson took the hint and moved elsewhere. Despite their great friendship, Bradlaugh was relieved to see him depart because his regular drunken binges were having a bad effect on Susannah who was also drinking heavily.

In control of the *National Reformer* again, Bradlaugh used its columns to call for the creation of a new organisation to bring local secular societies into one national union. His lectures up and down the country had encouraged the formation of new societies and he saw the opportunity of merging them. In 1866 the National Secular Society was formed with the *National Reformer* as its mouthpiece. There were several possible candidates for the Presidency but the only one who had serious support was Bradlaugh. So in September 1866 he became the first President with Charles Watts, his loyal and compliant colleague, as Secretary. Bradlaugh at the age of thirty-three had without any doubt consolidated his leadership of the freethought movement.

Chapter Fifteen

Despite the business problems that beset him in 1866 and 1867, Bradlaugh continued his regular lectures and expanded them beyond the topic of freethought to deal with two other matters: electoral reform; and the Irish question. Electoral reform became a key issue in 1866 and Bradlaugh was one of those who founded the National Reform League. Edmond Beales, a barrister, was its President and Bradlaugh one of its vice-presidents. Another vice-president was a clergyman, the Reverend W H Bonner, who was a radical Christian and a peace campaigner. Bradlaugh said at the time that he wished there were more clergymen like Bonner. Indeed in the Reform League Bradlaugh found himself surrounded by Christians (Beales also was an active churchman) and he had to be sure that he did not intermingle his atheism with his work for electoral reform.

Bradlaugh's contribution to the League consisted primarily in his mastery of the public platform and his effective advocacy of a wider franchise. This was the political question of the day and the Reform League made the most of it. The Liberal party led by Lord Russell wanted a new parliamentary Reform Bill to follow the Great Act of 1832 but were not adept at achieving this, largely because of obstruction in the House of Lords. There was consternation in the country and demonstrations and disturbances were being organised. These disturbances came to a head in the Great Hyde Park Rally of 22 July 1866. It was Bradlaugh who persuaded the Reform League to support this demonstration when Sir Richard Mayne, the Police Commissioner, gave notice that he would prohibit it. Beales and Bradlaugh led the demonstrators, from all parts of the country, to the gates of Hyde Park which were closed to them. Whilst Bradlaugh was always in favour of peaceful action, the demonstrators got out of hand and this was the historic occasion when several hundred yards of the park railings fell to the ground. This gave the crowd access to the park and led to a massive fight with the massed police who used their truncheons without hesitation to break heads and cut faces. The crowd gave the police as good as they got and the demonstration was quelled only when the military was called in. Bradlaugh was regarded as a ring-leader even though he consistently favoured orderly demonstrations and did his best to avoid breaches of the peace.

Ultimately the efforts of the Reform League were effective. The Russell cabinet resigned because the Conservatives defeated the draft reform with the help of dissident Liberals. It was then Lord Derby who formed a minority Conservative government and Disraeli who, with consummate political skill, enacted the Representation of the People Act 1867. The provisions of this Act, whilst still modest, went beyond those proposed by Lord Russell, giving the vote to all male householders thereby doubling the electorate and supplying for the first time a voting voice to the working classes.

Bradlaugh's service in the 7th Dragoon Guards had made him conscious of the suffering of the Irish peasantry and he was always concerned at what he saw as the English misgovernment of Ireland. The Irish question reached a crisis point in the years 1866 to 1868 and Bradlaugh spoke frequently and powerfully on these matters. Articles on the state of Ireland appeared regularly in the *National Reformer* and it was a frequent topic for his Sunday lectures. He referred alliteratively to three great curses of Ireland: her beggars, her bogs, and her barracks. As someone who had served three years in those barracks, he understood the oppression they maintained. His recommendation, expressed in a long article in the *National Reformer* in January 1868, was that a Commission be established, with extensive powers of amnesty, which would inquire into the grievances of the Irish people and furnish a pledge from the Crown that immediate steps be taken to redress all genuine injustices. His speeches on the Irish question often ended with a passage full of passion and rhythm of the type that made his perorations so powerful: 'On behalf of Erin, wan, weary and wretched, I plead to those who wield England's executive power to remember that exacting fierce legal vengeance for rebellion and sedition brings a halo of sanctity to the deeds of the punished and shame to the memory of the executioner.' Gladstone appreciated Bradlaugh's Irish article and wrote to him from Carlton Gardens to express his cordial agreement. This was one of the few occasions when Bradlaugh received Gladstone's approbation.

The response to Bradlaugh's speeches and his articles in his journal were polarised. His supporters had immense respect for his views and his uncompromising propagation of them. Many of those sympathisers travelled large distances to hear him. The power of his oratory, the persuasiveness of his rhetoric, his command of radical ideas expressed with unmatched eloquence, had a magnetic effect on his followers. But to the conventional, the creedbound, the straitlaced, that is to say the majority in mid-Victorian England, he was a figure to be hated, scorned and vilified. The authorities in particular were deeply concerned about his activities. He had not been prosecuted for his major part in the Hyde Park demonstration. There had been no legal proceedings arising from his passionate speeches on the Reform Bill though officers of the Crown had been consulted about a possible prosecution. Nor was it thought expedient to prosecute him for blasphemy. But the authorities were undoubtedly looking for an opportunity to make an example of this radical atheistic agitator.

Chapter Sixteen

THE ASSAULT ON BRADLAUGH BY THE authorities was made by way of the *National Reformer* which on 24 May 1868 appeared with a headline banner in heavy type stating proudly: PROSECUTED BY HER MAJESTY'S ATTORNEY-GENERAL. The Commissioners of the Inland Revenue had issued a writ against Bradlaugh for the recovery of penalties of £50 and £20 incurred in respect of the publication and sale of the *National Reformer* of 3 May 1868 without making a declaration and supplying sureties required, as they asserted, by two statutes of William IV in 1830 and 1836. The surety that was required was in the sum of £400. The payment of £50 was for each and every day, and the payment of £20 was for each and every copy, so the penalties sued for were enormous. If this claim were to succeed the journal would cease publication and Bradlaugh would be ruined. His public reply to the Commissioners was unqualified:

> With all humility, I am obliged to bid you defiance; you may kill the *National Reformer*, but it will not commit suicide. Before you destroy my paper we shall have to fight the question, so far as my means will permit me. I know the battle is not on equal terms: you have the national purse, I an empty pocket; you have the trained talent of the Law Officers of the Crown, I my own wits; but it would be cowardly indeed to shrink in 1868 from a contest in which my gallant predecessor, Richard Carlile, fought so persistently more than a quarter of a century since.

The writ served on Bradlaugh referred to the two William IV statutes but the prosecution was actually based on the Newspapers and Stamp Duties Act 1819 as Bradlaugh by application to the

Court forced the Crown to reveal. This Act was notorious. It was one of the 'Six Acts' of 1819 enacted by the Conservative administration of Lord Liverpool and which represented the high water mark of legislative repression. These Acts were passed because of the anticipated threat to public order from the economic depression following the French revolution and more immediately by concern about the 1818 Peterloo massacre. Because of its unpopularity there had been little effort to apply the 1819 Newspaper Act. The House of Commons in 1855 and 1857 had voted to repeal it but the Bills had been thrown out by the House of Lords. In 1868 no-one could remember when a surety for a journal such as the *National Reformer* had been required. The Act was directed against 'all Pamphlets and Papers containing any Public News, Intelligence or Occurrences' that were published for sale for less than sixpence. The *National Reformer* sold for twopence. Thus, as Bradlaugh wrote: 'If our price was 6d we should not be prosecuted; it is only cheap blasphemy and sedition which is liable to be suppressed.'

The information was served on Bradlaugh on 28 May 1868 and he decided to represent himself. The Crown was represented by the Attorney-General, the Solicitor-General, and a junior. Bradlaugh dared to stand alone against this strong legal team. But this one man proved himself a master of legal procedure and ran rings round his opponents. He first demonstrated that the information served on him was undated, so the Court ordered it withdrawn and properly presented. He then applied for further and better particulars, which revealed that the basis of the prosecution was the deeply unpopular 1819 Act rather than the statutes of William. He then pleaded his defence in four alternative pleas. When the Crown asserted that a statute of James I required there be only one plea, he showed that this statute was out of print, had not been invoked for many years, and in any case made no such provision. This was sloppy work by the Crown and the reputation of the Attorney-General was not improved by Bradlaugh's thorough approach.

The hearing was to be in the Court of Exchequer on 13 June. Before that date public meetings were held throughout the country in support of Bradlaugh. Despite widespread hostility to his atheism and to the *National Reformer* there was understanding that at stake was freedom of speech and of opinion. Many petitions were presented to the House of Commons and one organised by Bradlaugh was laid before the House by John Stuart Mill, the British philosopher and economist who had been recently returned as Liberal MP for Westminster. On the eve of the hearing the matter was raised in the House when several members questioned the press laws and their consequences. J. S. Mill in his speech sought repeal of the 1819 Act and immediate suspensions of all prosecutions under it.

The Crown asked for a special jury and when the hearing began only ten men answered to the jury call. The Attorney-General was then asked if he 'prayed a tales', the technical term for making up the deficiency of jurors. This was the opportunity for the Attorney to bring to an end a trial that would do the Crown and him personally no good so he replied, 'We do not pray a tales.' Neither did Bradlaugh wish to cure the deficiency, it was clearly not in his interest, and so the ten jurors were discharged and the trial collapsed.

Bradlaugh might well have expected that to be the end of the matter. But when the Liberals were returned in December 1868 to form Gladstone's first ministry, the new government decided to resurrect the prosecution. It is remarkable that a Liberal administration wished to reinstate such an anti-liberal prosecution, but Bradlaugh never received much support from the devoutly Christian Gladstone. So on 24 January 1869 the *National Reformer* once more carried its banner: PROSECUTED BY HER MAJESTY'S ATTORNEY GENERAL. When this second trial commenced in February Bradlaugh was again opposed by the formidable team of the new Crown lawyers. By a remarkable coincidence only ten special jurors were again available but this Attorney-General did call for two talesmen. As Bradlaugh fully expected, the Crown was successful in obtaining a jury verdict against him but he was given liberty to argue certain points of law.

The final stage took place in April 1869 when Lord Chief Baron Kelly and two brother judges heard the legal arguments. The most vital of these was whether the *National Reformer* was a newspaper within the meaning of the 1819 statute. Bradlaugh's argument was that the statute was not to be taken to mean that a publication which contained any news was a newspaper, but only one whose main or general object was to supply news. It is likely that Bradlaugh would have succeeded in this argument because he had a powerful precedent in his favour. But in the meantime the government had decided to repeal the statute. The solicitor to the Inland Revenue offered him a *stet processus*, that is an agreement for an absolute stay of proceedings. With reluctance, Bradlaugh agreed. As he wrote in reply: 'I never counted the cost, nor have I ever shrunk from it; but I have no inclination to carry it on; fighting the Crown is a luxury to be indulged in by the rich. I have fought from necessity, and have the sad consciousness that I retire victor at a loss I am ill able to bear.'

Within three months the government passed the Newspapers, Printers and Reading Rooms Repeal Act 1869 that repealed the statute under which Bradlaugh had been prosecuted together with eight more statutes, all of which had placed fetters on the expression of opinion. This indeed was a victory for freedom of communication. Particularly gratifying for Bradlaugh was a letter from J. S. Mill who wrote, 'You gained a very honourable success in obtaining a repeal of the mischievous Act by your persevering resistance.'

Chapter Seventeen

EVER SINCE BRADLAUGH HAD FIRST SPOKEN at Bonner's Field his ambition had been to become a Member of Parliament. He decided in 1868 that he should make his attempt at the General Election to be held in November of that year. So in the *National Reformer* of 5 July 1868, in the middle of the prosecution of that journal, appeared the notice:

> 'To the Present and Future Electors of the Borough of
> Northampton. In seeking your suffrage for the new
> Parliament I shall give independent support to that party of
> which Mr Gladstone will probably be chosen leader'

Then followed his election address including the following objects which he held to be essential to the progress of the nation: A system of compulsory national education; a change in the land laws and in particular the abolition of primogeniture and entail; a reduction in national expenditure especially by ceasing to employ hereditary nobles in public offices; an improvement in the relation between employers and employees and a system for the settlement of industrial disputes; a complete separation of church and state and the removal of Bishops from the House of Lords; the abolition of fetters on the expression of speculative opinions; and the abolition of hereditary peerages and their replacement by life peers selected as a reward for merit.

These purposes were well in advance of their time and yet also remarkably modest. Here he exhibited the themes that were to direct his political life. He naturally wanted a complete separation of church and state; in his opinion the state should play no part in matters of faith. He wanted freedom of thought with no curbs such as by way of taxes which his journal was currently fighting. He wanted an efficient labour market with fairness to both capital and labour. He was passionately opposed to hereditary power and influence. He held the view that a man should make his own way as he had done, and not benefit from formally entrenched privileges of birth. His proposal for life peerages was especially modest. He eventually came to understand that it was necessary to abolish the House of Lords. But Bradlaugh, though radical, was not revolutionary. He was ready to accept incremental progress in achieving his political aims.

The year 1868 was a good one to fight an election. The electoral reforms of 1867 had increased the electorate substantially. In Northampton, a borough of 55,000 persons, it had gone from below 3,000 to above 6,000. Bradlaugh had lectured there many times, had always received a warm welcome, and had a sponsor in Joseph Gurney, JP, now a borough councillor. Northampton was the right choice for Bradlaugh in many ways. It was a town wonderfully placed at the cross-roads of England. It was the centre of the boot and shoe industry. Gossip had it that when you were within a mile of the town you could smell the leather and hear the sound of the lapstones used by the shoemakers. These shoemakers were the single largest group of workers in the town and since most of them worked in their homes or in small workshops they were more independent than most workers. Northampton was a Liberal town but its voters more radical, less deferential, more in favour of freethought than most mainstream Liberals.

Bradlaugh stood for election as a radical candidate. The two sitting MPs were both Liberals; Charles Gilpin was a Quaker and Viscount Henley came from the Whig faction. There were two Conservative candidates, Merewether and Lendrick, and there was an eccentric candidate, Dr Frederick Lees, who campaigned as a radical and teetotaller. Bradlaugh had great respect for Gilpin who was an active member of the House, but little enthusiasm for Lord Henley and it was his seat he wanted. For Dr Lees he had nothing but contempt.

During his campaign, which extended from July to November, Bradlaugh was careful to make no mention of secularism. He well understood the importance of separating his secularist views from his political opinions. But of course everyone knew he was an atheist and consequently his electioneering engaged the national interest. Newspapers throughout the country followed his progress. Hostility to him was rampant. To the Christian majority the thought of such an overt atheist in the House of Commons was unthinkable. It was a fierce fight and Northampton became one of the most actively contested constituency battles.

Bradlaugh attempted to win the backing of Gladstone and John Bright but both made public their support of the sitting candidates. Many opponents of Bradlaugh came to Northampton to speak against him. One of his most virulent opponents was Hardinge Giffard, QC, a leading lawyer and Conservative candidate for Cardiff. He was a devout Christian of a conventional kind and bitterly against Bradlaugh and everything with which he was associated.

Bradlaugh had significant supporters too. Austin Holyoake, his printer, took charge of his election fund. Charles Watts was an indefatigable assistant, spending much of his time in the constituency and speaking at election meetings. Thomas Allsop, Bradlaugh's distinguished mentor, came to assist with door-to-door canvassing. He was a man who if he willed the end willed the means, even if it meant he had to spend days in house-to-house solicitation. John Stuart Mill came out strongly in support of Bradlaugh and at the end of August published an open letter in his favour and contributed £10 to his election fund. Mill was himself fighting hard to retain his seat in Westminster and received much criticism for his strong backing of Bradlaugh.

Many women of the town were Bradlaugh supporters. This strikingly large man, then only thirty-five, and with an immensely powerful voice, was always courteous to women, some said in the French manner, and they responded favourably to him. If the women of Northampton had enjoyed the vote he might well have been elected. It was the women who chose Bradlaugh's election colours: mauve, white and green, which were flourished wherever he went. These colours could be conveniently displayed in floral arrangements. There were many mauve and white blooms which, combined with green foliage, made attractive bouquets, nosegays and posies. Bradlaugh the robust platform orator seemed a gentler man when surrounded by his election flowers.

Like most parliamentary candidates, before and since, Bradlaugh invoked the support of his family in his cause. A week before polling day, Bradlaugh and Susannah, her father Abraham Hooper, Alice, Hypatia, and young Charlie, then aged nine, travelled together with Charles Watts to Northampton on the twelve o'clock express from London. They were met at the station by a tremendous gathering. There were banners galore, declaring 'Bradlaugh for Northampton', and a brass band to escort them to the Victoria Hotel for a tea party with a thousand supporters. Susannah conducted herself with commendable poise since by then she was a chronic alcoholic. Bradlaugh spoke a few appropriate words as did Charles Watts. That evening there was a Ball for the candidate in the Corn Exchange. It was a splendid day for the Bradlaugh family.

Polling took place on 17 November. Two days before that the *National Reformer* appeared with the notice, 'Edited by Charles Bradlaugh' rather than the usual statement, 'Edited by Iconoclast'. This was the hour for Bradlaugh to dispense once and for all with his nom-de-guerre.

The General Election was won handsomely by the Liberals and Gladstone formed his first administration. At Northampton Gilpin and Henley were returned with 2,632 and 2,105 votes respectively. The Conservative candidates received 1,625 and 1,378 votes. Bradlaugh had 1,068 votes. Dr Lees had retired from the contest but nonetheless drew 485 votes. There was an upset in the Westminster constituency which had previously been a Liberal stronghold. The seat went to W. H. Smith, a Conservative, who roundly defeated J. S. Mill and most people supposed this was a result of Mill's support for the Northampton radical.

Bradlaugh had lost, but he had lost honourably. Gilpin expressed his gratitude to him for the manner in which he had conducted his campaign and backed up these words by generously contributing £10 to his election fund. Bradlaugh had been defeated but his foot was in the parliamentary door and eventually that door would open for him.

Chapter Eighteen

IN 1867 BRADLAUGH BEGAN A LEGAL action to recover a debt owed to him by a business man, De Rin, with whom he had financial transactions. The litigation, which is fully reported in the law reports, is significant because it demonstrates the difficulties Bradlaugh had to contend with in doing business as an atheist; it shows his remarkable persistence as a litigant; and it resulted in two new statutes which changed the law, though not in any satisfactory or conclusive way.

In the course of business activities Bradlaugh was owed £280 pounds by De Rin. The debt was formally established by three bills of exchange that were drawn abroad, accepted by De Rin in London and then sent abroad again when, after several intermediate endorsements, they were finally endorsed in Paris to Bradlaugh. This complex process gave rise to complex litigation. Bradlaugh began his action against De Rin in the Court of Common Pleas in December 1867 before Mr Justice Montague Smith and a jury. At the trial Bradlaugh was due to give evidence on his own behalf but counsel for De Rin, who was instructed to put every possible impediment in the plaintiff's way, objected to Bradlaugh being sworn on account of his notorious opinions as an atheist. The judge to his credit favoured the objection being waived but De Rin's counsel firmly objected to Bradlaugh taking the oath or making an affirmation. The deadlock was eventually resolved by counsel admitting those facts that Bradlaugh was required to prove. It was then argued on behalf of De Rin that the endorsement of the bills in Paris, technically known as an endorsement in blank because not to a specified party, was invalid according to French law. The jury gave a verdict in favour of Bradlaugh but the defendant was given leave to pursue further the legal objections he had raised. When these issues came before the Court of Common Pleas in July 1868 the decision went against Bradlaugh. The court held that the bills were not validly endorsed by the law of France and hence could not be sued on in England.

In the meantime there was an enormous outcry about the incapacity of Bradlaugh to present evidence in the first trial. National newspapers expressed the view that it was clearly unjust to conduct a defence on the basis that the plaintiff, by reason of his freethought opinions, was unable to give evidence. Despite the hostility towards his atheism, Bradlaugh's difficulty struck a popular chord. So the government acted, and acted with haste. It introduced a new section, section 4, into a Bill currently before Parliament, which became the Evidence Further Amendment Act 1869. This section provided that a person objecting to taking an oath in any court of justice may, if the presiding judge was satisfied that the taking of an oath would have no binding effect on his conscience, make an affirmation instead. Like much hasty legislation this new provision was flawed in at least two respects. It failed to define what was a 'court of justice' or 'presiding judge'. And it did not recognise that those who objected to taking an oath may not have done so because the oath was not binding on their conscience but because they objected to the four simple imprecative words: 'So help me God.'

Bradlaugh soon demonstrated that this section was inadequately drafted. Undeterred by his defeat in the Court of Common Pleas he appealed to the Court of Exchequer Chamber. This court decided that a preliminary step was to determine as a matter of fact whether the endorsement on the bills took place in Paris or London. This question was referred by agreement to an arbitrator to decide. Bradlaugh appeared before the arbitrator and again De Rin objected to him giving evidence. The arbitrator asked Bradlaugh, 'Do you believe in God?' Bradlaugh replied, 'I do not.' Then from the arbitrator, 'Do you believe in a future state of rewards and punishments?' Bradlaugh replied, 'After death, certainly not.' Then said the arbitrator, 'I must refuse your evidence.' He had decided that as an arbitrator he was not a presiding judge within the meaning of s.4 of the 1869 Act and so could not authorise the making of an affirmation.

Bradlaugh went immediately to a judge in chambers to seek an order that the arbitrator hear his evidence but the judge held, and it was later confirmed by the court, that since the arbitrator had decided he was not a 'presiding judge' that decision could not be overturned. The general principle was that the parties having chosen their tribunal are bound by it on matters of law as well as fact. With his characteristic persistence, Bradlaugh nonetheless pressed for his appeal to be heard by the Court of Exchequer Chamber. The hearing was delayed until May 1870 in order that Chief Justice Cockburn, Chief Baron Kelly and five other judges could hear it. An impressive bench indeed, such was the importance attached to this case. This final Court of Appeal decided unanimously in Bradlaugh's favour by relying on the absence of evidence to show that the law of France imposed no bar on Bradlaugh's right to sue there. So if he could sue in France, the law provided that he could sue in England, and he had won at last.

This was in May 1870. In August Parliament enacted the Evidence Amendment Act 1870 which made one provision only: that the words 'court of justice' and 'presiding judge' be deemed to include any person empowered by law to administer an oath for the taking of evidence. The loophole whereby an arbitrator could not authorise the making of an affirmation had been closed. But this Act went no further. It did not amend the law as to affirmations for jurors, or affirmations in affidavits. A comprehensive amendment relating to the law of oaths and affirmations had to wait until Bradlaugh himself could introduce it in Parliament.

Once again Bradlaugh had won a case that resulted in the improvement of English law. And once again it was at a heavy price. He did not recover his costs of the litigation and he received nothing from De Rin. This defendant became bankrupt immediately after the final decision was given against him.

Chapter Nineteen

THE YEAR 1870 WAS A DECISIVE one for Bradlaugh. His activities of the last few years had brought him substantial debts. The heavy cost of the *National Reformer* prosecution, the expenses of his parliamentary campaign, the financial burden of the De Rin case and other litigation in which he had been involved had all left him with heavy liabilities. He had borrowed £600 on the security of machinery used by the Naples Color Company, had been lent £400 by his father-in-law Abraham Hooper and had other obligations. This put him in serious difficulties.

He also had to acknowledge that his ventures in business had not been a success. The De Rin litigation had persuaded him that he was unlikely to be able to operate successfully in the City. His notoriety as an atheist and radical politician meant that there was a general reluctance to do business with him. Most fundamental of all he had come to realise that his heart was not wholly dedicated to business. His prime interest was the public platform; it was there that his outstanding talents lay. His first concern was the promotion of freethought, of republicanism and of radical politics.

He was also influenced by a letter from his mentor, Thomas Allsop, who urged him to limit his activities. Allsop was a man who understood that ends must be matched by means and his wise counsel was that Bradlaugh's interests should be better focussed. This advice from a man whom Bradlaugh much admired, and who was one of his few older friends, must have weighed heavily in his decision to give up business and concentrate on his primary interest. The decision was announced in the *National Reformer* of the 22nd May 1870 under the Heading, 'PERSONAL':

As after five years' severe struggle so severe as to repeatedly endanger my health – I find it utterly impossible to remain in business in the City in the face of the strong prejudice excited against me on political and religious grounds, I have determined to entirely give up all business and devote myself solely to the movement. I have, therefore, taken steps to reduce the personal expenditure of myself and family to the lowest possible point in order that I may set myself free from liabilities as early as I can, and shall be glad now to arrange for week night lectures in any part of Great Britain.

He ended this notice by adding that 'All letters for me should in future be addressed to me at 29 Turner Street, Commercial Road, E.' Because of his financial predicament he had been forced to give up Sunderland Villa and sell the fine furniture he had collected there. His chose to live simply in two rooms in a small, four-storey terraced house just off the Commercial Road. For many years after Bradlaugh's death there was a plaque commemorating his residence there but the house no longer exists, having with its neighbours been converted into four houses. Young Charlie was being taught away from home at the headquarters of the 2nd Battalion Grenadier Guards and he remained there. Susannah, Alice and Hypatia went to live with Bradlaugh's father and mother-in-law at their cottage at Cocking, a village just outside Midhurst, Sussex. It says much for the admiration that Abraham Hooper had for his son-in-law that he accepted this arrangement.

It was not only business difficulties that prompted this resolute change in Bradlaugh's life. In recent years there had developed a distance between him and Susannah, well recognised by his friend James Thomson and by his two daughters. Susannah's growing alcoholism had become distressing to a man of his abstemious habits. Coupled with this alcoholism and fed by it was her financial extravagance, which added to his expenses. Something had to be done about that. Though Bradlaugh remained friendly with his wife, she had, from her excessive drinking, turned into a full-blown matronly figure and in recent times, no doubt to her mortification, they no longer lived as man and wife.

Bradlaugh paid £3 per week for his family's support at Cocking. His two rooms in Turner Street cost him no more than three shillings a week. He took with him to his new quarters only a few simple pieces of furniture, a bedstead, a washstand, a chest of drawers, a table for writing and six chairs. His most valued asset was his library, his collection of books on theology, on law and politics, on economics and on philosophy. These were the tools of his trade and covered the walls of his two rooms, He knew that, if he devoted all his energies to writing and speaking, he could earn by this means, from his pen and his tongue as he liked to put it, about £1,000 a year. So with this new modest way of life and his determination to pay off his debts he could avoid bankruptcy.

To illustrate Bradlaugh's resolution to succeed in his new life the *National Reformer* records that in July 1870 he gave twenty-six lectures in various parts of the country. But July was a tragic month for him. In June young Charlie, ten years old, was taken ill with scarlet fever and was taken to Midhurst to be nursed. Scarlet fever developed into kidney disease, the family weakness, and Charlie died on 15th July. The depleted family finances meant that Charlie could not be buried at Brookwood necropolis as Bradlaugh wished and was buried instead in Cocking churchyard on 20 July. There was a brief family reunion brought about in the saddest circumstances.

A day after Charlie's death Bradlaugh was due to speak at the Hall of Science. Many doubted whether he would fulfil this engagement. He threaded his way through the crowded hall, on time as ever, arranged his books and papers, and gave his lecture with a white face and a rigid body. He made no reference to his son's death in his lecture, and rarely mentioned it thereafter. Despite appearances he was a man of deep feelings, and maybe carrying on with his programme, conscious of his obligations, was for him a part of his grieving. He had now set his course, he knew where he was going.

Chapter Twenty

NOW THAT HE HAD DECIDED TO concentrate full time on the freethought movement, Bradlaugh's first task was to put the *National Reformer* on a sound basis. The journal was enjoying an increasing readership and its success owed much to Bradlaugh's faithful assistants, Austin Holyoake and Charles Watts, who also spoke regularly on freethought platforms. Watts had a second wife, Kate, an attractive, articulate and forceful young woman who contributed to the team. In the absence of Susannah she acted as hostess at functions held in the Hall of Science, an arrangement which worked well.

James Thomson, in his own way, was also part of the team, a frequent contributor to the journal. He kept in touch with Susannah at Midhurst and there was regular correspondence between these close friends. Bradlaugh missed his daughters and they missed him. As soon as he could afford it he took an extra room at Turner Street so they could stay with him. Sometimes they came together, sometimes they alternated. When they were in London together Thomson took them to popular music concerts, to the opera, to art galleries. He nurtured their education in music and the theatre. When his daughters were at Midhurst, Bradlaugh often wrote to them, and usually wrote in French, giving as his reason that they learn the language. He regularly addressed them as 'Mes bien chère filles', and ended his letters with, 'a vous, mes petites bien aimées'. Bradlaugh, powerful and eloquent as he was, also had a simple sensitivity where girls and women were concerned and it was as though he found it easier to express his immense affection for his daughters in French rather than his own language. In any case Bradlaugh loved all things French and had made a practice of visiting France on his business visits to Italy. The Franco-Prussian war, begun recklessly in 1870, awoke his interest in continental politics. He was naturally unsympathetic to Bismarck and equally unsympathetic to the French Emperor Louis Napoleon III. But with the French defeat, the departure of Napoleon and the declaration of the Third Republic on 4 September his concern was stimulated.

On 17 September Bradlaugh had a significant visitor to his insignificant rooms in Turner Street. He was working away at one of his speeches when a knock came to the door. This was the arrival of the elegant French aristocrat Madame La Vicomtesse de Brimont Brassac. She made this mysterious visit to seek Bradlaugh's help in speaking on behalf of France. She had heard that he loved France, she knew of his powerful oratory and she sought to recruit this eloquence in support of her country. Madame was a persuasive woman, but she had no need to exert her charms. Six days before she arrived the *National Reformer* had published an article welcoming the Third Republic. Already in the press was an article by Bradlaugh affirming that the *National Reformer* threw in its lot with republican France. But Mina (as she was known to her friends) acted as a spur to galvanise Bradlaugh into organising a substantial series of meetings dedicated to the French cause. The first of these was held two days later at the Hall of Science and attracted an audience of 1,400. A meeting at St James' Hall on 24 September was an even greater success, attended by 3,000, who with acclamation sent addresses to Mr Gladstone and the French National Government. At the end of this meeting a Frenchman rushed on to the platform and kissed Bradlaugh on both cheeks amidst loud cheers.

These two meetings were not all. Bradlaugh organised and spoke at numerous gatherings throughout the country always attracting full audiences. His efforts in support of France were deeply appreciated in that country. In February 1871 Monsieur Tissot, the French Charge d'Affaires in London, conveyed his country's thanks. He wrote, 'You have given your time, your energy, your eloquence, your mind – in a word, the best part of yourself. France, whom you alone have defended, will never forget it.' Madame de

Brimont became a friend for life of Bradlaugh and his daughters. She used her persuasion to prompt Bradlaugh to send Alice and Hypatia to school in Paris. They began there in September 1872 under the tutelage of an enlightened Directress, Mme Befrieres, who had no concern that her new pupils were without religion. 'Ah! Monsieur, that saves trouble,' she told their father. Mina had genuine affection for the daughters, acted in loco parentis, and welcomed them to her Paris house at weekends. This education cost Bradlaugh £70 a year in fees, a sum he could hardly afford, but it secured a sound education for his beloved girls.

When Mina stayed in London she occupied an apartment at the Grosvenor Hotel and one day whilst visiting her there he was introduced to a Frenchman with beard and whiskers with whom he enjoyed a scintillating conversation. This turned out to be Prince Jerome Napoleon, cousin of Louis Napoleon who on Louis' death became head of the Bonaparte family. Bradlaugh developed an agreeable friendship with Prince Jerome. They met occasionally and corresponded for many years. It might be thought they had little in common, this English working-class radical, and this aristocratic French Prince. Bradlaugh had a sense of prudence where women were concerned whereas the Prince ('Plom-Plom' to his friends) had a well deserved reputation as a playboy. In nationality, in upbringing, in education they were at odds. What united them was freethought and republicanism. Whenever the Prince visited London he regularly went to the Hall of Science to hear Bradlaugh speak and respected the uncompromising atheism he heard there.

The British republican movement reached its peak in the early 1870s. After the death of Albert in 1861, Queen Victoria had been in seclusion yet making heavy demands upon public finances for her large family. The creation of the French Third Republic gave impetus to republicanism and Bradlaugh took advantage of this conjunction of circumstances to press the republican cause. He was an opponent, not of Queen Victoria herself, but of the institution of monarchy, which for him was the symbol of hereditary advantage which he rejected in whatever form it took. He was an individualist and opposed any privileges not individually earned.

February 1871 saw the inauguration of a series of republican societies throughout England. The most important was the London Republican Club which was established on Bradlaugh's initiative. It was announced in the *National Reformer* of 2 April 1871 but its formation was delayed by the death of Bradlaugh's mother. She died in the family house of Bright's disease on 24 April. The first meeting of the Club was held in the Hall of Science on 19 May. Thomas Allsop, then seventy-five years old, was one of those on the platform. Bradlaugh was elected President, and Charles Watts, his acolyte as ever, became Vice-President. The secretary was George William Foote, twenty-one years old, who was to play a large part in the freethought movement. Foote came from Plymouth, the source of many freethinkers, and had arrived in London in 1868. Within a few weeks he had heard Bradlaugh speak and then regularly attended the Hall of Science. It was Bradlaugh's oratory that seized his mind. As he wrote later: 'He gave a full swing to his passionate eloquence. His perorations were marvellously glowing and used to thrill me to the very marrow.' Two years later Foote began writing articles for the *National Reformer* and eventually became a regular contributor.

At that inaugural meeting Bradlaugh explained that though he wanted a republican revolution, it should be a gradual, peaceful and enduring revolution rather than sudden, bloody and uncertain. He ended that speech with a rousing peroration of the kind that thrilled Foote:

> 'La Republique' has been carved as a woman, sculptor's chisel and artist's pencil have fashioned her as with a woman's beauty and woman's purity. Regard we pray you, the republicanism we preach as though the symbol were in truth the reality. Train the germ of republicanism as you would the daughter on your knees, nurturing it gently, healthily and hopefully. Protect it as it grows, from the attack or companionship of vice and rudeness as you would guard from like contagion the sister resting on your arm. Woo it, in its budding prime, with all the fervour and sincerity of passion with which you would seek to win the woman you love. And guard it as free from shame and blemish as you would the memory of the gentle mother who bore you.

The passion of this passage must have arisen from his thought of his mother who had died less than a month before.

In October Bradlaugh made his most notorious speech at the London Republican Club. Concerned at news that Queen Victoria was physically incapacitated from performing her duties and that the Prince of Wales might succeed his mother he said:

> Many of you are aware that I have lately repeatedly declared my most earnest desire that the present Prince of Wales should never dishonour this country by becoming its King. My thorough conviction is that neither his intelligence, nor his virtues, nor his political ability, nor his military capacity – great as all these are for a member of his family – can entitle him to occupy the throne of Great Britain. I am equally opposed to his ever being Regent of England. I trust that he may never sit on the throne or lounge under its shadow.

Many journalists were present at the meeting and this strong language was reported widely, not only in England, but in Europe and the United States. Bradlaugh became the object of immense hostility, was reviled up and down the country, and there were calls for his prosecution. But Bradlaugh's republicanism had not yet reached its zenith. He had been studying in detail the lives of the Hanoverian monarchs. On 27 July the *National Reformer* published the first of a series of lectures with the title: 'The Impeachment of the House of Brunswick'. This was the work that would generate the most intense hostility to his republicanism.

Chapter Twenty-one

AS WITH MOST OF BRADLAUGH'S WRITINGS, 'The Impeachment of the House of Brunswick' began as a series of lectures which were given in 1871 and 1872. The lectures were published as a pamphlet, the most notable that Bradlaugh ever wrote, in 1872 and were amended and reprinted many times. The lectures proved immensely popular in the Republican clubs and amongst republicans generally. They were given in the Free Trade Hall Manchester, the Town Hall Birmingham, the City Hall Glasgow, in the Town Hall, Northampton and on many other platforms.

The subject matter was the Hanoverian Kings, that is the four Georges and William IV. Bradlaugh used the term 'impeachment' because the pamphlet was designed to charge these five monarchs with gross misconduct which affected the Kingdom. He chose to refer to the Hanoverians as the House of Brunswick because these Guelphs (as he also called them) came from that duchy of North Western Germany.

Fifteen years before, Thackeray had given a set of lectures, also published as a book, entitled 'The Four Georges'. Thackeray's work was written in the fine literary language, replete with embellishments, that is all of a piece with his novels. He was able to amuse by revealing the absurdities, hypocrisies, and outlandishness of the Hanoverian Kings. Bradlaugh's pamphlet is different. It is a political tract, a polemic for republicans. Its literary style is based on sarcasm – bitter remarks and wounding taunts – stemming from a detailed discussion of the private and public acts of this bizarre succession of sovereigns.

From George I's ignorance of the English language, the constant indebtedness of George II, the madness of George III and his part in the loss of the American colonies, the dishonesty of George IV, to the ten illegitimate children, but otherwise harmlessness of William IV, Bradlaugh exposes all their weaknesses of intelligence and character in exhaustive terms. Bradlaugh was always concerned about wasteful public expenditure. In his thorough fashion he displayed in this pamphlet the massive increase in National Debt that occurred under the Hanoverians and attributed it to their mischievous policies.

The main purpose of the pamphlet, however, was not to discredit this Hanoverian line but to set out the manner in which the succession could be terminated after the death of Queen Victoria. Bradlaugh had the practical sense to see that no change could be made until the demise, or possible abdication, of the Queen. What he wanted was to avoid the succession of Albert Edward the Prince of Wales. His recommended method was repeal of the Act of Settlement of 1701 in so far as it concerned the continuity of the throne. He argued that the people, through their parliamentary representatives, could enact that the throne be no longer filled by a member of the House of Brunswick. His argument was 'that Parliament has full and uncontrollable authority to make any enactment and to repeal any enactment heretofore made, even if such new statute, or the repeal of any old statute, should in truth change the constitution of the Empire, or modify the character and powers of either Parliamentary chamber.' He ended his pamphlet with powerful language:

> I do not pretend to have pleaded for republicanism. I have only pleaded against the White Horse of Hanover. I loathe these breast-bestarred wanderers, whose only merit is their loving hatred of one another. In their own land they vegetate and wither unnoticed; here we pay them highly to marry and perpetuate a pauper prince race. If they do nothing, they are 'good'. If they do ill, loyalty gilds the vice till it looks like virtue.

Bradlaugh's lectures and the subsequent pamphlet caused consternation. There was deep concern in Parliament about this uncompromising attack on the monarchy. The nation was stirred by the tone and content of the pamphlet and there were rumours that Bradlaugh was to be arrested and prosecuted for treason. Wherever he lectured, police were drafted to maintain order. His audiences may have been delighted but the majority of the country was deeply offended. The editor of the monthly *Gentleman's Magazine*, the most influential periodical of the day, published in November 1872 a reply to Bradlaugh written by John Baker Hopkins. This author, who acknowledged Bradlaugh as 'the brains and soul of English republicanism', attempted to demolish the arguments of the Impeachment. He pointed out that any Act of Parliament had to be passed by both Houses and then assented to by the Sovereign. Thus Parliament as an enacting body includes the Sovereign and the Act of Settlement could not be repealed, in whole or in part without the concurrence of the Queen. This, said Hopkins, was a practical objection which Bradlaugh had ignored. Moreover, Hopkins argued, Parliament was not competent to amend in the way that Bradlaugh asserted. The monarchy is an hereditary institution and can be removed only by revolution not by Parliamentary decision.

Remarkably, Bradlaugh was given the opportunity to reply in the *Gentleman's Magazine* of January 1873. In a carefully expressed response Bradlaugh reaffirmed his view: 'That the British Parliament can prevent the succession of the "lawful heir to the throne" is certain.' 'I contend,' he wrote, 'that they [the House of Brunswick] are lawfully on the throne, and may be as lawfully ejected from it. I deny that by law or practice the throne of this country is hereditary, except so far as created by Parliament.'

He ended his reply with a personal statement:

> One word more and I lay down my pen. I am not the chief of the English republicans. I am only a plain, poor-born man, with the odium of heresy resting on me and the weight of an unequal struggle in life burdening me as I move on... . That I have ambition to rise in the political strife around me, until I play some small part in the legislative assembly of my country is true. If I live, I will; but I desire to climb step by step, resting the ladder by whose rounds I ascend firmly on Parliament-made laws, and avoiding those appeals to force of arms which make victory bloody and disastrous.

This final personal flourish was a mistake. It was unwise for Bradlaugh to express himself in such modest terms. The last word in this exchange was given by Hopkins in the February 1873 issue of the magazine. Reiterating his arguments in forceful prose he referred to Bradlaugh's final passage: 'Not lack of culture, nor humble birth, nor heresy will prevent him from sitting in the British Parliament. In no Republic, past or existing, is complete freedom to be found, and no Republic that can be devised can confer upon its citizens greater liberty than Mr Bradlaugh confesses he enjoys as a British subject.' In this combat between authors, honours ended even.

Chapter Twenty-two

BRADLAUGH'S NOTORIETY AS A REPUBLICAN BROUGHT him many offers to lecture in the United States and the poor state of his finances impelled him to undertake a visit in September 1873. Like many before him he saw a lecture tour of the United States as a means of earning money. His income was about £1,000 from his speeches and writings but most of this went to pay his debts and the interest on those debts. So he was pleased to accept an engagement with the Cooper Institute of Newark who undertook to organise an extensive American tour in return for 10% of his fees.

Before leaving for the United States he had to ensure that the *National Reformer* would be in good hands and that he would be ready to fight Northampton again in the expected 1874 general election. He relied heavily on Austin Holyoake (not well and increasingly fragile) to look after the journal, and on Charles Watts to carry out lecture engagements on behalf of the National Secular Society. These two, together with George Foote, would visit Northampton to nurse the constituency. Well in advance, Bradlaugh issued his election address, much the same as in 1868, emphasising radical parliamentary reform, including reform of the House of Lords, disestablishment of the Church of England, and strict discipline in national expenditure.

A splendid soirée was held in the Hall of Science to wish him farewell. It was the sort of departure which brought home to him the strength of his supporters' feelings. He left for Liverpool and on 6 September joined the Cunard Lines *Scotia* for a stormy voyage to New York arriving eleven days later. He spent time wondering what sort of greeting a radical infidel lecturer would receive in the USA. He need not have been concerned.

On arrival at New York the chief customs collector immediately recognised him and said, 'Mr Bradlaugh, we know you here, and the least we can do is to pass you through comfortably.' His assistant thereby scrawled the necessary chalk symbol on his luggage. Bradlaugh then discovered that the room reserved for him was in the finest hotel in the USA. The Fifth Avenue Hotel was in mid-Manhattan occupying a whole block between 23rd and 24th Streets, It was six storeys high (with the first lift to be installed in a US Hotel) and had six hundred rooms exquisitely provided with rosewood furniture and brocatello marble tops. This was the hotel chosen by the social, cultural and political elite of New York. It was a remarkable contrast to the three rooms in which he lived in dusty and dreary Turner Street.

He had not long to rest before the journalists descended. A reporter from the *Sun* newspaper, with the largest circulation in New York, was the first to interview him, followed by the *Tribune* and the *New York Herald* and all three gave Bradlaugh a good notice. The *New York Herald* the next day described him under the heading: A Rabid Radical Republican:

> The personal appearance of the man would make him noticeable in any assemblage of his peers where the English tongue is spoken. Over six feet in height, with a loose swinging gait, and his chest like the breast of an oak; his large blue eyes, brown hair, which thickly clusters back of his ears; his fair ruddy skin, and his thoroughly athletic proportions bespeak him as the pure-blooded franklin who, from the days of Runnymede, has been habitually creating trouble for the oppressor and the bloated aristocrat.

Not all the newspapers were so courteous. The *Boston Daily Advertiser* dealt with him in its editorial: 'In England practical politicians among the advanced Liberal party avoid him as honest men avoid a felon, as virtuous women avoid a prostitute.' The *Brooklyn Daily Times* recognised that he came as a republican and not as an atheist: 'He comes to our shores with the expressed resolution to leave the subject of religion alone. For Heaven's sake let us do the same, and forget the heretic while we welcome the orator and tribune of the people.'

Bradlaugh found New York in the midst of a financial panic. There had been overlending by the Banks, especially in regard to the development of the railways, and Wall Street was agitated. The US President, Ulysses Grant, had come to New York in response to the crisis and was lodged in the hotel in a room above Bradlaugh's. The monetary panic was everywhere to be seen and resulted in a contraction of the tour to avoid the smaller towns.

The first lecture, on 'The Republican Movement in England', was given to a distinguished audience in Steinway Hall on 3 October. The audience included many journalists, artists and actors including Bret Harte, the popular poet and storyteller.

The editor of the *New York Graphic* attended and gave Bradlaugh a splendid review:

> Charles Bradlaugh is probably today the greatest of living orators, with the single exception of Emilio Castelor. We have no one in the United States comparable to him as a public speaker. He lacks perhaps the humor and exuberant imagination of Henry Ward Becher, and the polished grace of Wendell Phillips; but for manly earnestness and straightforward and subtle power over the passions and sympathies of his audience, he is superior not only to those great speakers, but to any now living in America. He fairly carries his audience to their feet, and it is a singular circumstance that one of England's most gifted orators should be compelled to come to another country to claim the position denied to him by the press and ruling classes of his native land.

These comments captured exactly the nature of Bradlaugh's speaking – the moral earnestness which was the essence of his manner.

After New York, Bradlaugh travelled north to Boston. At his first lecture there Wendell Phillips, known as the silver-tongued Demosthenes of New England, was his chairman. Also there were the famous abolitionists William Lloyd Garrison and Senator Charles Sumner. In contrast to New York, most of the Boston audience were working men with the Irish well represented. Boston was followed by visits to the rest of New England, and then to Philadelphia. Bradlaugh then went West, via Buffalo, to Cincinnati and St Louis and as far as Kansas City.

On his way back East he lectured in Chicago and recorded that the Grand Pacific Hotel where he stayed 'beats for hugeness and splendour anything of the kind I have yet seen in the world.' When he arrived at the lecture hall he was stopped by a face which he had not seen for twenty-five years. He could not place it immediately but when the woman asked in an English accent, 'Don't you know me, Mr Bradlaugh?' his memory went straight back to those days in Warner Place when he shared scanty food with Eliza Sharples and her two daughters. Hesitating, he said, 'I am not quite sure, I think it is Hypatia.' He was wrong, it was Theophila. Here in Chicago he was face to face with one of the daughters of Richard Carlile and the other one, his first infatuation, lived nearby. Thousands of miles from home his thought was for his own two daughters and whether they, like the daughters of Carlile, would after his death live unknown in a strange land.

After lecturing at Kalamazoo in nearby Michigan, Bradlaugh was obliged to return to New York by the suicide, due to the monetary panic, of the agent in charge of his lecture arrangements. He then went again to Boston when on 31 December he was invited to a reception in honour of Ralph Waldo Emerson. Vice-President Wilson was there with many distinguished Bostonians to pay greetings to 'the sage of Concord' as Emerson was known. The hostess seated Bradlaugh next to Emerson and after the poet read aloud one of his recent poems Bradlaugh was called on to speak. Twenty-six years before, Bradlaugh had been too poor to purchase a copy of Emerson's essays and now he was contributing greetings to that self-reliant American.

Three weeks later, after many more lectures on the East Coast, Bradlaugh received a telegram from Austin Holyoake to tell him that Gladstone had dissolved Parliament and that a general election was imminent. Bradlaugh immediately went back to New York, cancelled all further lectures and caught the first available steamer to England. Thus the lecture tour ended prematurely. Bradlaugh had to pay cancellation charges for the broken engagements so he was no better off than when he began. But he returned with an affection for the USA, its character, its growing prosperity and its vigorous people.

Chapter Twenty-three

AS BRADLAUGH HASTENED BACK TO ENGLAND on the Cunard steamship *Java*, Charles Watts and George Foote were conducting his electioneering campaign in Northampton. The campaign was short, with only twelve days between announcement of the dissolution and polling day on 5 February. This brief period suited the Tories because they were fully prepared; since their defeat in 1868, Disraeli had made his party much more effective. This February election was the first to be conducted by secret ballot. The Ballot Act 1872 had at last, after long controversy, satisfied one of the main points of the Peoples Charter. Ballot secrecy may well have helped the Conservatives by allowing Liberal voters of 1868 to defect to Disraeli without publicity.

Lord Henley, the Liberal candidate implacably opposed to Bradlaugh, sought to have Bradlaugh's nomination declared invalid because he was out of the country but this manoeuvre was given short shrift by the mayor and town clerk. As before, Bradlaugh's principal nominator was Joseph Gurney, now a Northampton councillor. Watts and Foote ensured that every voter had a copy of the radical election address and held meetings to support their candidate. Austin Holyoake did what he could but was frail and his main task was to take care of the *National Reformer*. The election result was: Phipps (Conservative) 2,690; Gilpin (Liberal) 2,320; Merewether (Conservative) 2,175; Lord Henley (Conservative) 1,796; and Bradlaugh (Radical) 1,653. Bradlaugh was again bottom of the poll but in six years he had garnered 600 more votes. The Conservatives had gained a seat. The drop in Lord Henley's vote put Bradlaugh in a stronger position for it meant that unless the Liberals supported him there was a danger that both seats would go to the Conservatives.

Bradlaugh arrived back in London three days after polling and on 10 February travelled by train to Northampton with Charles and Kate Watts and George Foote. He was met at the station by a tumultuous welcome from a crowd of 12,000 that extended back to the town centre. A carriage and pair was waiting to take him and his companions in triumph to the market place accompanied by a brass band that every so often broke into the air of 'Bradlaugh for Northampton' to the satisfaction of the enthusiastic throng. Shops in the line of the procession had closed for the day and the colours green, mauve and white were seen everywhere. This welcome eclipsed all previous receptions. These supporters knew that, undaunted by defeat, their candidate would persist until victory was gained.

After the bustling American tour and the fervour of the welcome back, Bradlaugh returned to a heavy programme of lecturing. The *National Reformer* records that in March 1874 he lectured every Sunday morning and evening in the Hall of Science and spoke frequently in the provinces during the week. His topics ranged from 'The New Parliament' to 'The Existence of God', to 'Heinrich Heine' to 'The Theory of Evolution'. He also took up the reigns as editor of the journal with a wide range of articles. With the help of Austin Holyoake the journal had doubled its readership.

James Thomson continued as regular contributor always writing under his pen name 'B.V.'. On 22 March the journal printed the first part of his poem 'The City of Dreadful Night' and three further parts followed on 12 and 26 April and 17 May. This poem was Thomson's major work which had taken him three years to write and for which he became best known. It is a lengthy and striking poem, consisting of an elaborate expression of gloomy despair earning Thomson the label 'Laureate of Pessimism'. The poem's structure is complex. It begins with a Proem followed by twenty-one cantos, with alternating six- and seven-line stanzas, the cantos dealing with the present and the past. The final canto is a lyrical description of a figure overlooking the City of Dreadful Night, the statue of Melancolia depicted in the famous Durer etching.

There was a heavy demand for the issues of the journal containing the poem which then remained out of print for six years.

The editor received several letters of complaint about the work, its pessimism and negativity, and one was received expressing admiration for it but regretting that its publication was extended over so many weeks. This letter of approval was from Bertram Dobell, the well-known second-hand bookseller and collector, and it was he who organised the republication six years later. Thomson in replying to Dobell wrote: 'We must not forget that there is probably no other periodical in the kingdom which would accept such writings, even were their literary merits far greater than this one.'

The issue of the *National Reformer* which published the first part of the poem was also the one that reported the serious illness of the deputy editor, Austin Holyoake, then forty-seven years old. He had been ill for over a year with tuberculosis and was prostrate with little hope of recovery. He died on 10 April nursed by his wife, Jane Alice, at the room where the family lived, over his printing business at 17 Johnson's Court, Fleet Street. His funeral a week later was an impressive occasion. The hearse left Johnson's Court for Highgate on a day of fitful sunshine and was followed by a carriage containing his son Percy, his brother George Jacob and two other brothers. A further carriage contained Bradlaugh, Watts, Foote and Thomson. Many more followed on foot and were joined by other carriages and other walkers. The procession wound its way to Holborn, Tottenham Court Road, Hampstead and Kentish Town to Highgate Cemetery. At the graveside Charles Watts read the secular service that Austin Holyoake had himself written for secularists two years before:

> We this day consign to the earth the body of our departed friend; for him life's fitful dream is over…. He derived his being from the bountiful mother of all; he returns to her capacious bosom, to mingle again with the elements…. Noble he performed life's duties on the stage of earth; the impenetrable curtain of futurity has fallen, and we see him no more. But he leaves to his sorrowing relatives and friends a legacy in the remembrance of his virtues, his services, his honour and his truth.

Bradlaugh then gave a brief address, unusually for him from written notes for on this emotional occasion he did not trust himself without them. His final words were: 'A quarter of a century's recollections, and fourteen unbroken years of friendship, are now within that grave.' James Thomson stood quietly at the edge of the tomb as his friend was lowered into it, not realising that he himself would eventually be buried in that same grave.

Immediately after the funeral Bradlaugh opened a trust fund which was intended to raise £650. He had pledged at Austin's bedside to raise this money. The sum was to be paid to Austin's executors, on behalf of his widow and two children, in purchase of the printing and publishing business which was to be passed to Charles Watts to carry on, including printing the *National Reformer*. In the event some £500 was raised by subscription and Bradlaugh made up the difference himself by instalments.

Austin Holyoake had been Bradlaugh's closest friend and colleague. It was Austin who arranged Bradlaugh's first lecture in the Philpot Street Hall in 1850 and persuaded his more distinguished older brother to take the chair. It was Austin who remained loyal to Bradlaugh through several disagreements he had with George Jacob. It was Austin who had supported Bradlaugh by printing the *National Reformer*, acting as deputy editor and in a myriad of other ways. Bradlaugh had lost his most valuable supporter. But his life was about to be transformed by a new association.

Chapter Twenty-four

IN JULY 1874 A YOUNG MARRIED woman who was separated from her husband the Reverend Frank Besant, called at the shop of Edward Truelove, a freethought publisher and bookseller at 256 High Holborn. Whilst there she saw a copy of the *National Reformer* for 19 July and paid her twopence so as to read it while travelling to south-east London where she was living. That issue of the journal was a typical one. There was a statement by Bradlaugh replying cautiously to a long letter from the Reverend Thomas Arnold, one of his opponents in Northampton. There was an article by George Foote on 'The Crisis in France' and an imaginative article by 'B.V.' on 'A National Reformer in the Dog Days'. What particularly caught the attention of Annie Besant was an article by Charles Watts on the National Secular Society.

Annie Besant thereupon wrote to the journal asking if she could join the Society even though she was not an atheist. The reply to correspondents, given without identification in the issue of 2 August, was that to be a member of the NSS it was only necessary to accept the principles given in the journal of 14 June. These principles were straightforward and required no more than a declaration that the Promotion of Human Improvement and Happiness is the highest of human duties. Satisfied that she was qualified, Annie Besant sent her readership application form together with a shilling's subscription to the office of the NSS at 17 Johnson's Court. The *National Reformer* of 9 August records that a membership certificate was available to Mrs Besant (amongst others) and would be delivered at the Hall of Science by the President of the Society, Charles Bradlaugh, after his Sunday evening lecture. So it was that Annie Besant made her first visit to the Hall of Science to hear Bradlaugh speak. Twenty years later she recorded the occasion in her autobiography:

> The Hall was crowded to suffocation, and, at the very moment announced for the lecture, a roar of cheering burst forth, a tall figure passed swiftly up the Hall to the platform and, with a slight bow in answer to the voluminous greeting, Charles Bradlaugh took his seat. I looked at him with interest, impressed and surprised. The grave, quiet, stern, strong face, the massive head, the keen eyes, the magnificent breadth and height of forehead – was that the man I had heard as a blatant agitator an ignorant demagogue? He began quietly and simply, tracing out the resemblances between the Krishna and Christ myths, and as he went from point to point his voice grew in force and resonance, till it rang round the hall like a trumpet. Eloquence, fire, sarcasm, pathos, passion, all in turn were bent against Christian superstition, till the great audience, carried away by the orator's force, hung silent, breathing soft, as he went on, till the silence that followed a magnificent peroration broke the spell, and a hurricane of cheers relieved the tension.

At the end of the lecture Bradlaugh walked down the Hall with the NSS certificates in his hand and offered one to Annie with the question, 'Mrs Besant?' He knew immediately who she was because her elegance and her manner distinguished her from the usual members of that audience. There was an instant accord between the large, strong, confident lecturer, now forty years old, and this graceful and appealing woman of twenty-seven years. It is said that a woman is attracted to a man by what her ears tell her, and a man to a woman by what his eyes tell him. Annie Besant had just listened to a great orator, a master of spoken language. Charles Bradlaugh had in front of him a slim young brunette with well-modelled features and wistful grey-blue eyes. It is no surprise that there was a real attraction.

Bradlaugh invited this new member of the NSS to visit him to discuss the question of atheism and he proffered a book that he had used in preparing his lecture. She accepted both offers and two days later arrived at his cramped rooms at 29 Turner Street. Books were everywhere, on the table, on the floor, on the chairs.

He removed the books from the chairs and the two of them sat down to talk. Annie put to him question after question. She had brought with her a neat manuscript copy of an essay she had prepared on 'The Nature and Existence of God'. She read parts of it to him and it was his turn to be charmed by her mellow and carefully modulated voice. He made one important correction. She had written that 'the atheist says there is no God', whereas he pointed out that the atheist does not deny God but simply asserts that the word God has no meaning for him. At the end of the conversation Bradlaugh said to Annie, 'You have thought yourself into atheism without knowing it.'

As she left his rooms Annie invited him to call on her. With courtesy and prudence Bradlaugh declined her offer. Within two days she sent him an urgent note explaining that she had many more questions to ask and pressed again her invitation to visit. This time she was successful and Bradlaugh visited her at her residence in Colby Road, Upper Norwood, near the Crystal Palace. He had an eye for talent, recognised the contribution she could make to his journal, and before he left he had offered and she had accepted a post as writer on the *National Reformer*. She was to be paid a guinea a week, exactly the same sum as Charles Watts received as writer and sub-editor.

Annie lost no time in submitting her first article, which appeared on 30 August. Like many of the contributors she wrote under a pseudonym. She chose the name Ajax represented in the *Iliad* as second only to Achilles in bravery. There was a statue of Ajax crying for light in the centre of neighbouring Crystal Palace Park. To emphasise this new light she labelled her column 'Daybreak'. Her first article was well written with a light satirical touch. She commented on a wide range of subjects including cremation, spiritualism and especially a string of sarcastic observations on the Bishop of Lincoln.

The night that the *National Reformer* went to press with her first article, Annie Besant gave her first lecture at the Co-operative Institute, near Oxford Street, on 'The Political Status of Women'. Bradlaugh took the chair, the usual audience from the Hall of Science turned up and George Jacob Holyoake moved a vote of thanks in generous terms. It was her first public lecture and it was a success. Bradlaugh in his report of the meeting wrote, 'It was probably the best speech by a woman we have ever heard.' Life had moved fast for Annie Besant. In the middle of July she had seen the *National Reformer* for the first time. By the end of August she had become a member of the National Secular Society, had secured a post as weekly columnist and had lectured before the leaders of the freethought movement. This was a woman who made things happen.

Chapter Twenty-five

ANNIE BESANT WAS BORN ANNIE WOOD on 1 October 1847. Her father, William Wood, was from Ireland on his mother's side and her mother Emily (née Morris) was of pure Irish stock. Annie was always proud to say that she was three-quarters Irish. The family was prosperous, lived in comfortable circumstances in St John's Wood, and had a high regard for education. William's uncle was Sir Matthew Wood, twice Lord Mayor of London, and MP for the City. One of Sir Matthew's sons was William Page Wood, a barrister, who in 1868 became one of the less distinguished Lord Chancellors with the title Lord Hatherley.

When Annie was five her father died and the family fortunes changed for the worse. Shortly after that unexpected event Annie's younger brother Alfred also died and the family problem then became how to educate Annie and more especially her elder brother Henry for whom a glittering career was expected. Emily herself came up with an enterprising solution. Eschewing all but minor help from the wealthy Woods, she decided to move to Harrow, rent a large former vicarage with a commanding position at the top of Harrow Hill and earn her living by taking in boys from the College. The key to this solution was that Henry would be a 'town boy' and thus entitled to reduced school fees. The proposal had the approval of Dr Vaughan, headmaster of the College, and it worked well, securing Henry's education at Harrow.

A first-class education for Annie was also obtained in an unusual manner. One of the neighbours on Harrow Hill introduced Annie to Miss Marryat, a spinster of means and the favourite sister of Frederick Marryat the author of *Midshipman Easy*. Miss Marryat was a brilliant teacher and dedicated herself to the education of a few hand-chosen children. She took a liking to Annie and asked Mrs Wood if Annie could join her. After initial reluctance Emily Wood saw the sense in this and so Annie went to live with Miss Marryat at Fern Hill, near Charmouth in Dorset. Here Annie received the best possible homeschooling. All teaching was done by Miss Marryat and was based on a thorough study of language. Annie was taught to read the classics and to write well. Study of Latin gave a solid understanding of grammar, and she learnt to speak German and French. When Annie was fourteen Miss Marryat took her to Germany and France for several months and it was in Paris that Annie was confirmed in the Anglican Church by a visiting priest. This was an education of incomparable quality in which Annie was not only taught well but learnt how to learn for herself. Undoubtedly Annie's ability to study and write for long hours, the intensity of her intellectual powers, owed a great deal to this remarkable maiden lady.

When Annie was sixteen-and-a-half Miss Marryat decided she could do no more for her pupil so Annie returned to live with her mother. These were happy days for her as she mingled with the Harrow boys and younger masters. Her interest in Anglicanism had been fired by her confirmation and she regularly attended High Church. The colourfulness of the service, the incense-laden atmosphere, the high mystery of Anglo-Catholicism, all these appealed to her. At Easter 1866 Annie and her mother visited grandfather Morris at his house in Clapham and discovered that there was nearby in Stockwell a mission church devoted to high Anglicanism. There Annie met a young deacon, a recent mathematics graduate from Emmanuel College, Cambridge, who was teaching at Stockwell Grammar School. The Reverend Frank Besant came from a respectable family, his brother was Walter Besant the popular novelist, but not nearly so well-connected as the Woods. Frank had set himself to become a schoolmaster and to take holy orders. He had a precise mind, a methodical approach to everything, a sense of order that dominated his behaviour. But he was attracted to this approachable young woman who appeared to have an interest in the Church.

In the summer the Woods went on holiday for three weeks to

St Leonards on the Sussex coast. To everyone's amazement, in the middle of that holiday, Frank Besant turned up on a week's holiday himself. Annie and Frank spent that week together, walking and talking and sightseeing. An hour before he left for London Frank asked Annie to marry him. This was totally unexpected and Annie was confused and silent.

Frank took that silence for consent. He bound Annie to mention this to no-one until he had spoken to her mother. So their betrothal was founded on a mistake. In her own words much later, Annie said, 'I drifted into an engagement with a man I did not pretend to love.'

At first Mrs Wood was doubtful about the match but gradually warmed to it. Many months went by in which, if the right words had been spoken, the engagement could have been ended. In the 1860s a broken engagement was a serious matter and in any case Frank looked like a man with prospects. And Annie was at this stage deeply impressed by the Church and had romantic ideas about the priesthood. Twenty years later her friend William Stead, the editor of the *Pall Mall Gazette*, summed up the matter succinctly: 'She could not be the bride of heaven, and therefore became the bride of Mr Frank Besant. He was hardly an adequate substitute.'

They were married at St Leonards in December 1867 when Annie was twenty and Frank twenty-seven. The wedding night was disastrous. The innocent young Annie sustained a shock for which she was totally unprepared. One of Balzac's sayings is that the fate of a marriage is determined by the wedding night. The day after the wedding this marriage gave no hope of happiness.

The married couple moved to Cheltenham where Frank had obtained a teaching post as assistant master at Cheltenham College. They struggled as best they could, this ill-matched pair. Frank liked to be master in his own house whilst Annie was a spirited young woman with a mind that surpassed his. In January 1869 their son Digby was born and in August 1870 they had a daughter Mabel. Meanwhile Annie, unhappy in Cheltenham, took to writing short stories and articles, which she saw as the only way out of her difficulties. Annie had never wanted to be married to a schoolmaster, she thought she was marrying a priest. She decided to do something about this. In the autumn of 1871 she wrote to her father's cousin, Lord Hatherley, Lord Chancellor and Church Commissioner, to ask if he could find a Crown living for her husband. This family influence worked. They were given the choice of two livings and chose one in a small village of 800 souls at Sibsey in Lincolnshire which carried a stipend of £440 per annum.

Annie had advanced her husband's career, but that Frank owed this appointment to his young wife did not help their relationship. Annie later asserted that Frank threatened violence if she ever mentioned that he owed his living to her.

For a brief time Annie was less unhappy. She could help the poorer parishioners, play the part of a priest's wife in village life, and she had time to write and think. Thinking gave rise to doubts about the Church. She spent time making a systematic analysis of the account in the four Gospels of the Crucifixion and was troubled by the evident discrepancies. She was moving from Christianity to theism, denying the divinity of Christ.

It was in Sibsey church in the spring of 1873 that she took a step that affected her profoundly. She had been playing the organ, alone in the church, when she decided to discover what it was like to preach. She closed all the doors and climbed into the pulpit. Her imagination presented her with pews full of an attentive congregation. She spoke extemporaneously with a ringing voice in bell-like tones, filling every corner of that church. Her voice was powerful and carefully articulated. There was no congregation to be moved but she, Annie Besant, moved herself by her own eloquence and the understanding that she was a gifted speaker. This sense of vocal power never left her.

Troubled by her doubts on the divinity of Christ, she had the temerity to visit Oxford to meet Dr Pusey, an orthodox Christian and the most influential member of the Church of England, so as to place her doubts before him. Pusey gave her short shrift. He refused to discuss the divinity question. His response was, 'You are blaspheming. The very thought is a terrible sin.' His last words to her were, 'It is not for you to make terms with God.' It is probable that Annie received from this visit what she sought: the resolution to assert her own views come what may.

On her return to Sibsey she reached a compromise with her husband; she would attend the general Church services but would not celebrate communion. It was an agreement that could not last. Conflict between Annie and Frank grew without any let-up and in September 1873 the crisis came. In a fit of violent temper, Frank delivered an ultimatum. She must conform to the outward observances or she must leave. She chose to leave. A deed of separation dated 25 October was drawn up by lawyers but negotiated by her brother and Frank. Annie received one-quarter of Frank's stipend, £110 per year. Frank was to have custody of Digby and Annie custody of Mabel. The children were to spend one month's holiday with the other parent. Annie would take with her only her personal property. This was not a generous settlement though no doubt the best Henry could negotiate. Annie had the essential provision that she wanted: freedom from her husband.

In the previous year Annie had made friends with the elderly Thomas Scott and his young wife who lived in Upper Norwood. Scott was a venerable lion of a man, well educated and of independent means.. After an adventurous life he had retired to promulgate his views as a freethinker and rationalist. He kept an open house, an heretical salon, and assembled a group of writers, publishing their diverse pamphlets in a monthly series. There was strong sympathy between young Annie and the elderly Scott and he encouraged her to write for him. So on leaving Sibsey Annie chose to live in a small house in Colby Road, Upper Norwood, near to the Scotts. There she was among friends, could call on the Scotts any time to receive sympathy and understanding. She also had to make a living for herself since £110 a year was hardly enough to keep her and Mabel and her maid Mary found for her by Mrs Scott. Annie was never, even in the depths of financial hardship, without at least one servant girl. No doubt she was helped occasionally by her brother who was now doing well. But the real solution was to write and Thomas Scott was able to pay her modest sums to produce a series of tracts. So she spent days on research at the British Museum Library and she wrote, quickly and efficiently, with a trenchant vigorous style. And as she wrote she moved slowly from theism towards atheism.

The final essay she prepared for Scott was the one 'On the Nature and Existence of God', which she showed Bradlaugh when they met at his house. And it was on her visit to the British Museum in July 1874 to prepare that essay that she had made that first purchase of the *National Reformer* from Truelove's shop.

Chapter Twenty-six

IN THE FIRST WEEK OF SEPTEMBER 1874 Charles Gilpin, the Liberal member for Northampton, died. The resultant bye-election presented Bradlaugh with an opportunity and a difficulty. He might reasonably expect to succeed Gilpin who had always had sympathies for him. But Bradlaugh had pledged himself to visit the USA again in the autumn of 1874, partly to pay off the obligations incurred on his first curtailed visit. If he did not go he would be liable in substantial damages but it was also important that he stay and fight. To miss one Northampton election in 1874 might be regarded as a misfortune, to miss both would look like carelessness. He learnt with relief that the writ for the election was to be issued promptly, that nominations would be closed on 2 October and the poll held on 6 October. His calculation was that if he left Northampton immediately after the poll was declared he could arrive in New York in time to salvage matters there.

Merewether was once more the Conservative candidate and again Bradlaugh stood as a Radical. The moderate Liberals would not support Bradlaugh and wanted a candidate of their own. They offered the nomination to several, including Jacob Bright, brother of John Bright, all of whom refused. Eventually they found William Fowler, a quaker barrister and banker, who was ready to stand. Fowler was a tough candidate who regarded Bradlaugh as his main opponent. This was the most formidable fight Bradlaugh had yet experienced with statements about his morals and absence of religion flung at him. Had Bradlaugh's mother lived on parish relief? Were his two daughters illegitimate? These were the type of unsavoury anonymous questions that had to be dealt with.

Bradlaugh responded by strong attacks on Fowler, calling him 'a liar and a coward'. It was a bitter election.

Bradlaugh received his usual strong support from Charles Watts and George Foote who came to Northampton to speak and to canvass. They held several good meetings in the town and everywhere the green, mauve and white favours were in evidence. Annie Besant was in Northampton to report the election for the *National Reformer*. Councillor Joseph Gurney again nominated Bradlaugh and there was tremendous enthusiasm from his core supporters. The result was predictable: Merewether (Conservative): 2,171; Fowler (Liberal) 1,836; Bradlaugh (Radical) 1,736. Bradlaugh again came bottom of the poll but had increased his vote from earlier in the year.

The Northampton Radicals were deeply disappointed. When the results were announced there was a riot in the streets, an attack made on Fowler's campaign headquarters and on the plant of the *Northampton Mercury*, which had been hostile to the Radicals. Bradlaugh was able to pacify his supporters by personal persuasion, but when he left at 9.00 p.m. to get his ship to the USA, disturbances broke out again. The Mayor read the riot act not once but twice and soldiers were called in. Eventually, after midnight, the agitation subsided.

The Radicals had two sources of discontent: the personal attacks on their candidate by Fowler's supporters; and that the introduction of Fowler meant that a naturally Liberal constituency was now represented by two Conservatives. This election sent a warning to Liberal opinion in the constituency. Far-seeing liberals took note of Bradlaugh's persistence. His parting words to Northampton as recorded by Annie Besant were, 'I will fight the borough over and over again.' These Liberals saw that the choice for them was hard but had to be faced: either be represented by the infamous, atheistic Bradlaugh but with a genuinely radical programme, or be represented perpetually by two Conservatives.

Bradlaugh's journey on the *Parthia* to New York was not pleasant. The hard work of the election, the defeat in acrimonious circumstances, had tired him out and the ship proved a remarkably slow one as it ploughed through rough seas. Arrival in New York lifted his spirits by the welcome he received. The customs officer again recognised him and passed him through in advance of the other passengers. He travelled immediately by night express for his first lecture at Dartmouth College, New Hampshire. Once the process of lecturing was underway he took new heart; this was what he had come for and this was what he could do well.

Every week Bradlaugh sent a long letter to Charles Watts, who was acting as editor of the *National Reformer*, to describe his progress. After Dartmouth he moved up and down the East coast, to Cambridge, Massachusetts, Philadelphia, Delaware and of course New York. In Boston he gave a stimulating interview to a reporter from the *Boston Times*. Asked which English politician he most admired, he made an unusual but discerning choice of the radical Professor Fawcett who Bradlaugh thought was qualified to be Prime Minister were it not for his blindness. He told the reporter: 'I want to see a little more of the West than I did last time. So many people in England ask me for advice as to where they should go to in America, and they take my advice so confidently, that I want to fit myself to give the best information I can.'

Bradlaugh did go West – to Chicago, to Milwaukee, and to Iowa. He was offering lectures on a variety of subjects: the French Revolution; Republicanism in England; The Impeachment of the House of Brunswick; and the most popular one, Cromwell and Washington – a Contrast. Despite the heavy intellectual content, this was entertainment for his American audiences and they were absorbed. Bradlaugh's lecturing style was one they had never experienced before. The account of one of his lectures given in the Milwaukee Sentinel expressed this well:

> He is an orator of a class we are totally unaccustomed to here, but very common in England, whose fascination lies in the exquisite shading of salient points. At times thrilling and almost heroic, at times almost whispering, the perfect master of the art of expressing irony, and bitter sweet sarcasm, and a declaimer of wonderful passion, he is all we have been told, very nearly a perfect elocutionist and quite an apostle of the people.

So successful were these talks that he was often engaged for a second or third time in a city. Those who missed his first lecture wanted to be sure of hearing him next time.

Bradlaugh returned to England in the steamship *City of Brooklyn* at the beginning of March 1875. This return journey was even more stormy than the outward one. In the middle of winter the north Atlantic could be harsh and there were furious gales and powerful waves sweeping the decks. For twenty-four hours those on board feared for their lives. But for Bradlaugh this second American tour had been a success. He had earned enough to pay the remaining liabilities of his first trip and was able to put £1,000 to relieve other of his debts. Before leaving New York he had already arranged to return again in autumn 1875.

Chapter Twenty-seven

WHEN BRADLAUGH ARRIVED BACK IN LONDON in the middle of March 1875 he became fully aware of Annie Besant's commitment to the *National Reformer* and the freethought movement. In order to be nearer the journal's offices at Johnson's Court she had moved with Mabel to 19 Westbourne Park Terrace, Bayswater, sharing an attractive house with two woman friends. She wrote assiduously for the journal, not only her weekly 'Daybreak' column, but a variety of other articles and a spate of book reviews. Her diligence was unbounded.

With her new devotion to freethought she had undertaken a major lecture tour. Her pen was no less active but she understood that her greater talent was expressed on the lecture platform. In February she travelled to the north of England and across Scotland. Her first stop was at Birkenhead where her lecture was received with acclamation, before she took the mail train to Glasgow. There her talk at the Eclectic and Secular Institute was so successful that the secretary wrote to the *National Reformer* to say that her lecture had not been equalled in excellence and force by any of the better known lecturers. This northern trip was a preliminary to her first appearance on the platform at the Hall of Science on Sunday evening 28 February when she spoke to an audience of over 1,000 on 'The Gospel of Christianity versus the Gospel of Freethought'. This was an auspicious occasion and she was given top billing. The *National Reformer* reported that 'the immense audience cheered again and again, the lecturer winning golden opinions from all.' Heady stuff for this young woman.

Bradlaugh realised that he had recruited a remarkable talent for his movement. He acted as her mentor, guiding her as to how to prepare lectures, some of which advice she later recorded. He gave sound counsel: 'No steady work can be done in public unless the worker study at home for more than he talks outside.' 'Do not waste time by reading opinions that are mere echoes of your own; read opinions that you disagree with and you will catch aspects of truth you do not readily see.' 'You should never say you have an opinion on a subject until you have studied the strongest things said against the view to which you are inclined.' He was anxious that Annie adopt the same thorough preparation for her lectures that he did for his own.

Over the following months Annie continued with her lecture tours, concentrating on the North of England and the West country. Her future engagements were recorded weekly in the *Reformer* immediately below those of Bradlaugh and Charles Watts and she soon had to give notice that she was booked up for months ahead. These performances were a singular achievement for a woman of twenty-eight in the middle of the Victorian era when women of any age were not common on public platforms let alone heretical ones. Part of her success was her appearance. She had large brown eyes with a wistful look. Her full lips tended to droop at the corners giving her an air of tristesse. Her hair was parted in the middle and brushed close to her head to supply a delightful frame to her oval face. She wore expensive dark silk dresses that were tight at the waist but with full skirts that rustled with alluring femininity as she walked. She had fine hands, soft and delicate, but when she spoke she used few gestures, keeping her arms close to her sides. It was her voice on which she relied, and its bell-like quality, its precise modulation and careful articulation. Like Bradlaugh her speeches had weighty content and in a woman so young, so elegant, and so obviously well educated this was a prepossessing feature. What her presentations lacked was humour. She had no wit, no jocularity, it was earnestness all the way.

Annie's hard work was rewarded by the National Secular Society at its 1875 Annual Conference in Manchester on Whit Sunday 16 May. She joined Charles Watts, George Foote and the President on the platform of this organisation that she had joined only nine months before, and on Bradlaugh's proposal was unanimously elected one of the Society's vice-presidents. This rise to prominence of Annie was not achieved without some resentment by those who had been there many years. Though Charles Watts admired her industry and dedication, he was concerned that she had replaced him as Bradlaugh's closest colleague. Charles Watt's young wife Kate, about the same age as Annie, had more cause for resentment. She was the daughter of leading Nottingham freethinkers so her pedigree in the movement was impeccable and she was used to playing the part of hostess at the Hall of Science. Annie, lacking in tact and sensitivity, was a threat to that position. George Foote was similarly put out by the presence of Annie. His hostility was directed at Bradlaugh whose dominance he questioned. He wrote less for the *Reformer* and hankered after his own lighter and more unconstrained freethought journal.

The colleague of Bradlaugh who was most dismayed by the emergence of Annie was James Thomson. Early in 1875 Thomson told Bertram Dobell, his bookseller friend and supporter, that he was being crowded out of the *National Reformer* by Ajax who took up so much space. Thomson's last article in the journal was in June and shortly thereafter he and Bradlaugh had a rancorous argument. Bradlaugh, who had shown over the years a remarkable tolerance of Thomson's shortcomings, had now had enough of his unreliability and dipsomania, whilst Thomson had come to dislike Bradlaugh's manner of editing the *Reformer* and especially his promotion of Annie's contributions. Bradlaugh was ruthless when he considered the occasion required it and he gave Thomson a written notice of dismissal citing drunkenness as the cause. Thomson never forgave him for this and they never spoke again. The break was disastrous for Thomson who not only lost the occasional income from the journal, which he desperately needed, but also felt unable to maintain his friendly correspondence with Susannah or take Alice and Hypatia to concerts and the theatre. When he did occasionally see the daughters at the Hall of Science he felt unable to speak to them. That was a sad ending to twenty-three years of close friendship.

On 17 September Bradlaugh left for his third visit to America. The passage to New York was the best he had ever had. He sailed on the *City of Berlin*, the finest merchant vessel afloat which on this voyage crossed the Atlantic in seven days and eighteen hours, the shortest time then recorded. On board he made a friend of Dr Fessendon N. Olis, reputed to be the ablest physician in New York, and together they enjoyed a most pleasant journey. Though this trip started well, and Bradlaugh began his usual lectures by staying at the Fifth Avenue Hotel and lecturing up and down the East Coast, it ended disastrously. By early December he was seriously ill with typhoid plus an attack of pleurisy brought on by too much work and too little rest. He sought the advice of Dr Olis who arranged for him to be moved from the Fifth Avenue Hotel to St Luke's Hospital where he could get the best of care. The illness was serious and could easily have been fatal. He was strongly advised to abandon the remainder of his tour for he was told that it would be suicide to face a winter in Mid-West America. So Bradlaugh cancelled more than fifty engagements, thereby losing £1,300, and arrived back in England on 27 December. A visit that was intended to help him reduce his liabilities had placed him further in debt.

But Bradlaugh at forty-two was a strong man and within a month he was again undertaking a heavy lecturing programme. It was now more important than ever that he earn money. His friends had been deeply concerned by his illness in America and were delighted to see him back in action. On 29 February 1876 they organised a welcome-back tea and soirée at the Hall of Science. The Hall was decorated from top to bottom with flowers, all in his Northampton colours. There was music and there was dancing. The top table was occupied by Bradlaugh, Charles Watts and Annie. Kate Watts reigned over the tea urn, and was also given the task of presenting a congratulatory address. To balance this, Annie presented him with a purse of gold, contributed by his supporters, containing £169. There was a speech by Bradlaugh and a generous reply by George Holyoake. This evening all was sweetness and light amongst his followers.

Annie's hard work lecturing and writing had enabled her to earn significant money and in June 1876 she moved from Westbourne Park Terrace to a house of her own, Oatlands, Mortimer Road, St John's Wood. This was an elegant semi-detached house with many rooms and a large garden Annie had been born in St John's Wood and spent her first five happy years of life there. It was near Regent's Park where she could walk and ride. For her this was a homecoming.

The year 1876 had been a hard one for Bradlaugh but the year ended on a happier note. In August the previous year Henry Turberville, otherwise known as Henry Blackmore, the brother of R. D. Blackmore the author of *Lorna Doone*, had died leaving an estate of about £15,000. Turberville was a dedicated follower of Bradlaugh's and in April 1875 had made a will in his favour leaving him his residuary estate and appointing him as sole executor. He did this 'as a slight testimony of my immense admiration of that most truly noble of the human race, who is so grandly content with poverty for the sake of truth'. At Turberville's death it was revealed that there were other wills, one in favour of a Mr Essery and one in favour of a Mr Maggs. So there was a probate dispute complicated by R. D. Blackmore arguing that his brother had died intestate. Out of this confused situation a sensible compromise was reached between the disputants, and Bradlaugh in December received the sum of £2,500 plus his legal expenses. As Bradlaugh said to his daughters, 'this money has come just in time'.

Chapter Twenty-eight

IT WAS NOT ONLY BRADLAUGH'S COLLEAGUES on the *National Reformer* who resented the growing influence of Annie Besant. Alice and Hypatia were concerned about the expansive part she was playing in their father's life. They loved their mother, who was now seriously ill at Midhurst, but they were also aware of the unhappiness of their father. In recent years these two growing girls had been their father's most important feminine influence. This was changing and they had mixed feelings about it.

When Bradlaugh first introduced Annie to his daughters he chose to do it on neutral ground. He accompanied them to the Midland Hotel at St Pancras Station where Annie had taken a sitting room. The girls were shy but expectant. They had heard a lot about Ajax and were willing to be impressed by her. Annie may have been shy herself, though shyness was hardly one of her characteristics. She treated the girls perfunctorily. Alice and Hypatia sat together on a sofa whilst Annie and Bradlaugh were seated at a large round table some little way off. Annie spoke to Bradlaugh so softly that the girls could hardly hear what she said, whereas Bradlaugh spoke in his normal resonant tone continually endeavouring without success to bring his daughters into the conversation. Alice and Hypatia felt excluded. The gloom of the hotel room descended on the company. Taking their leave, as father and daughters descended the hotel steps, Bradlaugh asked, 'Well, how do you like Mrs Besant?' Hypatia was usually the responsive one, but Alice forestalled her without hesitation, 'I do not like her at all.'

That first meeting between the girls and Annie coloured their relationship ever afterwards and the girls never came to trust her.

They certainly saw a great deal of each other for Bradlaugh was always careful to use one or both of his daughters as chaperone when he would otherwise be alone with Annie. The relationship was outwardly friendly but beneath the surface there was a distinct lack of warmth. When Annie moved to Westbourne Park Terrace, Bradlaugh again took his daughters to have tea there. This was an occasion which certainly made him happy. He asked his daughters, 'What does one say when one likes being in a place?' Again Alice responded instantly. 'What does one say when one does not like it?' The daughters this time had not made the visit with great expectations and Annie again failed to hit it off with them.

The daughters resented any familiarity shown by Annie towards their father. One evening, the daughters, Bradlaugh and Annie were at the theatre with friends when Annie called to Bradlaugh in a loud voice, 'Charlie.' The daughters were shocked for this was a mode of address used only within the family by their mother and their grandparents. Annie, despite her insensitivity, realised that she had trespassed on unwelcome ground, and made sure that in the girls' presence she never took that liberty again. Undoubtedly Annie tried to befriend the children and interest herself in them. However, they felt this was always done for their father's sake and not a spontaneous flowering of affection. Occasionally they complained to their father about some tactlessness of hers towards them and he always promised to raise the matter with her but they were sure that he never did. The daughters realised they had little in common with Annie. They came from wholly different backgrounds and there was a mismatch, an essential misalliance.

What always puzzled Alice and Hypatia was the greater prosperity of Mrs Besant compared with their father. He lived in three cheap rooms in Turner Street adjacent to the dusty and smelly Commercial Road. She was able to take and furnish a substantial house with large rooms and a spacious garden in leafy St John's Wood. He depended on his daughters for housekeeping, whereas she employed a cook-housekeeper, a parlour maid and a part-time governess for Mabel. She dressed expensively. On one occasion, to the daughters' amazement, she purchased a splendid three-quarter length black silk coat at a cost of fifteen guineas. She didn't hesitate to hire a cab even if on occasion she had to ask the daughters to pay because she had left her purse at home. They could not understand why a woman who owed her employment to their father had a standard of living so much better than his.

The truth was that Bradlaugh was always short of money. His lectures and writings earned him about a £1,000 a year, he earned a little from the *National Reformer*, which was marginally profitable, and he had investments that paid annual dividends of £100. He also had some Italian bonds, acquired when he was in business, that had a substantial nominal value but supplied no worthwhile interest. This income was swamped by his expenses. He had to maintain his wife at Midhurst and supply her with regular nursing. He was responsible for maintaining his daughters. He was always ready to give financial assistance to his colleagues as necessary from time to time. Nursing his Northampton constituency was costly since he had to travel and stay there frequently at his own expense. His last trip to America had cost him dearly and altogether he had substantial debts and heavy interest on those debts. His greatest burden was litigation costs. He never hesitated to bring an action if it was necessary. He was regularly defamed in the press and as regularly brought defamation actions. He won most of these cases but when he won, it nevertheless cost him money. As he wrote in the *National Reformer*: 'If when I am libelled I take no notice, the world believes the libeller. If I sue, I have to pay about one hundred pounds for the privilege, and get the smallest coin the country knows as recompense.'

Annie Besant on the other hand had few liabilities other than her daughter Mabel. She had a maintenance allowance from Frank and a weekly income from the *National Reformer*. She earned substantial sums from her lecturing and writing. She came from a middle-class family that had significant wealth and it is likely that she received assistance from the Wood family, particularly from a great aunt who was in exceptionally comfortable circumstances. Annie may have spent freely but she fully understood the value of money. She was determined to live in a prosperous way and with style. Turberville had said of Bradlaugh that 'he is so grandly content with poverty for the sake of truth'. Annie fully intended to be grand but she was certainly not content with poverty.

Chapter Twenty-nine

ON 8 DECEMBER 1876 A BOOKSELLER name Henry Cook was arrested and summonsed in Bristol for selling a pamphlet named *The Fruits of Philosophy*. Cook was a rogue, well known for selling secular books above the counter and indecent books behind the counter, and had already served two years in prison for a previous offence. He had purchased 'The Fruits' from Charles Watts but had changed the title page and added two lewd plates. A week after this, Watts received a letter from Bristol informing him of Cook's arrest and seeking help with the defence. Annie Besant was at Johnson's Court when the letter arrived. Watts asked her if she would kindly read the pamphlet and give her opinion on whether it was indecent. Since the matter was urgent Annie promised to take the pamphlet away and give her opinion. Later that day she telegraphed to Watts: 'Book defensible as medical work.' When shortly afterwards Bradlaugh was consulted, he advised Watts to go to Bristol and inform the magistrates that he was the publisher.

Accordingly Watts travelled to Bristol, affirmed that he published the pamphlet, and deposed that the work was a scientific one containing nothing that was not available in medical works. But at the hearing before the magistrates when certain alleged indecent passages were read out, Watts decided immediately to withdraw from the defence and to destroy the printing plates. Cook was eventually convicted for selling an obscene work and was sentenced to a further two years' imprisonment, this time with hard labour.

The Fruits of Philosophy, subtitled 'The Private Companion of Young Married Couples', had been written in 1832 by Charles Knowlton, MD an American physician. It had found its way across the Atlantic and had been published in London in 1833 by the freethought publisher James Watson until his retirement in1853. It was then adopted by George Holyoake and his brother Austin until Watson's death in 1874 when Charles Watts bought the plates from Watson's widow and sold the pamphlet under his own imprint. So in 1876 the pamphlet had been sold in England for the modest price of 6d and in modest numbers for upwards of forty years.

Despite its grandiloquent title, *The Fruits of Philosophy* was a pamphlet which advocated contraception and described methods for practising it. Discussion of contraception, even under the euphemistic title of the population question, was regarded as improper and offensive in the 1870s. Knowlton himself had been sentenced to three months in a House of Correction for distributing the pamphlet. The work began with a 'Philosophical Proem', which contributed little but supplied a sophisticated veneer to the following four chapters. The first demonstrated the importance of limiting population 'without sacrificing the pleasure that attends gratification of the reproductive interest.'

The second was a detailed description of the female genitalia and reproductive organs. It was the third chapter which generated most objections. It described practical methods for preventing conception. The method preferred by Knowlton was the use of a syringe filled with a solution of zinc sulphate to supply a vaginal douche immediately after intercourse. The final chapter considered the human reproductive instinct and recommended that gratification of this instinct be enjoyed temperately. There is nothing in that pamphlet that would raise an eyebrow today, but it was written in a coarse and graceless style. Given that it was the first guide to contraception at a price to supply a mass market, it generated intemperate vilification.

In January 1877, as a consequence of his admission at Bristol, Charles Watts was arrested on a warrant in London and, after proceedings before magistrates at the Guildhall on 12 January, was committed for trial. On their return to Johnson's Court from the Guildhall, Bradlaugh said to Mrs Watts, 'The case is looking rather serious but we must face it. I would the prosecution had been against any other book for this one places me in an awkward position.' The awkward position, as Bradlaugh then saw it, was that the pamphlet was not a theological or political work and he was doubtful whether he could appeal to the freethought party for the funds to defend it. But that it should be defended he had no doubt. As he wrote in the *National Reformer* the following week, 'If the pamphlet now prosecuted had been brought to me for publication, I should probably have declined to publish it, not because of the subject matter, but because I do not like its style. If I had once published, I should have defended until the very last.' After that Guildhall meeting Bradlaugh invited Mr and Mrs Watts to Oatlands that evening to discuss with Annie plans for the defence.

As a preliminary to that evening meeting Bradlaugh had a frank discussion with Annie about the pamphlet and plans for the defence. To Bradlaugh's amazement, Annie was strongly in favour of defending the Pamphlet and establishing a defence fund from freethinkers. She reminded Bradlaugh that the masthead of the *National Reformer* included the word 'Malthusianism' as well as Atheism and Republicanism. In her eyes the pamphlet was a direct descendant of the work of Richard Carlile and what was at stake was the principle of freethought. She was passionately in favour of the defence. What is more she had, as usual, done her homework and already drafted a circular asking freethinkers to supply funds for the defence. Bradlaugh discovered that, when tested, Annie's backbone was as strong as his. She persuaded him.

At Oatlands that Friday evening Charles Watts and Kate were met by Bradlaugh and Annie and the two Misses Bradlaugh. They were pressed to defend the pamphlet as the only honourable course. Bradlaugh anticipated an acquittal but in the event of a conviction and a prison sentence he pledged himself to look after Watts' business and to support Kate and the family. Annie's draft circular was examined and approved by Charles and Kate. Faced with this barrage of persuasion and affected by the high emotion, Watts and Kate agreed to defend. Annie was due to lecture in Plymouth the next day and she said she would take a copy of the circular and begin the fund-raising.

The next day brought second thoughts. Kate read the pamphlet for the first time and was troubled by its content and coarseness. With her husband she decided they could not defend *The Fruits of Philosophy* as it stood. Contemplating the possibility of prison for Charles they changed their minds. On that Saturday evening Watts wrote to Bradlaugh saying he wanted to change the plan of defence. He also telegraphed Annie in Plymouth to warn her that the circular would have to be changed. This telegram deterred Annie not at all who proceeded to collect £8 for the defence fund from her Plymouth audience.

On Sunday morning Bradlaugh summoned Mr and Mrs Watts to 29 Turner Street and they arrived at 3 p.m. Watts handed Bradlaugh a paper headed 'Outline of Defence' setting out the facts in his favour and a testimony to his character. Bradlaugh immediately recognised this to be not a defence but a plea in mitigation. When he asked Watts if this meant he was to plead guilty, Watts answered, 'Yes.'

Bradlaugh was incensed. 'Oh, you coward,' he said. 'You had better make up your accounts on Tuesday morning and let us separate.' But Bradlaugh's temper cooled and it was arranged that the Watts should meet Bradlaugh and Annie on Monday after she returned from Plymouth.

At that meeting Watts repeated that he and Kate had read the pamphlet and decided not to defend. They were repeatedly advised not to yield. Bradlaugh put the crucial question: 'Are you actually going to plead guilty to indecency?'

'Yes,' replied Watts.

'But think what this implies; such a plea will disgrace you for the rest of your life. Under such circumstances I shall be obliged to take from you all my publishing.'

Annie was equally firm: 'I must withdraw my publishing since I cannot permit on my books the name of a man who has pleaded guilty to publishing an indecent work.'

Watts was sullen. Kate was angry.

Bradlaugh asked Watts, 'What notice do you consider fair?'

Watts: 'Three months if I am acquitted and three months after I come out of gaol if I am convicted.'

'That is absurd,' retorted Bradlaugh, 'I will let you have my decision in writing.'

On 18 January Bradlaugh wrote to Watts severing their business connection, removing Watts as sub-editor of the *National Reformer* as from that day, and giving notice that Watts was to cease publishing and printing the journal as from 25 March. He ended his letter, 'I desire to add, for your justification with the world, that except as to the defence of the Knowlton Pamphlet, I have no ground for determining the relationship between us.'

This dismissal was brutal. Watts had been Bradlaugh's loyal colleague for fifteen years. Recently he had been printer, publisher and sub-editor of the *National Reformer* and acted as editor when Bradlaugh was overseas. He had diligently supported Bradlaugh at Northampton. Severance of the connection was an immense blow to Watts's income and his self-esteem. On 8 February Watts appeared at the Old Bailey pleading 'guilty in law'. The judge accepted his evidence and released him on his own recognisance of £500 and by April the case against him was dropped.

Bradlaugh's treatment of Watts generated severe rumblings in the freethought movement. George Holyoake and George Foote expressed their sympathies for Watts who generated his own support committee. They were all troubled by what they saw as the bully Bradlaugh in action again. Bradlaugh published his own version of events under the title 'A Plain Statement' in the *National Reformer* of 11 February (printed ironically by Watts). Annie immediately sent back to Plymouth the £8 she had collected, saying, 'It was given to help Mr Watts to fight, not to assist him in running away.'

Kate Watts responded to Bradlaugh's 'Plain Statement' with a pamphlet of her own. She had never been in print before, but her husband's treatment prompted her first essay. Her attack was on Annie as much as Bradlaugh:

> He [Bradlaugh] evidently believes he is fully capable of guiding
> – I beg pardon, ruling the secular party, with, of course, the
> assistance of Mrs Besant, who, if she cannot lay claim to many
> years of service, has the gratification of finding that her brief
> connection with the movement and the *National Reformer*, has

resulted in her advancement to the post of sub-editor, which there are good reasons for believing she has long coveted.

It was clear from all the circumstances that in order for Bradlaugh and Annie to justify their actions they had themselves to publish and sell *The Fruits of Philosophy*. This they now set about doing.

Chapter Thirty

BRADLAUGH AND ANNIE MOVED FAST. ON 20 January 1877 they entered into a partnership agreement to carry on the business of printers and publishers under the name, style and form of The Freethought Publishing Company. The separate works of the partners were to be published on the same terms as before but author's rights were not to be included. Profits were to be divided equally. Annie was delighted to find herself a publisher. The partners raised money, most of it from Annie's friends, to take premises at 28 Stonecutter Street, a short passage running between Shoe Lane and Farringdon Street. The rent was £60 per annum and, though the building was dilapidated, when refurbished it provided space for printing, offices and a small shop. The partners persuaded William Ramsey, an atheist who sold books at the Hall of Science, to join them as manager. By necessity all this happened in double-quick time, for the presses had to be ready for printing the *National Reformer*.

On 21 February the partnership agreement was extended. The partners agreed to include in the partnership all their existing works with no allowance made for the copyrights. The exception to this was the *National Reformer* which Bradlaugh assigned to the partnership and for which he was credited with £1,000. If the partnership were dissolved the copyright reverted to Bradlaugh but in the event of his death it would become the sole property of Annie. By this agreement therefore Annie became co-proprietor of the *National Reformer* and she, rather than his daughters, would inherit it on his death. This was a remarkable advance in Annie's position.

The intention was to publish *The Fruits of Philosophy* as soon as possible. The partners organised a defence committee and a defence fund which was advertised in the journal. Amongst the supporters was Thomas Allsop now eighty-two but willing to travel to London occasionally from his home in the West Country to give his 'thorough' friend his full support.

Bradlaugh made a number of small but sensible alterations to 'The Fruits'. He changed the subtitle to 'An Essay on the Population Question', he arranged for Dr George Drysdale ('G.R.'), an experienced doctor and occasional contributor to the *National Reformer*, to contribute a few footnotes to bring the medical information up to date. And Bradlaugh and Annie added a publisher's preface. This was carefully composed to show that they did not endorse all of Knowlton's views but were motivated to enable discussion 'since progress can only be made through discussion'. The preface ended on a powerful note: 'We publish what others fear to issue, and we do it, confident that if we fail the first time we shall succeed at last, and that the English public will not permit the authorities to stifle discussion of the most important social question which can influence a nation's welfare.'

The pamphlet, bearing the imprint of The Freethought Publishing Company and priced at 6d, was ready for sale on Saturday 24 March and Bradlaugh sent copies to the Chief Clerk of Magistrates at Guildhall, the City Solicitor, and the Head of London Police, advising that the book was on sale at Stonecutter Street and inviting prosecution. On that Saturday sales were immense, 500 purchased in the first twenty minutes. Bradlaugh did the selling and Alice and Hypatia were kept in the back office, away from the scandal, busily packing and wrapping. Amongst those who purchased were plain clothes policemen.

Bradlaugh and Annie were expecting immediate arrest but the police were in no hurry and the arrests were not made until early April. Committal proceedings began in the Guildhall before Alderman Figgins and fellow aldermen on 12 April and adjourned until the following week. The arrests were made under the provisions of the Obscene Publications Act 1857 (known as Lord Campbell's Act) and the offence was the common law misdemeanour of unlawfully publishing and selling a certain obscene book called *The Fruits of Philosophy*. The committal proceedings were conducted in a friendly manner and counsel for the prosecution, with great chivalry, offered to remove Mrs Besant's name from the indictment. Bradlaugh would certainly have preferred to stand alone but Annie would have none of it. This was drama and she was determined to play the Queen. The two defendants were freed on their own recognisances of £200 to appear at the Old Bailey on 7 May.

This was now the time for Bradlaugh to exercise his mastery of legal procedure. He had no wish to appear with Annie in the dock at the Old Bailey so he applied for a writ of certiorari to remove the indictment to the Court of Queen's Bench and for it to be heard by a special jury. This would render the hearing a great deal more tolerable. The basis of his application was that there were legal complexities in the case and serious questions of admissibility of evidence. The application was heard by Lord Chief Justice Cockburn and Mr Justice Mellor, and Bradlaugh argued the matter brilliantly. Having read the pamphlet over the weekend the judges gave their decision: 'We have looked at the book which is the subject matter of the indictment, and we think it really raises a fair question as to whether it is a scientific production for legitimate purposes, or whether it is what the indictment alleges it to be , an obscene publication.' Accordingly the court granted the writ and ordered the trial to be by special jury. This was a success for Bradlaugh and at that moment the auguries were good. It called for celebration. That evening Bradlaugh, Annie and the two girls took a box at the Lyceum to see Henry Irving play Richard III. The winter of their discontent had for the moment been made glorious summer by this decision of the Lord Chief Justice.

The trial was set down to be heard at Westminster on 18 June and, good omen again, the Lord Chief Justice decided that he would preside. From the date of the committal to the day of the trial Bradlaugh and Annie devoted themselves full-time to preparation. They cleared the decks; all provincial lectures were cancelled. They spared no effort making themselves ready. The burden was especially heavy on Bradlaugh for he had a double load of work. In addition to his own preparation he had to train Annie, to show her how to present her case, what arguments to use and which to avoid. His was the responsibility, he was the architect of the defence, and he was always aware that if the case were lost he might be leading Annie into prison. After the trial was over he wrote, 'I have often faced hard toil, but I have never had to encounter persistent, wearying, anxious labour greater than that of the last three months.'

On 27 May in the midst of the stress of preparation, Susannah Bradlaugh died. It was Bradlaugh's sad task to arrange for his wife's body to be brought to London from Midhurst and make arrangements for her funeral at Brookwood Cemetery, Woking on 31 May. Susannah was forty-five years old and she died from heart disease brought on by heavy drinking. Her early death was not unexpected because she had long been ill and had recently required constant nursing. Ten days before her death, in weak handwriting, she wrote to Alice saying, 'My heart is very sick. With great love to dear Papa.' She loved her husband to the end and never once expressed anything but affection for him.

The last three days before the trial Bradlaugh spent with Hypatia, advising her what to do if he and Annie were sent to prison. Hypatia was nineteen and Alice twenty-one but Bradlaugh judged the younger girl more capable of acting as temporary editor of the *National Reformer*. It was Hypatia who had the greater measure of her father's courage and resolution. There was no-one else who could act in Bradlaugh's stead for all his close colleagues had gone, one way or another. This was a difficult time for the two girls, especially since they wished to conceal from their father their belief that it was Annie, his zealous co-defendant, who had led them into all this trouble. So Hypatia sat with her father, anxious and pale, taking pages of notes. On the final day before the hearing, Bradlaugh took Hypatia to his bank manager and gave her authority to sign cheques on his behalf. This brought home to them what was at stake.

Chapter Thirty-one

THE MORNING OF 18 JUNE WAS sunny and warm as Annie and Bradlaugh and his two daughters pushed their way through the crowd to attend Westminster Hall for the trial. The Press, both national and local, had given notice of the occasion. The question of family limitation, rarely mentioned in the press before, had been served up with the morning newspapers on thousands of breakfast tables. The Knowlton pamphlet, which in four decades had sold only a few hundred a year, had sold more than a hundred thousand in the previous two months. It was anticipated that the trial would be sensational. Those hostile to Bradlaugh were hoping that this time he had gone too far and was making the unchivalrous mistake of entangling a clergyman's wife in a perilous business.

The Court was crowded and there were no vacant seats. Several young barristers, expecting an exciting forensic duel, had chosen to attend and perhaps hoped to learn something from Bradlaugh's advocacy, for of course he and Annie were representing themselves. At their father's request, Alice and Hypatia did not sit in the Court. They were worried and restless and together paced continually up and down and around Westminster Hall dressed in black in mourning for their mother.

The special jury consisted of twelve men of whom seven described themselves in the Court records as 'gentlemen', the term which in Victorian times meant they were of independent means. One of these gentlemen was Arthur Walter, son of the proprietor of *The Times* newspaper which in its editorial columns was deeply hostile to the actions of the defendants. The importance of the trial was revealed by the presence of the Solicitor-General, Sir Hardinge Giffard, QC, as prosecuting counsel supported by two experienced juniors, Douglas Straight and Mr Meade. Sir Hardinge was a daunting opponent, the leading lawyer of his day. He was a Conservative member of Disraeli's government and so strongly Conservative as to border on the eccentric. He was short and stout with a square face which usually wore a severe expression. It was said of him that he never on any matter doubted that he was right. He detested Bradlaugh and his views with an intensity he never chose to conceal.

The defendants faced an indictment in the following terms:

> that Charles Bradlaugh and Annie Besant on the 24th day of March, in the City of London, unlawfully, wickedly, knowingly wilfully and designedly did print, publish, sell and utter a certain indecent, lewd, filthy, and obscene libel to wit, a certain indecent, lewd. filthy, bawdy and obscene book called Fruits of Philosophy thereby contaminating, vitiating and corrupting the morals.

Before the jury was sworn, Bradlaugh rose to his feet to make an application that this indictment be quashed on the ground that it was defective in law. Lord Chief Justice Cockburn, sitting with Mr Justice Mellor, agreed to reserve that legal question for later consideration. This was the way in which Bradlaugh preferred to proceed: to have the jury trial first, which he might win, but if he lost it could then be followed by argument on legal objections.

The Solicitor-General's case was that the Knowlton pamphlet was clearly obscene because of its content, and because its price allowed it to be purchased by anyone whatever their age, whatever their condition, married or single, whatever their mode of life and whatever their means. The Solicitor-General cited a reported case, *R, v. Hicklin*, decided by Lord Cockburn himself in that same Court of Queen's Bench in 1868. In that case the Court had ruled that the publication of an obscene pamphlet was not justified or excused by innocent motives; the publisher must be taken as intending the natural consequence of his acts. In this case the Court had also defined the meaning of obscenity; the test was 'whether the tendency of the matter charged with obscenity is to deprave and corrupt those whose minds are open to such immoral influences and into whose hands a publication of this sort may fall.' The prosecution argument was that because of its price the Knowlton pamphlet could fall into anyone's hands. This was a strong opening speech though one of its features was the frequent interruptions by the Lord Chief Justice.

Annie began her opening speech before lunch on the first day. It was a lengthy address, the transcript amounting to some 40,000 words. This young woman was dressed becomingly in black and spoke unhurriedly and with the most careful articulation. She was evidently at ease, dealing with Lord Cockburn's occasional comments deftly and courteously. The long hard hours she had worked had given her complete command of the material. She dealt mainly with social aspects of the case, on the importance of free discussion of contraception and the necessity of family limitation to poor people. Her speech was largely uninterrupted except by appreciative comments from Lord Cockburn. She continued until halfway through the afternoon of the second day, finishing with these words to the jury: 'Unless you are prepared, gentlemen, to brand me with malicious meaning, I ask you as an English woman, for that justice which it is not impossible to expect at the hands of Englishmen – I ask you to give me a verdict of "Not Guilty" and send me home unstained.' This final emotional appeal was received with loud applause, quickly suppressed by the Court officials.

Bradlaugh's opening address was not much more than half as long as Annie's and dealt with the legal meaning of 'obscenity'. He compared the Knowlton Pamphlet with a wide variety of other books to show that the medical information it presented was described in more detail elsewhere. He dealt, as Annie had done, with the position of the poor who had to choose between large families or late marriages. He asked these special jurors, men of independent means, to consider the agricultural labourers:

> Sometimes mere sexual gratification is the only pleasure of their lives. They cannot read Virgil; they cannot read Dante. They cannot listen to Beethoven; they cannot listen to Handel. They have no time to run occasionally across the Alps. They are limited to their narrow parishbound, and their bound is only the work, the home, the beerhouse, the poorhouse and the grave.

He finished on a personal note:

> I know the poor. I belong to them. I was born amongst them.
> Such little ability as I possess today has come to me in the hard
> struggle of life. I have had no University to polish my tongue;
> no Alma Mater to give me an eloquence by which to move you.
> I plead here simply for the class to which I belong, and for the
> right to tell them what may redeem their poverty and alleviate
> their misery.

Again at the end of this address there was applause which again
was quickly curbed.

The defendants called three witnesses to give evidence on their
behalf. These were Dr Alice Vickery, a specialist in midwifery, Dr
Charles Drysdale, a consultant physician, and Henry George Bohn,
a publisher and librarian who was most anxious to supply
supporting statements. Not one of these was cross-examined. On
the morning of the fourth day, Annie and Bradlaugh gave their
final speeches, received again with applause.

The final address from Sir Hardinge Giffard was again subject
to frequent intervention by Lord Cockburn who clearly disliked
his manner of presenting the prosecution case. It was in this final
speech that Hardinge Giffard used the words by which this
prosecution has been recalled by subsequent commentators: 'I say
that this is a dirty, filthy book, and the test of it is that no human
being would allow that book to lie on his table; no decently
educated English husband would allow his wife to have it, and
yet it is to be told to me, forsooth, that any body may have this
book in the City of London, or elsewhere, who can pay sixpence
for it.'

Lord Cockburn's summing up was markedly helpful to the
defendants. He began by saying: 'A more ill-advised and more
injudicious proceeding in the way of prosecution was probably
never brought in a court of justice.' He added, 'I should very much
like to know who are the authorities who are prosecuting, because
that has not yet transpired.' Throughout the summing up it was
apparent that he favoured free discussion. He advised the jury 'that
if they thought the matters dealt with by Knowlton may fairly

be discussed – that the proper answer to them is by argument and not by prosecution – the defendants are entitled to your verdict.' So favourable was this for the defence that one enterprising young barrister made a book, and bets were laid at twelve to one that the verdict would be not guilty.

The jury retired at 12.45 and returned at 2.20 p.m.; it had taken them no longer than an hour and thirty-five minutes to reach their verdict. When the Clerk asked the foreman whether they found the defendants guilty or not guilty, he replied, 'We are unanimously of the opinion that the book in question is calculated to deprave public morals, but at the same time we entirely exonerate the defendants from any corrupt motive in publishing it.' For a moment Lord Cockburn was perplexed. This ambiguous verdict was not what he had expected. Then he said, 'If you find that the book is calculated to corrupt and deprave public morals you must find that they have a corrupt motive in publishing it. Of course your exoneration of them will be taken into account at the proper time, but I am afraid you must find a verdict for the Crown.' The foreman bowed to the judge, turned to his fellow jurors, some of whom signified acquiescence, but the majority gave no sign at all. The foreman bowed again to the judge and a verdict of guilty was recorded by the Court.

This was an unsatisfactory decision in a momentous case. The verdict returned by the jury was an exercise in fence-sitting. The opinion that emerged subsequently was that this decision was strongly influenced by Arthur Walter and by an equally hostile foreman. Afterwards two of the jurors, disappointed at what had happened, refused to accept their attendance fees. It seemed clear however that Lord Cockburn in all the circumstances was likely to deal with the defendants leniently. The case was adjourned for a week so that Bradlaugh could than challenge the legality of the indictment and if that failed for the defendants to be sentenced.

Chapter Thirty-two

ON THE EVENING OF 24 JUNE, the Sunday following the adjournment of the obscene libel case, there was a meeting at the Hall of Science addressed by Bradlaugh and Annie. Fourteen hundred persons paid for admission and hundreds more were turned away Many copies of 'The Fruits' were sold that evening. It was an occasion of high emotion Bradlaugh told the meeting that they would continue to circulate the pamphlet. Annie took Lord Cockburn's name in vain, saying that his summing up was weighed towards the defendants and that his highly trained brain had declared in favour of their Malthusian views. These two speeches were a grave mistake.

At the resumed hearing on 28 June Bradlaugh invited Alice and Hypatia to attend the Court because he felt confident of a favourable outcome. He was expecting a fine, but had withdrawn £250 in notes from his bank, placed them in his pocket book to give to Hypatia to return to the bank if the decision was to be imprisonment. That morning Bradlaugh presented three propositions to Lord Cockburn and Mr Justice Mellor. The first was a motion for a new trial, the second was a motion for arrest of judgment, and the third was a motion to quash the indictment. Lord Cockburn swiftly dismissed the first two but the legality of the indictment required extensive consideration. After lengthy argument, with submissions from Bradlaugh and Harding Giffard, Lord Cockburn declined to quash the indictment himself and after Bradlaugh indicated that he would appeal to the Court of Error the judge decided that he would proceed with the sentencing and leave the legal issue to be decided on appeal.

After the luncheon adjournment Sir Hardinge Giffard sprung

a crushingly effective surprise on the defendants. With no warning he presented two affidavits to the Court. One was sworn by a newsagent deposing that he had, three days before, purchased thirty-six copies of 'The Fruits' from William Ramsey, Bradlaugh's manager. The second affidavit was sworn by a journalist and had as attachment a copy of the *Morning Advertiser* reporting the Hall of Science meeting. The content of these two affidavits was taken as an affront by Lord Cockburn. He was deeply annoyed that Mrs Besant had purported to present his views to the meeting and that the pamphlet was continuing to be sold. From a Lord Chief Justice who had been sympathetic, Bradlaugh and Annie now faced a judge who was incensed.

Lord Cockburn conferred with Mr Justice Mellor and then said:

> This case has now assumed a character of very, very grave importance. We were prepared, if the defendants had been ready to submit to the law and do everything in their power to prevent the further publication and circulation of a work declared by the jury to deprave public morals, to discharge them on their own recognisances to be of good behaviour in the future. But the defendants instead of submitting themselves to the law have set it at defiance.

The sentence then passed was that Charles Bradlaugh and Annie Besant be imprisoned for six months; that they pay a fine of £200 each; and that they enter into recognisances in the sum of £500 to be of good behaviour for two years. Bradlaugh, standing in the dock, went white as he realised that he and Annie were to be imprisoned. But his voice remained firm and unfaltering as he asked his Lordship if he would entertain an application for a stay of execution. 'Certainly not,' snapped the judge. Bradlaugh responded with a dignified bow.

The Court Officer moved forward to take Bradlaugh and Annie into custody. Bradlaugh indicated to Alice and Hypatia that they should accompany them and quietly gave his pocket book with the £250 to Hypatia. The four of them, the defendants and the daughters, all dressed in black, moved slowly with the Court Officer to the door which led to the cells. It was a slow involuntary walk as if through a haze. The courtroom was silent as everyone watched this procession. As they reached the door Lord Cockburn broke that silence with a voice that had softened:

> On consideration [he said] if you will pledge yourselves unreservedly that there shall be no repetition of the publication of this book, at all events until the Court of Appeal shall have decided contrary to the verdict and our judgment; if we can have that positive pledge and you will enter into recognisances that you will not avail yourself of the liberty we extend to continue the publication of the book we may stay execution, but we can show no such indulgence without such a pledge.

Bradlaugh replied: 'My Lord, I meant to offer that pledge in the fullest and most unreserved sense, because although I have my own view as to what is right, I also recognise that the law having pronounced sentence, that is quite another matter so far as I, a citizen, am concerned.' Lord Cockburn: 'I wish you had taken this position sooner.' Bradlaugh: 'If the sentence goes against us, it is another matter. I should not like your Lordship to be induced to grant this request on the understanding that in the event of the ultimate decision being against me I should feel bound by this pledge.' Lord Cockburn: 'I must do you the justice to say that throughout the whole of this battle your conduct has been straightforward since you took it up.'

This was an extraordinary exchange between two men in vastly different positions but with fundamental respect for each other. Bradlaugh and Annie both pledged not to circulate the pamphlet until the decision of the Court of Error. But beyond that they had given no undertaking. For the time being they were at liberty.

Chapter Thirty-three

THE KNOWLTON PROSECUTION RECEIVED IMMENSE PUBLICITY. The newspapers were full of it. Some few, like *The Times*, included long extracts from the speeches at the trial whilst most of them were satisfied with printing brief selections. *The Exeter and Plymouth Gazette* regretted the lengthy excerpts printed by some papers and added: 'The moral ordure served up in the case of Mr Bradlaugh and Mrs Besant has been spread out upon the breakfast tables of thousands of English families.' *The Newcastle Chronicle* on the other hand was sympathetic to the defendants: 'Everyone who heard the trial speaks in the warmest terms of the ability with which the defence was conducted. It is commonly said that a man who acts as his own counsel has a fool for his client, but this certainly has not been the case with Mr Bradlaugh and Mrs Besant.' Previously, newspapers had been silent on the question of contraception; the trial broke through this constraint and the cause of family limitation was discussed more openly. Even those papers strongly opposed to 'The Fruits' were unable to forbear from reporting the case and thereby giving publicity to the cause they considered abhorrent. The purpose of the trial was to prevent publication of a work considered obscene, but the process of prosecution resulted in the sale of many thousands of copies.

Annie Besant had an eye for opportunity and she recognised the unacknowledged demand for a pamphlet on contraception. Having pledged not to sell 'The Fruits', Annie wrote at speed, with the industry that came naturally to her, a new pamphlet which she called 'The Law of Population' with the sub-title, 'Its Consequences and its Bearing upon Human Conduct and Morals'. This work was ready for sale by the end of 1877. It was dedicated to 'the poor in great cities and agricultural districts, dwellers in stifling court or crowded hovel' and was about the same length as Knowlton and also sold for 6d. It contained no new information but was more dignified in tone and more up-to-date. It sold in many tens of thousands and proved a money-spinner. For several years she regularly produced new editions and it was purchased around the world. The English version was sold in India, Australia and New Zealand and it was translated into French, German, Italian, Swedish and Dutch. There were occasional rumblings that sellers of this work too would be prosecuted, especially in Australia, but nothing came of them.

The Writ of Error in the Knowlton prosecution was heard in the Court of Appeal on 29 January 1878. Bradlaugh and Annie again appeared in person, the Crown was represented by Sir Hardinge Giffard and Mr Mead, and the judges were Lord Justice Bramwell, the Senior Lord Justice of Appeal, and Lord Justices Brett and Cotton. The Writ of Error was an instrument then used for appealing against a procedural error or, as in this case, an alleged defect in an indictment. The defect that Bradlaugh asserted was that the indictment being for the publication of words supposed to be an obscene libel, those words ought to have been expressly set out.

The appeal hearing lasted for the best part of three days. Detailed arguments on the legal question were presented by Bradlaugh. Judgment was reserved and given on 12 February with Bradlaugh and the two girls there to hear the decision. Each of the three judges had before him many volumes of law reports; this was a judgment to be supported by ample citations of authority. The judges were unanimous that the indictment was defective. Lord Justice Bramwell in particular pulled to pieces every reason given by Lord Cockburn when dealing with the issues. Two American cases on which Sir Hardinge relied were judged to be 'rather in favour of the defendants than in favour of the Crown'. Bramwell put the Court's decision with utmost clarity: 'The indictment is wholly defective, not merely doubtful but wholly defective: not only are there no words set forth, and no description of any sort or kind given, but it contents itself by saying that the defendants uttered a certain indecent, lewd, filthy, and obscene libel.' LJJ Brett and Cotton agreed. Accordingly the judgment of Lord Cockburn was reversed, the sentences on the defendants were annulled and the whole proceedings were at an end.

This was a sound victory for Bradlaugh. It was said to be a technical victory and that was so in the sense that it did not remove the finding of the jury that the Knowlton pamphlet was obscene. But it was a technical victory of great importance. The indictment had simply averred that an offence had been committed and in the procedure in libel cases at that time it was a vital error. It was an error that Bradlaugh had noticed as soon as he saw the indictment. Sir Hardinge Giffard could have cured the defect but had declined to do so. On this technical legal question Bradlaugh had proved himself a better lawyer than the Solicitor-General. This triumph sent a clear message: anyone who tangled with Bradlaugh in the law courts was likely to be worsted.

Successful though the final result proved to be, there were damaging consequences. There was no escaping the fact that a special jury had found that Bradlaugh had published a pamphlet they held to be obscene. This would haunt him for years to come. His reputation was damaged and his parliamentary ambitions endangered. One of his first steps was to visit Northampton to explain his activities at a meeting of supporters presided over by his faithful friend Alderman Gurney. This meeting of radical supporters gave him their continued backing but the chance of support coming from the Liberal Party in Northampton was now diminished.

The Knowlton case also lost Bradlaugh some friends, at least for a while. The National Secular Society had been divided about the advisability of its President publishing a work that had little connection with secularism and which might bring the Society into disrepute. Certainly this was the view of George Holyoake and George Foote. But success breeds its own approval, and within two years Foote and Holyoake were more or less reconciled with him. They had to recognise that Bradlaugh was clearly the biggest beast in the freethought jungle. Over the next few years the aftermath of the Knowlton prosecution impinged on Bradlaugh's life in many ways. But of all consequences the most serious and the most immediate was endured by Annie Besant.

Chapter Thirty-four

THE REVEREND FRANK BESANT WAS ENRAGED by his wife's activities. He abominated her authorship of atheistic writings, he detested and distrusted her association with Bradlaugh, and he was ashamed of her prosecution for publication of an obscene pamphlet. In his view the name of Besant was being disgraced. The focus of his concern was his daughter Mabel who was not receiving the Christian education which he considered was due to the daughter of a clergyman. He deeply regretted that in the Separation Deed of 1873 he had consented to Annie's custody of Mabel. In August 1875 when Mabel spent a month at Sibsey, Frank had refused to let her return to her mother, but a prompt threat of a writ of habeas corpus soon resolved that matter for Annie. Frank was determined to regain legal custody of his daughter and the outcome of the Knowlton prosecution provided the opportunity.

Frank waited to see if Annie was to be sent to prison. When that seemed unlikely he acted. In April 1878 he filed an action in the Chancery Division to recover custody of his daughter and he briefed a distinguished barrister, Mr Ince, QC, to represent him. This was expensive and some of his parishioners raised money to help him. He was supported by the Bishop of Lincoln who had been the victim of Annie's sharp pen a few years before. The judge who heard the action was no less than the Master of the Rolls, Sir George Jessel. He took the case because it was the first action under the Custody of Infants Act 1873 and therefore likely to raise some nice legal points. The purpose of the Act was to enable custody of an infant to be given to the mother. It also provided that no court should enforce a separation deed between the father and mother of an infant if the court was of the opinion that it would not be for the benefit of the infant. Thus the key to the case was Sir George Jessel's view of Mabel's best interests.

Sir George Jessel was the first Jew to be appointed a judge and the irony that he was to decide on the Christian education of an infant was not lost on the press. He was a man of prodigious memory and was said to dislike the written word and never reserved his judgments which were delivered without advice and without taking time to consider. He was an impatient man who tended to be brusque with counsel and witnesses. He liked to deal rapidly with matters and 'the law's delay' was not to be tolerated in his court.

The first proceeding in the case of in re Mabel Emily Besant was held on 4 May when Mr Ince applied for the hearing of the petition to be held over for two weeks for the production of affidavits. Annie being a married woman, a *feme covert* as the law described her, had to act through a next friend and Bradlaugh served that function, sitting next to her throughout the hearing. Behind her were Alice and Hypatia and a bevy of her women friends. This was an occasion for feminine support.

It was at this hearing that Mr Ince revealed that Annie would appear in person.

> *His Lordship*: Appear in person? a lady appear in person? never heard of such a thing! Does the lady really appear in person?
> *Mr Ince*: I believe so.
> *His Lordship*: This is certainly not a case to be argued by a lady in person.
> *Mr Ince*: It is not for me to express an opinion on that.
> *His Lordship*: But it is for me; I consider it would be a shocking waste of time of the court; it would be useless for the lady to attempt to argue the case, as it involves some nice points of law.
> *Mrs Besant*: I am the respondent to the petition my lord, Mrs Besant.
> *His Lordship*: Then I advise you, Mrs Besant to employ counsel to represent you if you can afford it, and I suppose you can.

> *Mrs Besant*: With all submission to your lordship, I am afraid I must claim my right of arguing my case in person.
>
> *His Lordship*: You will do so if you please, of course, but I think you had much better appear by counsel. I give you notice that if you do not, you must not expect to be shown any consideration; you will not be heard by me at greater length than the case requires, nor allowed to go into irrelevant matter, as persons who argue their cases generally do.
>
> *Mrs Besant*: I trust I shall not do so, my lord; but in any case I shall be arguing under your lordship's complete control.

These remarks by Jessel were downright discourteous. They were also unwise. They suggested partiality, a disinclination to hear argument coming from Annie in person, though she was entitled to give it. It is hard to disagree with Hypatia who, years later, described Jessel's behaviour as 'brutally intolerant'.

At the main hearing on 18 May all the evidence was given by affidavit. After reading this and listening to the arguments by Ince and by Annie, Jessel delivered his judgment. Whilst he had the grace to admit that 'You have conducted your case very ably and temperately', and whilst he acknowledged that Annie had been kind and affectionate in her conduct and behaviour towards Mabel, his judgment was as brutally intolerant as were his previous remarks. He referred to her writings on atheism and commented: 'I know, and must know as a man of the world, that her course of conduct must quite cut her off, practically, not merely from the sympathy of, but from social intercourse with, the great majority of her sex. I do not believe a single clergyman's wife in England would approve of such conduct, or associate with Mrs Besant.' Jessel was doing his best to make her a social outcast. Finally he referred to the Knowlton Pamphlet:

> The pamphlet itself, even if it had been couched in the chastest and most refined language, would be grossly immoral; and it

would be subversive of all human civilised society if the female population of our country were once imbued with the idea that they might safely indulge in unchaste intercourse without fear of any of the consequences such intercourse entails upon them.

After referring again to his opinion that 'one cannot expect modest women to associate with her' he ordered that 'the custody of the infant be forthwith given up to the father'.

When Bradlaugh heard this word 'forthwith' he acted swiftly, anticipating that Frank Besant's advisers would claim immediate custody. So Bradlaugh arranged for his daughters to go immediately to Oatlands and carry off Mabel. Later that day Annie was travelling to Manchester to fulfil a lecture engagement. This gave an opportunity for a tearful parting at Willesden Junction. At this dreary station, with trains rattling by, Annie and Mabel were able to enjoy a brief uninterrupted farewell.

This was by no means the end of the legal tribulations suffered by Annie. She naturally appealed against Jessel's judgement but when this was heard in March 1879, L.J.J. James, Bramwell and Baggalay condemned her as an infidel and confirmed the judgment though with a graciousness not shown by Jessel. Frank then with both Mabel Emily and Arthur Digby in his custody stopped all payments to Annie and refused her access to the children. Annie responded with an application for judicial separation which if it had been granted she could have readily converted into a divorce. In order to make this application she had to put together a case. Since she could not plead adultery or desertion it had to be cruelty. And a case based on cruelty Annie did not hesitate to make. She averred that in various ways and at various times when they had lived together Frank had been violent towards her, even threatening to kill her if she revealed that it was she who had obtained for him the Sibsey living. Frank of course denied all these charges but his denial was less than convincing since he also pleaded that the violence, if there was any, 'had been done in the heat of the moment'.

In the end all these claims, made back in the Chancery Division before Jessel, were of no value. The only assistance Jessel could give her was an order for access to her children to see them once a month, and to enjoy three weeks holiday a year with them, accompanied by a guardian. After consideration Annie decided not to see or correspond with her children until they reached the age when they could understand and choose for themselves. This was no doubt a wise decision for when they reached maturity both Mabel and Digby opted to leave their father and live with their mother.

As for the divorce, Jessel ruled that the obstacle was the Separation Deed of October 1873. He held that this voluntary agreement constituted a condonation of any matrimonial offences there may have been and was an absolute bar to a petition for dissolution. In legal language Annie was estopped from petitioning for divorce. That separation agreement amounted for her to a charter of oblivion. Frank and Annie were thus yoked together in an unwelcome harness until Frank died in 1917. Annie used the name Besant for the rest of her life.

Chapter Thirty-five

THE TURBERVILLE LEGACY THAT ARRIVED PROVIDENTIALLY at the end of 1876 enabled Bradlaugh to leave 29 Turner Street. In February 1877 he moved to 10 Portland Place, Circus Road, an address which soon thereafter was simplified to 20 Circus Road, St John's Wood. Here Bradlaugh lived for the rest of his life. The house was at the end of a terrace and like all of Bradlaugh's other residences has long been demolished, in this case to make way for the St John's Wood public library. From paying 3s/6d a week at Turner Street his rent was now £50 a year. Apart from leaving the dusty and noisy Commercial Road for the leafy St John's Wood the house was not a vast improvement. Bradlaugh had the top floor and the basement with a bathroom on the first floor. The ground floor and most of the first floor were occupied by a firm of music sellers. In 1880 Bradlaugh was able, for an increased rental of £75 to take over the whole of the first floor which became his study. Here at last he had space for his growing library. The kitchen was in the basement and the family ate there. Bradlaugh's bedroom was small, ten feet by nine feet, with the same simple furniture that he had at Turner Street. There was no garden to the house, not even a backyard. In this unusual house, Bradlaugh was looked after by his daughters with the assistance of one young servant girl, who according to Hypatia was given to much fainting. The advantage of the house, and undoubtedly the reason why Bradlaugh chose it was its proximity to Oatlands. A walk of three quarters of a mile would bring him to Annie.

A normal day for Bradlaugh, when he was not lecturing in the provinces, was to rise early and spend most of the morning writing letters and supplying advice to the many who sought it from him.

Although he was not an MP he conducted what amounted to a daily surgery, dispensing sound counsel to members of the National Secular Society, to freethinkers in general and to all manner of other working people facing problems. His advice was always to the point and based on an understanding of the law. Strangely, this leading advocate of atheism was consulted by several clergymen who as young men had adopted a clerical career and then as their understanding matured had lost their faith. What should they do? Bradlaugh's advice to single men was to renounce their religion and find alternative employment, but to those with wives and children his recommendation was to proceed slowly, putting the support of their families as their first consideration.

In the late morning Bradlaugh would collect the books and papers he required and walk to Oatlands where he and Annie worked intensively in her spacious study on their speeches and their writings. They would break briefly for lunch and dinner, prepared by Annie's housekeeper, and work on until ten when Bradlaugh walked back home. Occasionally after an intensive day they would play a game of cards; the American game of euchre was their favourite. Sometimes they would take a day off and travel outside London to walk along the Thames at Windsor, or in the park at Richmond or take tea at a little restaurant in Kew. Bradlaugh liked to take Annie to his favourite spot at Broxbourne where he could fish in that river where he had learnt the art from his father. He would fish most of the day with Annie at his side and in the evening they would have dinner at the Crown Hotel, Broxbourne Bridge, the Inn at the riverside. There in the dining room for many years was a preserved fish in a glass case; at 14 pounds 12 ounces it was the largest carp ever taken with rod and line in England. Bradlaugh had caught that carp. On these expeditions Bradlaugh would share his intimate thoughts and hopes with Annie. How he would persist until he was Member of Parliament for Northampton in order to pursue radical reform. He told her of his love of England, a country that honoured justice for its citizens, and that one of his aims was to assist the Indian people in their struggle for freedom. These were splendid days of relaxation when he could express his private thoughts to a young woman with the intelligence and sympathy to understand him.

In this quasi-domestic life Alice and Hypatia often joined their father and Annie at Oatlands. They acted in part as chaperones but their company and their welfare was important to their father. Annie's lifestyle was more prosperous than Bradlaugh's; she had a large house and an ample garden. She did her best to make the daughters welcome but there was always a suppressed coolness in the air. The girls took German lessons at Oatlands from a teacher Annie found for them. Annie bought a piebald Irish mare, named Kathleen, which she rode in neighbouring Regent's Park, but soon tired of it leaving Hypatia to give it daily exercise.

Bradlaugh was a dog lover and when he had lived at Tottenham he always had a dog or two. One day when all four of them went to Crystal Palace for the dog show, Annie bought a St Bernard puppy for £10. This was in the late 1870s when St Bernards were popular, particularly amongst the nobility, and Annie had room for it at Oatlands. This dog, named Lion, was a splendid specimen and became immensely fond of Bradlaugh, always keeping his large ears cocked to welcome his arrival. When fully grown, Lion was large enough to put his front paws on Bradlaugh's shoulders and look him in the eye. In some ways this dog resembled Bradlaugh. They were both large and imposing, they both had massive heads, and the same qualities of power and endurance.

There was inevitably much gossip and innuendo about the relationship between Bradlaugh and Annie. Despite their closeness there is no evidence that they were sexually intimate. They had an intellectual affinity, they were soul mates rather than physical intimates. This restraint was doubtless due to Bradlaugh. Though he pioneered the publication of works on contraception, he had the Victorian attitude of modesty and propriety in sexual matters. Propriety was the means that allowed him freedom of expression. He believed in freethought and not in free love. His priority was a career as a radical politician and he would allow nothing to impair or impede his political aims. He sometimes expressed this metaphorically to his close friends: 'I have not a passion that I could not crush like an egg shell in my hand.'

Nonetheless it is clear that at one stage Bradlaugh would have married Annie if they had both been free. In his last letter to Kate Watts, when he and she were in dispute, he complained in strong but courteous terms of her remarks about his friendship with Annie that she had expressed in her open letter. He said, 'If you want to do your very worst say that I love her dearly and esteem her very highly and hope the day may come when I have the right to share with her my home and give her the protection of my arm.'

Annie was at that time perhaps the keener to marry. She had written to a correspondent in Edinburgh, 'Mr Bradlaugh and I are engaged to be married. There is no secret about the attachment between Mr Bradlaugh and myself; his daughters know it and are on terms of great friendship with me.' Of course there was no engagement, nor could there be with a married woman. When Bradlaugh's daughters learnt of this letter they were bitterly angry – 'outraged' is the word Hypatia used – and raised the matter with their father. Soon after that Annie came to dinner at Circus Road and when Bradlaugh had left the room Annie remained behind to speak about the letter. She knelt by the girls, admitted the letter was hers, and added, "Although it is not true now, I hope it will be true." But the decision of Sir George Jessel that Annie could not divorce her husband meant that the hope expressed in that letter could never be realised.

Chapter Thirty-six

AT THE BEGINNING OF 1879, THE Knowlton prosecution being over, Annie Besant was ready for new endeavours. The year before, London University had for the first time allowed women to take degrees and Annie decided she would become a graduate. She had shown an ability to grasp legal principles and act as her own advocate and so she chose to read law. She might then be of assistance in the litigation in which Bradlaugh was constantly embroiled. The first step was to matriculate and Hypatia decided to join her in her studies. An announcement appeared in the *National Reformer* of 9th February:

> Mrs Besant, thinking it may add to her usefulness to the cause, intends to take advantage of the opportunity recently afforded for women obtaining degrees in the London University. The necessary studies in preparing for the very severe examinations will take up much of her time, that for several months to come she will only be able to lecture on Saturday and Sunday. Miss Hypatia Bradlaugh is studying with Mrs Besant for the same object.

Annie had a thorough knowledge of languages but matriculation required mathematics and science, so a science tutor was necessary. Alice and Hypatia had already been studying at the City of London College and had met Dr Edward Bibbins Aveling, one of the teachers. It was therefore natural for Annie and Hypatia to enrol with Aveling, so as to study the necessary science subjects. Aveling was a remarkably successful teacher. He was born in north London, the son of a congregational minister and was a precocious scholar. He was four years younger than Annie and passed himself off as possessing Irish blood (as had Annie) and as having been educated at Harrow (as had Annie's brother) but there was no evidence that either assertion was true.

A short, stocky man, Aveling was physically unprepossessing and had eyes that were sometimes described as reptilian. His best quality was his magnificent voice, which was deep, dark, powerful and with a velvety resonance. Women loved his voice, and Aveling did not hesitate to use it as a seductive tool. His two failings were his predilection for women and his tendency to be always in debt. Those who knew Aveling well, when asked about him would reply with a question, 'How much have you lent him?' He was known to borrow money, large sums or small, from anyone who had it.

However, Aveling was a superb educationalist. He could learn and he could teach. He graduated in biological sciences at University College in 1870 and six years later became a Doctor of Science. He lectured regularly at the London Hospital and at King's College. He taught his students by a carefully planned systematic method. He forbade note-taking while he was lecturing. At the end of the lecture he gave headings to the students which they then expanded to form their notes. The students were required to go over this material at home. At the next lecture the students would each read this material aloud in class and it would be corrected by the class as a whole. This triple traverse method, as he called it, was outstandingly successful and secured excellent results for all his classes.

Alice and Hypatia were certainly not bowled over by Aveling. It took a long time for any man to gain the confidence of these two innocent girls and Aveling never did. He did not attempt to borrow money from them but flattered them both with the object of winning their good opinion so that he might become a writer for the National Reformer. Alice and Hypatia did not like him and nor did Lion. One evening in Annie's house when the two girls were there and Aveling was a guest, the St Bernard was stretched at Bradlaugh's feet and growled continuously whilst Aveling was present. That dog was a good judge of character.

Aveling soon managed to become a contributor to the National Reformer. Bradlaugh was always looking for new talent and a Doctor of Science with an ability to render complex ideas clearly and lucidly was a useful acquisition. His first article in January 1879 was entitled 'Darwin and his Views' and was written under the pseudonym 'E.D.'. This was followed by articles on a wide variety of subjects: 'On Educating Women' , 'On Personal Influence', and on 'Playgrounds for the Children'. Aveling had a versatile pen.

On a freezingly cold day in March 1879, Hypatia was exercising Kathleen, Annie's temperamental mare. As they passed Regent's Park Zoo an elephant trumpeted loudly and this set Kathleen off in a wild gallop, and it was not long before horse and rider had come to grief. Hypatia was knocked unconscious and was housebound for many weeks. As a result Annie and Aveling, student and teacher, were alone together at the science tutorials. When Hypatia returned to the classes she discovered that Annie, instead of studying law, now intended to become a Bachelor of Science. No doubt Aveling had persuaded Annie to read science, but she in turn had persuaded him to come out as a declared freethinker. He announced this at the end of July in an article in the *National Reformer*, 'Credo Ergo Laborati', by declaring 'in a manner as public as possible that I am a Freethinker' and signed this with his own name. As a result he was dismissed from his lectureship at the London Hospital but was welcomed wholeheartedly into the freethought movement. It was an advantage for him to align himself with someone as stable and dependable as Bradlaugh. He was now able to lecture throughout the country to freethinkers, and from then on his forthcoming lecture engagements were published weekly in the *National Reformer* below those of Bradlaugh and Besant. Those freethinkers with a waggish tongue referred to them as 'The Trinity'.

It also meant that Aveling was welcome as a lecturer in the Hall of Science. His first lecture there was in August on 'Shelley'. This occasion was reviewed by Annie under the heading: 'A new Soldier' in which she wrote: 'I had the pleasure, in Mr Bradlaugh's absence, of taking the chair and spoke but brief words of introduction…I may fairly congratulate the party on our acquisition of Dr Aveling as a lecturer. His language is exquisitely chosen, and is polished to the highest extent, so that the mere music of the speech is pleasant to the ear.' Soon after that lecture Aveling wrote a flattering, flowery letter to Annie which ended: 'For the sake of my own future as well as for the sake of the world's I desire that your life may last for many years to come and that throughout such as those years as form part of my life I may be able to sign myself as I do now, Your affectionate friend, Edward B Aveling.'

Bradlaugh was far more wary of Aveling than was Annie but he recognised his talents as a writer and lecturer and especially as a teacher. Bradlaugh arranged for him to give classes in one of the rooms of the Hall of Science and these were both well attended and successful. They were organised under the auspices of the Science and Art Department, South Kensington, which meant that the classes attracted a government grant and Aveling received an income from this work.

Towards the end of 1879 Bradlaugh became increasingly absorbed by the likelihood of a General Election and with hopes for success at last in Northampton. The Conservative government was faltering; there was a deepening agricultural depression and the Irish question was becoming ever more troublesome. After his defeat in 1874, Gladstone had passed leadership of the Liberals to Lord Hartington. But in 1879 Gladstone was selected as Liberal candidate for Midlothian and this gave him new vigour.

He embarked on a major series of speeches, the Midlothian campaign, to acclamation throughout the whole country. It was clear that Disraeli would have to call an election in 1880 and that the Liberals were likely to win. Bradlaugh understood that his prospects in Northampton depended upon unity between the Radicals and the moderate Liberals. He made this point forcibly in the *National Reformer* with an article entitled, 'Who are to be the Members for Northampton?' in which he recognised that the apparently immovable objections of the moderate Liberals was his stumbling block. Bradlaugh was without God but he appreciated that he needed a *deus ex machina* to unite the Northampton Liberals.

Chapter Thirty-seven

DISRAELI ANNOUNCED THE DISSOLUTION OF PARLIAMENT on 8 March 1880 and polling day in Northampton was fixed for Friday 2 April. Between those two dates Bradlaugh worked full time at his fourth attempt to become a Member of Parliament in the Radical cause. He had already announced the cancellation of all lecturing engagements and he moved to the George Hotel in Northampton where he stayed during the campaign. The number of registered electors in the borough had increased from 6,829 in 1874 to 8,189 in 1880. This significant increase was judged to be in Bradlaugh's favour since a high proportion of them were freeholders and their independence would lead them to support the radical candidate.

The two sitting members, Phipps the local brewer and Merewether the London barrister, were again selected as the Conservative candidates. Thomas Wright, a respected local solicitor who was also a councillor in Leicester, was the Liberal candidate and had a popular following. But those Liberals who were hostile to Bradlaugh, the moderate Liberals as they were known, wanted a second Liberal candidate. Their first choice was Mr A. S. Ayrton who was actively seeking the candidature but had an accident three weeks before polling day that put him out of contention. A Mr Hughes was then approached but he also fell out, this time because of illness. Mr Balfour was then invited to stand, but he declined because he thought he could not possibly win if there was to be no unity with the Radicals. Still the moderate Liberals sought their own candidate.

Bradlaugh was working hard. Apart from speaking at meetings throughout the constituency, he had to organise the campaign.

He marshalled his canvassing team, known as the 'Radical Two Hundred' to arrange the production of posters, to assemble a card index of every elector, and to canvass the constituency with thoroughness. There were also the newspapers to be kept informed. Northampton had six local newspapers, two weeklies and four dailies. Two of these were captive Conservative newspapers but the others reported the campaign fully and fairly.

On 19 March Bradlaugh organised a major meeting at the Town Hall. Annie Besant and Aveling and the two daughters travelled to Northampton and sat with Bradlaugh on the platform. Aveling spoke first and showed that he could speak effectively on political issues as well as on his usual subjects. Annie in her vigorous style roundly condemned the foreign policy of Disraeli which tapped a deep seam of support in the audience. At the end of the long applause which followed her speech the Chairman said: 'To listen to such speeches would soon convert those who objected to Lady Members of Parliament.' Finally, Bradlaugh roused his audience with his usual polemical style. The leading newspaper reported the meeting as 'a threefold feast of eloquence'.

Meanwhile a prominent Northampton Liberal, Mr M. P. Mansfield, had decided to act. He travelled to London to see the Liberal Chief Whip to ask for a candidate who could unite Radicals and Liberals. The response was, 'I have just the man for you – Henry Labouchere.' So it was that Labouchere descended on Northampton to assess his prospects. He was decisive. He recognised immediately that accord between Liberals and Radicals was the key to the election and he agreed to be the candidate if they would unite. This was the pivotal action on which success turned. Thomas Wright, recognising the new situation, generously retired as candidate, and at last Northampton had two candidates whom Radicals and Liberals could support. The election message then became 'no plumping', that is no voting for Bradlaugh or Labouchere, but voting for Bradlaugh and Labouchere.

Henry du Pre Labouchere was of French Huguenot extraction but thoroughly anglicised. He was a small man with an impish manner, highly intelligent and highly strung, a chain smoker. He was two years older than Bradlaugh and had been an MP in the

1860s for the County of Middlesex. He was a man of the world, widely travelled in North and South America, and with ten years experience as a diplomat. His reputation had increased substantially since 1877 by his founding of a weekly journal, *Truth*, which was highly popular with the educated classes.

Bradlaugh and Labouchere apparently had little in common. One had left school at twelve and then educated himself. The other was a product of Eton and Trinity College, Cambridge. One was from the working class and always short of money. The other was the nephew of Lord Taunton, who had left him a fortune which he had increased by shrewd investment. Bradlaugh had little small talk and not much sense of humour whereas Labouchere was a racy wit and raconteur. The differences between the two men were illustrated by the journals they owned and edited. The *National Reformer* was serious and weighty, consisting of articles on theology, philosophy, politics, science and history, together with news of the freethought movement. *Truth* was largely gossip, under the heading 'Entre Nous'. It was gossip about royalty, about the aristocracy, about Society. It contained a lightweight short story every week, and a puzzle section. Its news was about horse-racing and stock exchange investments. These journals were as different as porterhouse steak and pate de foie gras.

Despite these differences, the two men came to enjoy a fundamental rapport. They were both radicals, they were both reformers. Their political objectives were aligned. Labouchere's radicalism, like that of Bradlaugh, was based solidly on reason. He was not anti-religious, he was non-religious. He wanted to see separation of Church and State. He objected to the hereditary principle, not because it was unjust but because it was absurd. He was in favour of the abolition of the House of Lords. Like Bradlaugh he was deeply opposed to the brutal practice of flogging in the British Army.

These two different men developed great respect for each other. Labouchere wrote in *Truth* of his first visit to Northampton:

> I had never heard of Mr Bradlaugh before. He is a massive man, physically and intellectually, and after listening to one or two

of his speeches I was not surprised at the influence he has acquired here. A more effective speaker at electioneering meetings I have never come across in America or in England. After calmly replying in detail to some of the trash that forms the staple of Conservative oratory, he raises his voice until the very walls re-echo with it and winds up with a fierce appeal to the electors to do their duty.

It took a little longer for Bradlaugh to understand and respect Labouchere but he came to recognise the underlying sincerity of the man behind the façade of cynicism, and he deeply appreciated the loyal support he was receiving.

So for the last week of the Northampton campaign Radical and Liberal were running a joint operation. There were combined meetings at which both candidates spoke, new shared posters were designed, the red election colours selected by Labouchere were mixed with the mauve, white and green of Bradlaugh. All went smoothly for this united effort. The Conservatives faltered for they recognised the likelihood of defeat.

The eve of poll meeting held by this Radical/Liberal combination was a remarkable success. More than 5,000 persons, many of them women, were crammed inside and outside the Corn Exchange. Results already coming in from elsewhere in the country indicated a swing to the Liberals and added fervour to the occasion. Bradlaugh spoke first and made an emotional appeal: 'Twelve years of my life have I spent – twelve years of my life have I sought you – twelve years of my life have I endeavoured to win you. Yet in all that long time I have never flinched. I have never faltered, I have never cringed, and I ask you to believe that in the House I will be the same.' Labouchere wound up the meeting with his own appeal: 'I do not ask you to vote for me. I ask you to vote for those principles which I represent.' Then, a call for unity. 'I do not ask you to plump for me. I call upon you to register the two votes the Constitution has given you tomorrow – one for Mr Bradlaugh and one for myself.' There was thunderous applause from the crowd. But it was action the speakers sought for the next day.

Chapter Thirty-eight

ON POLLING DAY ANNIE BESANT, AVELING and the Misses Bradlaugh travelled from London to Northampton, arriving in time to have a light lunch with Bradlaugh at the George Hotel. That morning he had completed the circuit of committee rooms and polling stations several times. His thorough organisation was paying off as one thousand of his supporters had voted before nine a.m. That afternoon his visitors hired a cab and toured the constituency admiring all the Bradlaugh colours and banners. At half-past three they returned to the hotel to find Bradlaugh tired but satisfied. 'All our men have polled,' he said. 'I'm a poor candidate who has no work to do.'

Bradlaugh was right to be confident of victory. Emptying of ballot boxes and counting of votes began at five p.m. and by the middle of the evening Mayor Joseph Gurney, JP, the Returning Officer, announced the result: Labouchere: 4,158; Bradlaugh: 3,827; Phipps: 3,152; Merewether: 2,826. The turn-out was high: more than ninety per cent of the registered electors had voted. Labouchere and Bradlaugh were respectively the senior and junior members for Northampton. For Bradlaugh this was the summit, the culmination of twelve years of hard political effort. Labouchere took it nonchalantly. When the news that Bradlaugh had been successful was brought to him in his hotel he was smoking a cigarette; he chuckled quietly and remarked, 'Oh! They've swallowed Bradlaugh after all, have they?'

Now it was the time to celebrate. The two new MPs had supper with Annie and Aveling and Bradlaugh's daughters. Annie was delighted with everything and sat between the two men smiling and chatting alternately with each of them. The following morning at the George Hotel, Bradlaugh, Annie and Aveling and the two Misses Bradlaugh climbed into a cab to travel to the station to catch the 10.40 train to London. There was a crowd all along the streets, a mass of heads to say goodbye. A brass band accompanied them playing 'See the Conquering Hero Comes'. There was a huge banner travelling with them, in mauve, white and green colours, carrying the Liberal election slogan, 'Unity, Peace, Retrenchment and Reform'. Everyone in that crowd struggled to shake Bradlaugh's hand. There were tears in the eyes of many. One supporter shouted, 'We have fought for you for twelve years, now we have got you.' Others said, 'Come back soon, Charlie.' Northampton was pleased to be Radical once more.

Back in London there were further celebrations at the Hall of Science on Sunday morning. As many were left outside the Hall as managed to get inside. The London Secular Choral Union had mustered in full force and were wearing charming little bows of mauve, white and green. The Hall was decorated with appropriate flowers: lilac, green leaves and white blossoms. The choir sang for their hero, Mendelssohn's 'Victors Return' and Trouselle's 'Men of England'. A few words were required of Bradlaugh. He told them of the straightforward way Labouchere had acted towards him throughout the election and described how the campaign had been won. All the five thousand inside and outside the Hall queued up to shake his hand.

Celebrations over, now was the time for relaxation. Bradlaugh escaped from the incessant greetings of eager freethinkers to rest and recuperate at his favourite spot on the Lea where, as he said, his surroundings were the peaceful ones of rod and line and trophies of other, finny, victories. Whilst he was there the newspapers were reporting the results, for the election was of interest not only in Northampton but all over England and beyond. *The Times*, not a lover of Bradlaugh, expressed the news with neutrality: 'Northampton has always been strongly Liberal, as becomes a town under the special patronage of St Crispin, but it has never before shown its Radical tendencies so boldly as with the return of Mr Charles Bradlaugh and his colleague Mr Henry Labouchere.' The *Worcester Daily Times* wrote more roughly, 'Mr

Bradlaugh advocates a despotic Republic.' The *Sheffield Telegraph* described him with hostile alliteration, 'Bradlaugh, the bellowing blasphemer of Northampton.'

Thomas Allsop, who had been in feeble health for some time, died on 12 April. Atheist to the last, he chose to be buried at Brookwood Cemetery, because it provided unconsecrated ground. As much as anyone, he had been Bradlaugh's mentor. In 1868 and in the two elections of 1874 he had come to Northampton to supply support but in 1880 had been too weak to make the journey. His last words to Bradlaugh expressed his hope to see him in the House before he died. The only mitigation of Bradlaugh's sense of loss was that Allsop had lived long enough to learn of the election success.

In the *National Reformer* of 11 April Bradlaugh wrote the leading article, reviewing his twelve-year fight to become an MP. The article ended, 'The battle was over and won.' The battle to become an MP was clearly over but the struggle to take his seat in the House of Commons and play a full part in its deliberations had only just begun. One of the first to recognise this publicly was the London correspondent of the *Sheffield Independent* who wrote on 17 April to suggest that difficulties lay ahead. 'Tenets which constitute the religious faith of Mr Bradlaugh are understood to present an insuperable difficulty in the way of his being duly sworn a member of "the faithful commons" and a large number of worthy and orthodox people take a morbid interest in speculating upon what they conceive to be a constitutional problem which it will not be easy to solve.' There was indeed a constitutional problem, created by worthy and orthodox people with morbid interests, which Bradlaugh now had to face.

Chapter Thirty-nine

THE IMPRESSIVE LIBERAL RESULT AT NORTHAMPTON PROVED to be part of a major victory for Liberals throughout the country. Gladstone's Midlothian campaign had led to an outstanding electoral success. The new House of Commons contained 353 Liberals, 253 Conservatives and, significantly, a rise to 61 seats for the Irish Home Rulers. A previous Conservative majority of 50 had been transformed into a Liberal majority greater than that. This was the product of a well-organised campaign with fewer uncontested seats than ever before.

The Marquess of Hartington (Harty-Tarty as he was affectionately known) had been opposition leader in the Commons and Earl Granville the leader in the Lords. Gladstone made it clear to them that he would oppose any administration not led by him and so, much to her dislike, Queen Victoria asked him to form a government. This was an inevitable choice. Gladstone dominated the House by his oratory, his energy (extraordinary for a man of seventy-one), by his patience and his immense grasp of detail. So it was that he formed his second administration.

The new Cabinet of fourteen was an unusual one since more than half were peers or sons of peers. Granville became Foreign Secretary, Hartington was Secretary of State for India, and Gladstone, glutton for work, decided to be his own Chancellor of the Exchequer. If this was a government stronger in the Lords than the Commons, the same could be said of the opposition with the latent influence of the Earl of Beaconsfield and Lord Salisbury. The Conservative leader in the Commons was Sir Stafford Northcote, an admirable man but uncertain and with little political imagination. As a leader he was uninspiring, quite out of

Gladstone's league. Hesitant and ineffective, he disliked opposing Gladstone whom he had served as private secretary twenty years before. It was said of Northcote that when he spoke Gladstone would fix his eyes on him to such powerful effect that the opposition leader would become confused and flustered. Northcote relied for assistance on two businessmen turned politicians, W. H. Smith who had helped his father found the great newsagent business, and Sir Richard Cross, a successful lawyer and banker before becoming a politician. Here was the Conservative party beginning to be influenced by business rather than landed interests.

Bradlaugh fully understood that as a declared atheist there would be opposition to his swearing the oath of allegiance. The newspapers, in London and the country, were discussing the question and it was a matter of gossip among all parliamentarians. Bradlaugh's decision was to seek to affirm and he was supported in this choice by the new Attorney-General and Solicitor-General. It was also a matter of esteem. As an atheist he wanted to avoid the charge of hypocrisy that would follow on his swearing on the Bible. When the new Parliament assembled for the first time on 29 April he sat next to Labouchere and told him, 'I shall ask to be allowed to affirm, as with my views this would be more decorous than to take the oath.' Labouchere replied, 'Are you sure that you can legally affirm?' 'Yes,' answered Bradlaugh, 'I have looked closely into the matter and I am satisfied of my legal right.' But Bradlaugh was wrong. His normally sound legal judgment had misled him.

Bradlaugh had written to the newly re-elected Speaker of the Commons, Sir Henry Brand, and to Sir Erskine May, the distinguished Clerk to the Commons, to inform them of his wish to affirm. Brand immediately sought an opinion from one of his experienced legal assistants. The advice was clear: Bradlaugh could not affirm. The governing legislation was the Parliamentary Oaths Act 1866 which provided that 'Quakers, and every other Person for the time being permitted to make a solemn Affirmation or Declaration instead of taking an oath may make and substitute a solemn Affirmation'. Bradlaugh was relying on those words and on the fact that for nine years he had made an affirmation in various judicial courts under the terms of the Evidence Acts 1869 and 1870. But the better view was that he did not come within the class of persons who could affirm under the Parliamentary Oaths Act. These two sets of Acts had different functions and the oaths they established were for different purposes. They were not to be confused. The Speaker passed this legal opinion on to Gladstone and Northcote who were thereby apprised of the difficulty. The former law officers on the Conservative side, Sir John Holker and Sir Hardinge Giffard, learnt of the opinion. So Bradlaugh was walking into a trap and the Conservatives were quietly aware of it.

By agreement with the Speaker, Bradlaugh delayed his entry to affirm until 3 May. After prayers, several members were reaching for the Bible, sometimes two or more holding it at once, swearing their oaths and consummating the act by kissing the book. As Bradlaugh marched, in his ponderous and dignified style, to the table of the House, the curious members all gave way to him. He presented a paper to Erskine May on which was written: 'To the Right Honourable the Speaker of the House of Commons: I the undersigned Charles Bradlaugh, beg respectfully to claim to affirm as a person for the time being permitted by law to make a solemn affirmation or declaration instead of taking an oath.' Erskine May passed the paper to the Speaker who invited Bradlaugh to make a statement to the House. Bradlaugh briefly submitted his view that he was permitted by law to affirm and cited his frequent affirmations under the Evidence Acts as support for this. He finished, 'I am ready to make the declaration or affirmation of allegiance.' The Speaker asked Bradlaugh to withdraw from the Chamber and informed members that he had grave doubts on the matter and that he wished to refer it to the judgment of the House. The senior Minister present, Lord Frederick Cavendish, moved on behalf of the government that the question be referred to a Select Committee. Sir Stafford Northcote seconded the motion and the appointment of a Select Committee was agreed.

On 11 May the Liberal Whip announced to the House the names of the nineteen members proposed for appointment to the Select

Committee. They were all highly respected members of the House with a preponderance of lawyers and included the Attorney-General, the Solicitor-General and the previous Attorney-General. This motion by the Government was opposed by Sir Henry Drummond Wolff, Conservative member for Portsmouth, and led to a debate. Wolff expressed his serious disagreement with the proposed policy which he described as 'inconvenient, unprecedented and irregular'. He had no hesitation in opposing a policy which his leader Northcote had commended. Drummond Wolff was supported from the Conservative benches by Sir Hardinge Giffard, long an opponent of Bradlaugh's on the platform and the courts. He urged that the question should be determined by the House rather than a Committee and that any Report of the Committee would not be the end of the matter. Another fierce opponent of the proposal was Charles Newdigate Newdegate, a solemn Conservative dressed always in black from head to toe. He was a strict constitutionalist, a protestant evangelist, a defender of the Established Church against all other religions and with an unusual slow and stately style of speaking. He held that affirmation was illegal. He agreed with Giffard that a question which so affected the constitution and dignity of the House should not be delegated. Bradlaugh, technically outside the Chamber but listening to the debate, learnt who were to be his main opponents. The motion to appoint a Select Committee was eventually agreed by 171 votes to 74. What was remarkable was that Conservatives spoke so forcibly against the policy agreed by their leader and that so few voted. Here at the beginning of this Parliament were signs of Conservative dissatisfaction with Northcote who chose not to vote in the division.

On 11 May, before the decision of the Select Committee was announced, the National Secular Society held its Whitsun Annual Conference at the Hall of Science. This was a further opportunity for celebration, that the President was now a member of the House of Commons. It was also an opportunity for Bradlaugh to make clear, as he had already stated in the *National Reformer*, that when arrangements for his lectures were made and posters and placards printed, the letters 'MP' were not to be added to his name.

Bradlaugh was determined not to muddle his atheism with his work in the House of Commons. At this meeting Bradlaugh congratulated Aveling on his sterling efforts for the Society. Aveling had delivered 116 lectures, spent 60 evenings on instruction in the science classes, and written numerous articles. Wary as Bradlaugh was about Aveling, he appreciated hard work and nominated Aveling as a Vice-President of the Society. This was the same rapid promotion that Annie Besant had achieved and Aveling was delighted to join her on the platform.

In his closing speech to the Conference Bradlaugh spoke to his members in personal terms:

> The Central London branch has decorated this room with the Northampton colours: let me hope that none of you in the years to come may be ashamed that your Society wore them today. 1849 to 1880. It is a large part of a man's life. From Bonner's Field to Westminster Hall. It is a long stride. And I have climbed, not crawled; marched, not crept; I have held clenched fist, not silken hand. But, friends, do not expect too much now. Man can do only what man may. I will try and do my best. [And then pointing to the banner behind him] Thomas Allsop gave me that motto of 'Thorough'. It is a good motto for without that a man is nothing. [And then his peroration] I have hope in the future, hope in the deliverance from the fears, shackles, the fetters of the past. The age is not far off when men shall be free and equal, not in the dead level of that equality which can never come, but the age when men rank higher than kings, and priests are not.

The Select Committee appointed by the House acted expeditiously and completed its work at a single meeting. The question for it to answer was whether persons entitled under the Evidence Acts to make a solemn declaration in Courts of Justice were permitted to affirm under the Parliamentary Oaths Act. Bradlaugh was invited to attend its meeting but gave no evidence. The Committee was evenly divided, mainly on party lines, though one Liberal voted with the Conservatives. The decision was therefore up to the casting vote of the Chairman who decided that Bradlaugh was not entitled to affirm. Bradlaugh had sensed the way the wind was blowing and was prepared for the result. He had already decided that he would be ready to take the oath.

Chapter Forty

THE HISTORY OF OATHS IS A complex subject and it was not surprising that the oath gave rise to formidable difficulties in Bradlaugh's attempt to take his parliamentary seat. An oath is a solemn appeal to a divinity to warrant the truth of a statement or the performance of a promise. This definition reveals the two types of oath: the assertory or testimonial oath, designed to aver the truth of what is said or written; and the promissory oath, such as one which pledges allegiance. The intention of these oaths is different: the one has the past or present as its object; the other is directed to performance in the future. Undoubtedly Bradlaugh understood the essential difference in these forms of oath but chose to confuse them thereby giving himself serious problems.

The manner in which oaths usually invoke the deity is by the words of imprecation, 'So help me God'. These four monosyllabic words are what caused so much trouble: to dissenters whose religion prohibited them from taking the Lord's name in vain, and to atheists for whom the words had no meaning. The main application of the testimonial oath was to the administration of justice where witnesses were normally required to give evidence on oath and it was most unsatisfactory that those whose religion forbade the oath were unable to testify. It deprived the courts of their testimony and subjected them to possible punishment for contempt of court. Accordingly the Evidence Act 1828 permitted Quakers and Moravians to give evidence by solemn affirmation and an Act of 1833 extended that privilege to Separatists.

This privilege of affirmation was further extended, by the Common Law Procedure Act 1854, to all those who had genuine conscientious objection to being sworn. But this objection had to be based on religious grounds and did not apply to atheists, who were outlaws for this purpose. This was the difficulty that Bradlaugh had experienced in the de Rin litigation and largely as a result of his endeavours the Evidence Further Amendment Act 1869 and the Evidence Amendment Act 1870 were enacted to extend the privilege of affirmation to atheists. Bradlaugh affirmed on many occasions before a judge under these provisions.

However, these two Acts were seriously flawed. A witness could affirm only 'if the presiding judge is satisfied that the taking of an oath would have no binding effect on his conscience'. This reservation was included as a safeguard, to ensure that a religious person did not affirm in order to lie with an easy mind. The provision was used by some judges for the humiliating examination of an atheist who wished to affirm. More seriously, it had the effect of asserting that an unbeliever was a person on whom the oath had no binding effect. This placed an atheist in a trap, precisely the trap that Bradlaugh was in when, after failing to affirm, he chose to take the oath of allegiance.

Promissory oaths on the other hand resulted from the sensitivity of the Crown to loyalty from its subjects. At one time a member of Parliament had to swear three oaths: an oath of abjuration, renouncing the claims of any Pretender; an oath of supremacy, to exclude a foreign power or prelate; and an oath of allegiance, of fealty to the Crown. An Act of 1858, applying to Protestants, substituted a single oath of allegiance for these triple avowals. Specific relief had already been given to Quakers, Roman Catholics and, rather later, to Jews. The Parliamentary Oaths Act 1866 simplified the procedure by providing one form of oath. It provided also 'that Quakers and every other Person for the time being permitted to make a solemn Affirmation or Declaration instead of taking an oath may make a solemn Affirmation omitting the words "So help me God".' Whilst other terms of the 1866 Act were left unchanged the Promissory Oaths Act 1868 simplified the text of the oath.

It was those words of the 1866 Act, 'every other Person for the time being permitted to make a solemn Affirmation or Declaration', whose interpretation was in doubt when Bradlaugh attempted to affirm. The 1866 Act also provided that if a member of the House of Commons voted in the House without having made and subscribed the oath he would be liable to a penalty of 500 pounds for each and every vote he made. This was the onerous penalty that Bradlaugh would come to face.

Chapter Forty-one

DISRAELI'S GOLDEN RULE FOR POLITICIANS WAS: 'Never apologise, never explain.' In a letter to *The Times* of 20 May Bradlaugh made the mistake of breaching that rule. The letter was by no means an apology, but it was a misjudged explanation of why he planned to take the oath. He began with an explanation of his decision to affirm: 'The oath, although to me including words of idle and meaningless character, was and is regarded by a large number of my fellow countrymen as an appeal to the Deity to take cognisance of their swearing. It would have been an act of hypocrisy to voluntarily take this form if any other had been open to me.' After setting out the decision of the Select Committee and his decision not to appeal against it, Bradlaugh then explained why he had decided to take the oath: 'My duty to my constituents is to fulfil the mandate they have given me, and if to do this I have to submit to a form less solemn to me than the affirmation I would have reverently made, so much the worse for those who force me to repeat words which I have scores of times declared are to me sounds conveying no clear and definite meaning.'

It was not obvious to whom this letter was directed, but it was certainly clear that publishing it was an error of judgment. Some freethinkers disliked it, considering that Bradlaugh should persist in his attempt to affirm. George Holyoake, always an uncertain ally, distanced himself from the decision to swear the oath, just as he had distanced himself from publication of the Knowlton pamphlet. But the major consternation produced by this letter was from MPs, Liberal as well as Conservative. Bradlaugh's description of the words of the oath as idle and meaningless was widely considered an affront. This letter of explanation generated irritation rather than sympathy.

Later that day Bradlaugh went to the House and after prayers proceeded with sedate steps up to the Table. As the Clerk began to administer the oath, Sir Henry Drummond Wolff addressed Sir Henry Brand, the Speaker: 'I object, Sir, to the oath being administered to the hon. member for Northampton. I protest against him being sworn.' The Speaker replied: 'It will be the duty of the Clerk to administer the oath to new members as they come up one by one; but if the hon. member for Portsmouth has any objection to offer now will be the time.' He then asked Bradlaugh to withdraw and added: 'I am bound to say that I know of no instance where, a member offering to take the oath in the usual form, any interposition has been allowed in the House to his doing so.' It was here that Brand made his crucial error. He was aware, as he had said, that no interposition between a member and the oath had been made before. His willingness to allow an intervention at this juncture was to cause enduring trouble: to Bradlaugh, to the Government, to Parliament and to the Speaker himself. This was the moment for firm action and Brand muffed it.

Drummond began a lengthy speech by saying that Bradlaugh was 'a professed atheist, and by the common law of England an atheist is not entitled to take an oath'. He then brandished a handful of pamphlets including 'A Plea for Atheism' written by Bradlaugh. He followed this with a reference to that morning's letter: 'It is perfectly clear from the letter written by the hon. member which appears in the newspaper today, that he regards the taking of an oath as a proceeding of a meaningless character, and he says it will be much the worse for those who have forced him to repeat words which carry to his mind no clear and definite meaning.' Wolff then made his central point: 'When the hon. member tells the House that he has been admitted to make affirmation in Courts of Justice, he must know that such an affirmation could only be administered to a witness when the presiding judge was satisfied that the oath would not be binding on his conscience.' Wolff then proposed a motion: 'That, in the opinion of this House, Mr Bradlaugh, member for Northampton, ought not to be allowed

to take the oath in consequence of his having previously claimed
to make an affirmation.'

By this motion Wolff launched a debate lasting for two days.
Gladstone followed him by a cogent speech in which he made the
fundamental point that the question raised by Wolff was a judicial
one: 'The hon. gentleman introduces, I think erroneously and
mistakenly, a political and constitutional question which is, in the
strictest sense, of a judicial character.' Accordingly, Gladstone's
solution, manifestly prepared in advance, was an alternative
proposal: 'That the question be referred to a Select Committee
to consider and report whether the House has any right to prevent
a member who is willing to take an oath from doing so.'

Sir Stafford Northcote gave his support to Wolff, and Labouchere
spoke in favour of his Northampton colleague. John Bright, an
elder statesman of the Liberal party and a member of Gladstone's
cabinet, spoke strongly in favour of Bradlaugh. As a Quaker, Bright
was one of those entitled by statute to affirm. He said: 'If he
[Bradlaugh] were to come to the Table and take the oath as it is,
I have no doubt that it would be as binding on his conscience as
my simple affirmation is binding on mine.'

The debate was adjourned until 24 May which gave time for
the gravity of the matter to be appreciated and for the preparation
of a powerful speech against Bradlaugh by a young, ambitious
back bench Conservative, Lord Randolph Churchill. He began
quietly, expressing the opinion that a further Select Committee
was undesirable. What was required, he said, was what Disraeli
once described as the 'unerring instinct of the House of Commons'.
His oratory gathered pace: 'If the House admitted that members
of the House might declare, with the authority which a
Parliamentary position gave, with right law and justice on their
side, that the words "So help me God" were merely a ridiculous
and superstitious innovation, utterly void of moral force, the whole
connection between the proceedings of Parliament and a divine
sanction was in danger.' Churchill then asserted that Bradlaugh's
ideas of loyalty were analogous to his ideas on religion. He drew
from his pocket a copy of 'The Impeachment of the House of
Brunswick' and scornfully quoted its notorious closing passage

which began 'I loathe these small German breast-bestarred wanderers whose only merit is their loving hatred of one another.' After reading this he threw the pamphlet towards Gladstone, marched down to where it had fallen, and vigorously stamped on it to the accompaniment of wild cheers from his side of the House.

Finally, Churchill appealed to Gladstone. He said that there was not another member of the House who viewed Bradlaugh's opinions with greater horror and revulsion than Gladstone. The Prime Minister had a great majority behind him and he asked him not to deal with the matter lightly: '"Do not," he would say to the right honourable gentlemen, "let it be in men's power to say that the first use you make of that powerful weapon was to mark it with an indelible stain, and that the first time you lead the Liberal party through the lobby in this new Parliament was for the purpose of placing on those benches opposite an avowed atheist and a professionally disloyal person."'

This was a potent point, because Gladstone undoubtedly did regard Bradlaugh's views with deep distaste. Gladstone's wish was to distance himself from his atheistic Liberal colleague and to have the matter of the affirmation and the oath dealt with by the Courts rather than by the House of Commons.

There were many speakers after Churchill, most of little interest or relevance. Charles Newdigate Newdegate asserted that if Bradlaugh took the oath he would do so with mental reservation and quoted from the old Oath of Supremacy by which those taking the oath had to do so 'without any equivocation, or mental reservation, or secret evasion'. Sir John Gorst was, like Churchill, against appointment of a Committee and, like Churchill, quoted Disraeli: 'A Committee of the House of Commons was an elaborate machinery to find out something which everybody knew.' Sir Hardinge Giffard added his authority as former Solicitor-General against the appointment of a Committee. He did not wish the House to sanction what he regarded as a gross irrelevance. 'Bradlaugh,' he said, 'used no disguise.' By the letter he had published 'he had asserted a right to go through the words prescribed by statute while he avowed and wished to make the

House a party to his avowal, that these words were not binding on his conscience'.

This debate had been set ablaze by the dramatic oratory of Lord Randolph Churchill. Historically the debate was significant because it saw the effective birth of the 'Fourth Party'. This party within a party was so named because it came after the Liberals, the Conservatives and the Irish Home Rulers. It was also a party of four: Churchill, Drummond Wolff, John Gorst and Arthur Balfour. These four sat together below the gangway and acted as a Tory ginger group. They were contemptuous of Northcote whom they considered spineless. They had no separate political programme and no clear positive agenda. Their policy was the negative one of harassing Gladstone and impeding the government programme.

Lord Randolph, at thirty-one, was the youngest of the fourth party but quickly took the lead. He was the third son of the seventh Duke of Marlborough and Member for Woodstock by the grace of his father's control of that constituency. He was excessively ambitious, impetuous and imperious, frustrated by being in opposition and anxious to make a major impact. He used the opportunity of the Bradlaugh affair as a means of establishing his reputation. Sir Henry Drummond Wolff, baronet, was forty-five years old, experienced as a diplomat and he it was who first recognised the opportunity for trouble-making that Bradlaugh was to supply. Sir John Gorst, also in his forties, was a lawyer as well as a politician and had reorganised the Conservative party in the country for Disraeli, thereby winning for him the 1874 victory. He had never benefited politically from this endeavour and thus had cause for resentment. Arthur Balfour, only a year older than Churchill and best described as a semi-detached member of the fourth party, was the nephew of Lord Salisbury and had the best prospects of all, eventually succeeding his uncle as Prime Minister in 1902.

Despite the vigorous Conservative opposition in the debate, Gladstone had his way. His proposal for a second Select Committee was approved by 289 votes to 214. These figures reveal the poor turn-out of Liberals; a significant number shared the dislike of the Conservatives for their atheistic colleague. A few days later the composition of the Committee was presented to the House. It consisted of the nineteen members of the first committee plus four additions. After some parliamentary skirmishing, in which Churchill took the lead, Northcote indicated he had no objections. The Committee was ready for its work.

Chapter Forty-two

ON 1 JUNE THE TWENTY-THREE members of the Select Committee assembled in Committee Room 13 of the House of Commons for their first meeting. The proceedings of this second Committee were much more substantial than the first and extended over six days. The Committee decided it should be an open one, and so the large room was filled to overflowing with members of the public, reporters and various members of Parliament who came and went through their own door. Edward Aveling was there to report the proceedings for the *National Reformer*. The Committee sat round a large horseshoe table at the open end of which there was a table and chair for those giving evidence. This was not a horseshoe that would promise good fortune for Bradlaugh. He sat at his own table, off to one side, and piled with musty law books.

Sir Erskine May, Clerk of the House, gave evidence first and supplied a long list of precedents illustrating the practice of the House with regard to the taking of oaths. Bradlaugh joined in the examination of Erskine May and by persistent questioning was able to establish that there was no precedent where the Oath of Allegiance had been refused to any duly elected member respectfully presenting himself to be sworn. His case was new.

Bradlaugh was the only other witness and in moving from his table to the table at the base of the horseshoe he made several journeys to transfer his books. He did not hurry but he did not linger. He was imperturbable, calmly detached from the fascinated interest of all those in the room. His manner towards the Committee was courteous and respectful but at the same time conveying independence and authority. He began his opening statement slowly, speaking in low measured tones, This was not what was expected from someone labelled as a bellowing blasphemer. His first reference was to a statute of the reign of Richard II. 'I claim to be sworn and take my seat by virtue of my due return, untainted by any illegality, and in pursuance of a statute of 1382 which puts upon me the duty of coming here to be sworn under a penalty of fine and imprisonment.' He then dealt comprehensively with all the precedents and concluded: 'There is no case in which the Oath of Allegiance has been refused to any Member respectfully tendering himself to be sworn.'

Members of the Committee then examined him in turn. As he replied to the questions, his quiet manner and the logic of his reasoning won increasing respect. As the examination progressed, so more and more MPs visited the room to observe how their new notorious colleague was performing. Members of the Committee were increasingly impressed. Beginning by observing him with curiosity, they gave him growing attention, and many ended up with discernible admiration for the way he was conducting himself.

The first question to him, from the Attorney-General, went straight to the heart of the Committee's concern. He was asked whether he was aware that when he made an affirmation in Court under the Evidence Acts 1869 and 1870, the judge had to satisfy himself that taking the oath would have no binding effect on his conscience. Bradlaugh's reply had been carefully prepared. 'My interpretation of these statutes is that upon certain answers being given by the witness, the judge is bound to take his affirmation, even supposing that the judge himself should not be of opinion that the oath is not binding upon him.'

Bradlaugh was asked about his letter of 20 May. He first objected to answer the question claiming the letter was an extra-parliamentary utterance on which he should not be examined. But after pressure from the Committee he agreed that the letter might be put in evidence and it formed an Appendix to the Committee's Report. Bradlaugh dealt with the letter by repeating several times in response to questions: 'Any form that I went through, any oath that I took, I should regard as binding upon my conscience in the fullest degree. I would go through no form, I would take no oath, unless I meant it to be so binding.'

One member of the Committee suggested that the affirmation and the oath were exclusive alternatives, and that the first Committee having decided that he could not affirm he had thereby excluded himself from the oath. Bradlaugh gave short shrift to that fanciful proposition. Aveling in his report in the *National Reformer* remarked that it were as if a man proposing to one of two ladies and refused by the first could not then propose to the other. This was a suggestion that would never appeal to Aveling.

After a series of votes the Committee published their agreed Report on 16 June. They were of the opinion that Bradlaugh, by regularly making claims to affirm in Courts of Justice, had voluntarily brought to the notice of the House that he was a person to whom judges must have been satisfied that an oath was not binding on his conscience. Accordingly the House could and should prevent him from swearing the Oath of Allegiance. The Committee added as a rider their recommendation that he be permitted to affirm at his legal peril.

So Bradlaugh, as he must have anticipated, was no further forward by the decision of this second Select Committee. Their decision was a mean one. They had used words in the Evidence Acts, intended to prevent the evasion of the oath by religious rascals, to suggest that Bradlaugh was untrustworthy, whereas they well knew he had been straightforward from the first. The words in the statutes were a snare and the Committee had used them for their own purposes and in so doing had themselves demeaned the value of the oath.

Chapter Forty-three

ON 21 JUNE, FIVE DAYS AFTER the second Select Committee had reported, Labouchere presented a motion before the House of Commons, consistent with the appended recommendation that Bradlaugh be allowed to affirm at his legal peril. Crowds were gathered outside the Commons that day. The strangers gallery was full though containing only a small proportion of those wanting to hear the debate. Bradlaugh sat under the gallery just beyond the bar of the chamber but able to see and hear all that took place. Gladstone was at first uncertain whether Labouchere was the right person to present the motion but after discussion the Cabinet swung behind him. The precise terms were: 'That Mr Bradlaugh, Member for Northampton, be admitted to make an affirmation or declaration, instead of the oath required by law.' Labouchere opened the two-day debate by reviewing the case as it had developed so far and then attempting to put the legal arguments for Bradlaugh to affirm. But Labouchere was not a lawyer, he was a satirist and publisher of a society journal, and his presentation was unconvincing. He was not the man to deal with complex legal argument. When he turned to practical considerations however, his foresight of what might happen if Bradlaugh were not allowed to affirm was faultless:

> I will suppose that, not being allowed to affirm, he goes to the Table and asks to be allowed to take the oath. He is ordered to retire. If he does not retire I presume he would be taken into custody. He would I presume be put in confinement. We will assume that at some time he will be let out. He would then come again to the Table. I think it possible the House would get tired of this and would say – "We can declare the election

164

void". Mr Bradlaugh would go down to Northampton. He would
be re-elected.

There were loud cries of 'No!' at the suggestion that Bradlaugh
would be re-elected. But Labouchere knew better. He had fought
Northampton alongside Bradlaugh and understood the loyalty that
constituency had for its junior member.

At the conclusion of Labouchere's speech, Sir Hardinge Giffard
rose to loud cheers from the opposition, and moved an amendment:
'That, having regard to the Reports of two Select Committees
appointed by the House, Mr Bradlaugh be not permitted to take
the oath or make the affirmation.' Giffard's speech in support was
clever. He began by saying, 'There was no member of this House',
then a bitter pause, 'save the member for Northampton', pause,
'who did not heartily regret that this question had been raised.'
He then referred obliquely to the letter of 20 May and suggested
that if Bradlaugh had come to the Table to take the oath in the
ordinary manner no question would have been raised. But as
he had challenged the House to say whether he was entitled
to take the oath it was impossible for the House of Commons
to shield itself by saying that each man must be guardian of his
own conscience. Bradlaugh was shifting to them the responsibility
which he should have kept to himself. Giffard then made the
lawyerly point that the recommendation attached to the second
Report went beyond the terms of reference of that Committee.
The second Committee in essence had said: 'Do what is unlawful,
and leave it to the courts to say whether it is right or not.' That
in Giffard's view was unacceptable. This was a powerful speech,
in its tone and manner deeply hostile to Bradlaugh. It transformed
the debate.

John Bright spoke at length in Bradlaugh's favour. He avoided
the legal issues and used his thirty-seven years experience of the
House to generate sympathy for his atheist colleague. He began
with a gentle rebuke to the Speaker for referring the question to
the House: 'Well, it would have saved us a great deal of trouble,
Sir, if you had decided the matter for yourself.' He then rebuked
those members who had paraded their consciences: 'It is no

business of mine to set myself up – perhaps it is no business of yours to set yourselves up – as having a conscience and honour superior to that which activates Mr Bradlaugh.' And then a rebuke to Northcote for his surrender to the Fourth Party: 'The front opposition bench appears to have abdicated its function entirely, and has shown, I will not say an abject, but a remarkable submission to gentlemen who sit in the lower part of the House.' He ended his speech with a warning: 'I am certain that the course which it is proposed to take in dealing with this rigid measure to a gentleman honestly, openly, fairly, and legally elected to a great constituency will be productive of great evils and may bring this House into conflict with at least one constituency and may bring us ultimately to humiliation.'

The debate was adjourned until the next afternoon when one of the speakers was Charles Newdegate. As he rose from his place there was a stampede for the exit. His speech was largely irrelevant. One view he expressed was that the matter of the affirmation could not properly be left to the courts who would decline to act in contravention of the House. 'What right had the House,' he cried, 'to expect an individual to incur the risk and expense of initiating proceedings at law if the House threw every impediment in the way of its success?' A discerning listener would have recognised that Newdegate was the individual who intended to incur that risk and that expense.

Gladstone spoke for one hour in his usual magisterial style to a Chamber in which every seat was filled. By this time he must have realised that the debate was not going his way and have regretted that he had not used his whips to garner support. He began by saying that he spoke only because he foresaw difficulty and did not want difficulties to ensue without giving the House his advice. He pointed out that the difficulties were not of the government's making and re-iterated the position he had held from the beginning: that the decision whether Bradlaugh could affirm was not within the jurisdiction of the House. Even if the House had jurisdiction it was not one it should exercise. He ended with a clear statement of the difficulties he foresaw:

If we undertake to interfere for the first time with a gentleman who proposes to fulfil at the Table of this House what he thinks is his statutory duty, we may find ourselves engaged in two conflicts, into neither of which do I feel either bound or disposed to enter, not being led there by obligation or precedent. I am not wishing to enter into conflict with the courts of law, nor am I willing to enter into conflict with the constituency of Northampton.

The debate did not finish until after midnight. The House divided in high emotion on all sides. As the tellers came forward to announce the result the uproar was so great that they could not be heard for two minutes. Gladstone described it in his letter of that day to the Queen as 'an ecstatic transport which exceeded anything which Mr Gladstone remembers to have witnessed'. Labouchere's motion had been lost by 230 votes to 275, and so Giffard's amendment, without further division, became the substantive resolution of the House. The opposition was beside itself with triumph. Members screamed their delight, waved their hats, stood on the benches, danced in the gangways and embraced each other. By a majority of forty-five the House had decided that Bradlaugh could neither swear the oath nor affirm.

This was the first significant division of the new Parliament and Gladstone had lost it. The majority included thirty-six Liberals and thirty-one Home Rulers though Parnell, the Irish leader, had gone through the government lobby. Bradlaugh was used to setbacks and regarded this as no more than a temporary defeat. That early morning he determined that the resolution of the House would eventually be rescinded.

Chapter Forty-four

BY APPROVING THE HARDINGE GIFFARD RESOLUTION, the House of Commons had acted shamefully. The first Select Committee had denied Bradlaugh the affirmation, the second had denied him the oath but recommended that he be allowed to affirm. The House had selected those decisions that were adverse to him and rejected the recommendation that assisted him. Bradlaugh's response was to claim at the earliest opportunity what he considered his right to swear the oath.

Accordingly at 12.30 p.m. after prayers, less than twelve hours after the Resolution had been approved, Bradlaugh, accompanied by shouts of 'Order, Order!', walked to the Table with the intention of taking the oath. The House was full and the public gallery was overflowing. Edward Aveling, with his usual diligence, was up in the gallery to report the proceedings. The Speaker read to Bradlaugh the Resolution and requested him to withdraw. Bradlaugh replied: 'Before withdrawing Sir I ask through you if this House, faithful to its traditions, will hear me before putting the Resolution into force?' Speaker Brand, unwilling to make this decision himself, replied: 'That is a question for the House and I call upon the Member to withdraw in order that the House may consider it.' Bradlaugh thereupon withdrew and Labouchere moved that Bradlaugh be heard. This was agreed, but with shouts of: 'At the Bar. At the Bar.'

So the Serjeant-at-Arms, the small and elderly Captain Gossett, drew the long brass octagonal bar from its cylindrical tube where it was normally held and extended it across the Chamber. The Bar was a symbol, it meant that Bradlaugh was technically outside the Chamber. But it had for Bradlaugh a distinct advantage. If he

had been speaking from a seat inside the Chamber he would have
been facing only half the members. Here he was able to face the
Speaker directly and look into the 600 pairs of eyes that were
watching him. He stood, erect and dignified, one hand resting on
the Bar as he spoke. It was not the manner in which he had
expected to deliver his maiden speech, but he was determined to
make the most of it. He began by appealing to the traditions of
the House and asserting that there was no case in which the House
had judged a member in his absence. He continued:

> Do you tell me I am unfit to sit amongst you? [Cries of 'Here,
> Here!' and 'Order, Order!'] The more reason, then, that this
> House should show the generosity which judges show to a
> criminal and allow every word he has to say to be heard. But I
> stand here as no criminal. I stand here as the choice of a
> constituency, with my duty to that constituency to do. I stand
> here returned duly, ready to fulfil every form that the law permits
> this House to require, ready to do every duty that the law makes
> incumbent upon me.

He referred to the relative positions of himself and the House:
'At present I am pleading at the Bar for justice. By right it is *there*
[pointing to a seat inside the Chamber below the gangway] that
I should plead.' As regards his atheism he observed:

> "I am no more ashamed of my opinions, which I did not choose
> – opinions with which I have grown – than any Member of the
> House is ashamed of his; and much as I value the right to sit
> here and much as I believe that the justice of the House will
> accord it to me before the struggle is finished, I would rather
> relinquish it for ever than it should be thought that by any
> shadow of hypocrisy I had tried to gain a feigned entrance here
> by pretending to be what I am not."
> [Cheers, and cries of 'Order!']

Bradlaugh then considered the future action of the House. 'It
is perfectly true that by a majority you may decide against me.'
He paused, leaned on the Bar, looked slowly round the House
and said, quietly: 'What are you to do then? Are you going to

declare the seat vacant? The moment I sit there [pointing again to the seat below the gangway] I admit the right of the House, of its own good will and pleasure, to expel me. But as yet I am not under your jurisdiction. As yet I am under the protection of the law.' He referred to his solitary position: 'It is said you may deal with me because I am isolated. I could not help hearing the ring of that word in the Lobby last night. But is that a reason, that because I stand alone the House are to do against me what they would not do if I had 100,000 men at my back? [Cries of 'Oh, Oh!'] That is a bad argument, which provokes a reply inconsistent with the dignity of this House.' His ultimate support, he asserted, was public opinion. 'You have the power to send me back; but in appealing to Northampton I must appeal to a tribunal higher than yours – not to courts of law for I hope the days of conflict between the assembly which makes the law and the tribunals which administer it are past. But there is a court to which I shall appeal; the court of public opinion, which will have to express itself.'

His peroration was a plea for justice: 'I beg you, not in any sort of menace, not in any sort of boast, but as one man against six hundred, to give me that justice which on the other side of this Hall the judges would give were I pleading before them.' This twenty-minute speech was delivered with passion, without notes, and like all of Bradlaugh's speeches had not been rehearsed. It was reasoned, carefully controlled, and never deviated from its purpose. Though it was too late to have any effect on the Resolution, it won him many admirers from Liberals in the House.

A brief debate followed Bradlaugh's withdrawal. Northcote expressed the view that no further action was necessary yet looked to Gladstone for advice. But Gladstone sat aloof, making no attempt to assist the House. Whereas the previous evening he had been dressed in his usual parliamentary clothes, he now wore a light coloured suit, carried a summer hat and a walking stick. This was the attire of detachment; he did not propose to deal with a problem created by the opposition. He told Northcote: 'I am one of the minority in the House who objected to the

Resolution. For that reason I abstain from offering my advice to the House.'

Labouchere attempted to move a motion to rescind the Resolution made not more than twelve hours before but was persuaded to withdraw it. The Speaker called Bradlaugh to the Table and informed him that the House had nothing to say beyond asking him to withdraw.

Bradlaugh replied, 'I beg respectfully to insist on my right as duly elected Member for Northampton, and I ask you to have the oath administered to me that I may take my seat. I respectfully refuse to withdraw.'

Mr Speaker again insisted that the Orders of the House were that he withdraw.

Bradlaugh: 'With great respect, Sir, I refuse to obey Orders of the House which are against the law.'

The Speaker, now bereft of authority, appealed to the House to compel the execution of its Orders. There were cries from the opposition benches of 'Gladstone, Gladstone'. But the Prime Minister simply sat back in his seat, his hands resting on his walking stick.

After a long and noisy pause, Northcote said: 'I take upon myself the responsibility of moving the motion.' The Speaker told him that the motion should be: 'That the hon. Member do now withdraw'; precisely the order the Speaker had given Bradlaugh and which he had rejected. The House divided and there were 326 in favour and 38 against. When the Speaker informed Bradlaugh that the Order of the House was that he now withdraw, Bradlaugh simply replied: 'I submit to you, Sir, that the Order of the House is against the law and I positively refuse to obey it.' This was not unthinking resistance on Bradlaugh's part. He knew what he was doing. He wanted the House to have no choice but to imprison him if they pursued a course on which as a matter of law they had no jurisdiction.

The Speaker then instructed the Serjeant-at-Arms to remove Bradlaugh below the Bar. The diminutive Captain Gossett reached up and touched the massive Bradlaugh lightly on the shoulder, requesting him to withdraw. Bradlaugh: 'I shall submit to the Serjeant-at-Arms, but I shall immediately return.' He went to the

Bar and then returned to the Table speaking with a voice rising above the clamour and uproar around him: 'I claim my right as a Member of this House [Cries of 'Order, Order'] to take the oath and to take my seat. I admit the right of the House to imprison me; but I admit no right on the part of the House to exclude me and I refuse to be excluded.'

The Speaker's response to Bradlaugh was to inform the House that it now had to deal with a grave matter, and to ask the House to advise what course should be taken. Again, everyone looked at Gladstone, who remained impassive in his seat. Eventually Northcote had to act. He moved the motion: 'That Mr Bradlaugh, having disobeyed the Orders and resisted the authority of the House, be for his said offence taken into the custody of the Serjeant-at-Arms.' At last Gladstone spoke: 'I have thought it more advisable that recommendations should be made to the House by those who have been parties to the original decision. I can enter no objection to the motion.' Labouchere could not restrain himself from adding his word. He pointed out that a citizen was being sent to prison for doing something that eminent legal authorities considered lawful.

So members filed out of the Chamber to cast their vote to imprison Bradlaugh which they did by 274 votes to 7, Gladstone included. Whilst the members were voting in the Lobby, Bradlaugh, the member not permitted to take his seat, stood with quiet dignity in the Chamber, next to the Table and adjacent to the mace that was the symbol of the House's authority. For a few minutes he and the Speaker had the Chamber to themselves. As the members filed back, one of the first to return was Peter Taylor, a radical member for Leicester, one of the few middle-class supporters of the Reform League. He was the one member who before returning to his seat went to Bradlaugh and shook his hand.

All was then anti-climax. Bradlaugh went quietly. Within the hour the Serjeant-at-Arms, called upon by the Speaker, was able to tell the House that 'in pursuance of their Order and Mr Speaker's warrant, I have taken the Member for Northampton into custody.' Bradlaugh was the last member of Parliament ever to be imprisoned in the Clock Tower.

Chapter Forty-five

BRADLAUGH WAS BY NO MEANS UNCOMFORTABLE in the Clock Tower for Captain Gossett proved a considerate gaoler and the atmosphere was convivial. The room in which the prisoner was confined was U-shaped and on the second floor. Bradlaugh was able to receive visitors and Parnell was one of many who came to shake his hand. That evening Bradlaugh dined in his room with Annie, Aveling, Alice and Hypatia and a few other guests. He slept at night troubled by nothing more than the chimes of Big Ben above him, for he was satisfied that his uncompromising stand had forced the House of Commons to face up to its responsibilities.

Others were busy that night. Gladstone wrote his regular letter to the Queen, telling her about Bradlaugh's speech at the Bar: 'His address was that of a consummate speaker.' Gladstone revealed in his letter his own view of the matter: 'Bradlaugh challenged the legality of the act of the House, expressing hereby an opinion in which Mr Gladstone himself, going beyond some other members of the minority, had the misfortune to lean towards agreeing with him.' The letter was written in tactful terms because of Victoria's deep dislike of the republican Bradlaugh.

Annie and Aveling were busy that night. After leaving the Clock Tower they hurried to Fleet Street to supervise the printing of a special edition of the *National Reformer* with Aveling's vivid description of the day's events. Annie, with her fluent pen, rapidly prepared a leaflet, distributed in thousands the next day, addressed 'To All Law Abiding Citizens' and headed, 'Law Makers and Law Breakers'. In this she wrote: 'The House of Commons has sent to prison a citizen of this country and a duly elected representative of the people, not for breach of the law, but to prevent him from obeying the law. Law is thus polluted at its fountainhead, and the source of law becomes the source of disregard of the law.'

Northcote that night will have pondered on his decision to move for Bradlaugh's imprisonment. The next morning he had a meeting with Disraeli (the Earl of Birkenhead) who advised him, definitely and decisively, not to make a martyr of Bradlaugh by a lengthy period in prison. In Disraeli's view the episode was a storm in a teacup which should be ended without delay. That next morning Bradlaugh, expecting a long confinement and dressed in an informal grey suit, was going through his large pile of supportive letters when he learnt he was to be liberated. He hurriedly changed into his parliamentary black frock coat and hastened to the House.

Soon after prayers that day Northcote asked Gladstone whether the government planned to make a statement in the case of Bradlaugh. Gladstone replied that he had no advice to tender. Northcote had no choice but to move the motion himself: 'That the House having committed Mr Bradlaugh to the custody of the Serjeant-at-Arms, and having thereby supported its Order and asserted its authority, Mr Bradlaugh be discharged from custody.' Northcote had marched his troops to the top of the hill and was now marching them down again. With much discomfiture for the leader of the Opposition, and loud laughter from the Government side, the motion was agreed. Bradlaugh was free.

Now that the Opposition had been humiliated, Gladstone decided that it was time for the Government to resolve the matter. It was too urgent for legislation, so the Cabinet solution was for a Standing Order which would provide: 'That every person returned as a Member of Parliament who may claim to be a person for the time being permitted to make a solemn affirmation instead of taking an oath shall be permitted, without exception, to make and subscribe a solemn affirmation. in the form subscribed in the Parliamentary Oaths Acts, subject to any liability by Statute.' There were two important features of this resolution: it was to apply without exception; and it provided that any person affirming be liable to the statutory penalties.

Gladstone knew that neither the Speaker nor the House would approve a Standing Order which rescinded the Resolution of 22

June. The Order had been carefully drafted to avoid this problem and Gladstone cleared it with the Speaker ahead of the debate. Gladstone then used his masterly command of Parliament to ensure that his resolution was passed. He used his whips effectively to persuade as many Liberals as possible to vote for it. He was assisted by a rumour that if the Government were defeated they would go to the country.

In the debate Gladstone made an effective speech, both masterful and emollient. He explained that action was necessary to avoid repetition of the painful parliamentary scenes of the previous days and to ensure the dignity of proceedings. He emphasised his fundamental view that the House had no jurisdiction in the matter and that it should be resolved in the courts. Gorst was one of the main opposers. In a bitter manner he described the Resolution as disorderly, one that the Speaker ought not to put from the Chair. He argued that if a question had been considered by the House and judgment made, then substantially the same question could not be put again during the current session. The Speaker was prepared for this. He said he found essential differences between the two Resolutions. One was a restraint upon a particular individual, the other applied without exception to every member. Moreover Gladstone's Resolution provided for a member's statutory liability. Drummond Wolff supported Gorst and claimed Gladstone was evading all his responsibilities. Many Irish Catholics spoke against the Resolution, revealing their growing antipathy towards Bradlaugh. Parnell made a speech that faced both ways; he said he would vote for the Resolution but it would be a personally odious task for him. This man, who had sought out Bradlaugh only a few days before, to shake his hand, was now more concerned with not offending his Irish colleagues. Despite further opposition, Gladstone had prepared well. He won the division by 303 votes to 249.

The next day Bradlaugh attended the House to make and subscribe his affirmation. There was a good deal of preliminary business, the issue of a new parliamentary writ, the presentation of private Bills, and half a dozen Reports on provisional Orders. Then Bradlaugh strode in silence to the Table, spoke to the Clerk, shook the hand of the Speaker, and went to his seat. Up in the Ladies Gallery, Annie Besant observed the scene.

The next business was a debate on a motion that the Speaker issue a warrant for the election of a member for the Borough of Tewkesbury. The debate ended in a division in which Bradlaugh entered the 'Aye' Lobby to record his vote. As he came out of the Lobby, Charles Newdegate drew that to the notice of one of the clerks: 'This may become the subject of enquiry hereafter.' Later that afternoon Bradlaugh was served with a writ asserting that he was not a person entitled to affirm under the statutes and claiming a penalty of £500. The writ was in the name of Henry Lewis Clarke, Plaintiff. The first step in the action of Clarke versus Bradlaugh had begun.

Chapter Forty-six

BRADLAUGH WAS DELIGHTED TO TAKE HIS seat in the House and be able to play his part in debates. But he was cautious and appealed to his supporters not to display too much enthusiasm. 'Now that the fierce struggle is over, and that I am really in full enjoyment of the right and privilege which the people of Northampton gave me on the day of the poll, I beg my friends not to mar this grand triumph by any undue words of exultation or ungenerous boast.' The fierce struggle was by no means over, it had just begun, for Bradlaugh now had hanging over him the action begun by Clarke. The potential penalties were enormous. The Parliamentary Oaths Act 1866, under which he was being sued, provided a penalty of £500 for every vote he made and every debate in which he sat. Since he took care not to miss a vote or forgo a debate, he was contingently liable for mammoth penalties.

Apart from this conditional liability, Bradlaugh had substantial debts flowing from his litigation and his parliamentary campaign. He was exceptionally busy with constant attendance at the House (on one occasion he was there for forty-one hours out of fifty-one) and had a mountain of correspondence to deal with every morning. Becoming an MP had increased his postbag substantially and he spent every morning, with Alice and Hypatia as his secretaries, dealing with it. And he had to earn his living. He must have been one of the few MPs who had no private income. In September, soon after Parliament rose for the recess, he wrote: 'I have this week had two rambles to the riverside as some slight off-set against the excessive labour which closed last Tuesday; but the necessities of life limited each of these pleasure trips to a brief space indeed. My own needs compel me to relax neither pen nor tongue, for the mere battle of life has its bread and cheese demands which permit but little relaxation and no idleness.' To earn this bread and cheese he lectured three times every Sunday and frequently on weekdays, often travelling long distances. He had chosen a hard and taxing life.

The *National Reformer* was doing well, with an increasing circulation. That its proprietor was now an MP no doubt generated extra interest. Bradlaugh provided a weekly column, 'Parliamentary Jottings', and Annie and Aveling wrote regular articles. Alice and Hypatia supplied a weekly 'Summary of News', collecting events and happenings of interest to freethinkers. George Foote was also an occasional contributor. He was now reconciled with Bradlaugh, again no doubt due to the parliamentary success. Foote was an effective journalist, incisive, aggressive and uncompromising in his atheistic viewpoint. He was never really easy working for another and was planning to start his own journal. In the meantime his contributions added sparkle.

In November 1880 there was an opportunity for a social gathering of freethinkers when Derobigne Mortimer Bennett visited London on his way back to America from a round the world trip. D. M. Bennett was the leading American freethinker and founder and publisher of the New York journal *The Truth Seeker*. This was an occasion for 'The Trinity' to play host to this distinguished American. Annie organised several dinner parties for him at Oatlands, Aveling took him to an expensive restaurant and to the theatre (no doubt at the expense of the National Secular Society) and there was a formal dinner for him at the Hall of Science with Bradlaugh presiding. Bradlaugh wrote an address for Bennett which Annie delivered and which included the splendid line, a favourite of Bradlaugh's: 'Better a thousand fold abuse of free speech than denial of free speech.'

Aveling reported the evening in the *National Reformer* and equated this journal to *The Truth Seeker*: "The Truth Seeker and the *National Reformer* were really synonymous terms, for how could the truth seeker be ought but a national reformer and which does a national reformer seek save the truth?" Bennett travelled back to America overawed by the generous hospitality and, as he called it, the 'aristocracy' of English freethinkers.

In the House of Commons, Bradlaugh played an effective part immediately. The day after he took his seat he made a speech on the Relief of Distress (Ireland) Bill, appealing to the Government to assist unstintingly the distress of the Irish people. Support for Ireland was one of his major interests as was backing for the better governance of India which captured his attention that first session. He spoke also, and with passion, against the flogging of soldiers, a subject on which he was able to give to the House the benefit of his army experience.

> He had been a private in the army during the time that flogging was permitted for offences now described as trivial. He had seen the lash applied – the man tied up and stripped in the sight of his comrades; he had seen the body blacken and the skin break; he had heard the dull thud of the lash as it fell on the blood-sodden flesh, and he was glad to have the opportunity of making his voice heard against it today; and trusted that nothing would induce the Government to retain under any conditions such a brutal punishment.

Of all the subjects Bradlaugh raised in his first few months in Parliament the one he made his own was the subject of perpetual pensions. In the autumn of 1880 he published a pamphlet, *Perpetual Pensions*, based on detailed research of the kind he enjoyed doing. Here he analysed the hereditary pensions of large amount paid to the descendents of those to whom the original grant had been made. In some cases the grant was for significant service to the nation, in others there had been no discernible public benefit. Bradlaugh detested hereditary privileges of any kind and here he had alighted on a cause that met with a general sympathetic response.

One of the perpetual pensions he treated in detail was that enjoyed by the Churchill family. The original grantee was the first Duke of Marlborough whom Bradlaugh described as 'possibly a great general, but scarcely a great man, unless exceeding baseness may stand for greatness'. For his military service, the Manor of Woodstock was given to him and his heirs and assigns for ever. The great House of Blenheim, built at the cost of the nation, went along with the title. What Bradlaugh objected to was that the seventh Duke of Marlborough, father of Lord Randolph Churchill, should receive in addition a perpetual pension which had subsequently been fixed at £4,000 per annum free of tax. In December 1880 at Portsmouth Churchill spoke of Bradlaugh in terms which were less than polite. Bradlaugh's riposte was to declare: 'I would appeal to his honour. As I cannot do this, I shall next session direct my argument to his sensitive part. I shall menace his pocket.'

Bradlaugh was not content to write a pamphlet. He wanted action. He organised a string of petitions against perpetual pensions which he presented to Parliament. These petitions asserted that in every case the amount already paid on a pension far exceeded any service alleged to have been rendered to the nation. By the middle of March 1881 there were 848 petitions with 251,332 signatures in favour. At the same time Bradlaugh gave notice that he intended to move for the appointment by the House of Commons of a Select Committee to enquire whether perpetual pensions ought to be continued having regard to any just claims of the recipient and to economy in public expenditure. This last phrase was important. During the whole of his parliamentary career, Bradlaugh was concerned with the importance of economy in public expenditure. There was wide support for his proposal for a Select Committee; it was said that one hundred Liberal members were in favour. And hearty assent was forthcoming from many sections of the press; here he had a proposal that met with general approval. But his intention to move for a Select Committee proved to be premature. It was overtaken by the hearings in the *Clarke v. Bradlaugh* litigation.

Chapter Forty-seven

BRADLAUGH WAS WELL AWARE THAT THE writ served on him by Henry Lewis Clarke on 2 July was actually motivated by Charles Newdegate and that the unknown Clarke was acting as a common informer. The writ had been served immediately after Bradlaugh's first vote in order to pre-empt any friendly legal action. During the rest of 1880 Clarke served his Statement of Claim and Bradlaugh his Statement of Defence and there were a series of legal skirmishes. The pleadings in the action took the form of demurrers, a procedure that Bradlaugh favoured. It was a rapid and effective method of determining a point of law between the parties which could if necessary be followed by a full trial on the facts. The hearing on the cross-demurrers was held on 7 March 1881 before Mr Justice Matthew, a Roman Catholic who had been sworn in as a judge only that morning. Bradlaugh was representing himself and Clarke was represented by Sir Hardinge Giffard and his junior Mr Kydd.

Bradlaugh appeared at the Hearing with his usual punctuality. Giffard it turned out was engaged elsewhere. Mr Kydd applied for an adjournment on the ground that he did not feel able to argue the case himself.

Bradlaugh told the judge: 'This is not a friendly action. I cannot consent to an adjournment.'

Mr Justice Matthew: "Very few actions are friendly. It is rather a question of consulting the convenience of Sir Hardinge Giffard. It is a very important case and he should have the opportunity of arguing it.'

Bradlaugh: 'Sir Hardinge Giffard has, on more than one occasion, refused to consult my convenience.'

Mr Kydd, deeply concerned that he may have had to proceed himself, sent for Giffard who appeared within a few minutes.

The case proceeded on the lines that both parties had argued before. Giffard simply contended that Bradlaugh on 2 July 1880 had sat and voted in the House of Commons without having made or subscribed the oath and was therefore liable for the statutory penalty. Bradlaugh's case was that before voting he had made a solemn affirmation in the form prescribed by the Act and that as someone who had been permitted to affirm in courts of justice by the Evidence Amendment Acts he came within the class of persons entitled to affirm.

The vital judgment was delivered on 11 March. Mr Justice Matthew complimented Bradlaugh on 'an argument which in vigour and clearness left nothing to be desired' but his decision was unmistakeable: 'I see no ground whatever for supposing that the legislature intended that the Evidence Amendment Acts of 1869 and 1870 should qualify the Parliamentary Oaths Act 1866, or that all these statutes should be read together as if they were one. It is impossible to attribute to the legislature the intention to blend the Acts together in one scheme of legislation.'

Failing on the main point, Bradlaugh yet won on a subsidiary but significant matter. Giffard had argued that the Parliamentary Oaths Act should be construed as if it contained a proviso that none but a person of religious belief could make and subscribe an oath. The judge held that the statute could not be interpreted that way. This was important; Bradlaugh was able as a matter of law to take the oath despite his alleged want of religious belief. Judgment was entered for Clarke on the main point and for Bradlaugh on the subsidiary question

The very day that judgment was delivered, Gorst, acting for the Fourth Party, gave notice of a motion requiring Bradlaugh's seat in Parliament to be vacated and a writ issued for a new election in Northampton. Gladstone opposed this on the ground that Bradlaugh had decided to appeal. Lord Randolph Churchill intervened to express his concern that Bradlaugh might not appeal for many months. A less arrogant man would have been chastened by Bradlaugh's reply that he was required to prosecute the appeal within twenty-one days, a matter 'the noble lord could have discovered on reference to any ordinary law book'. On the next day Bradlaugh travelled to Northampton to speak at a meeting in the Town Hall so as to inform his supporters of what was happening. He explained the judgment of Mr Justice Matthews and his decision to appeal. He explained also his conclusion that while it was his duty to sit and vote as long as he remained a Member it was also his duty to offer the Government his resignation so as to fight a fresh election at which his constituents might decide the question. The meeting passed unanimously a resolution expressing full confidence in their Member.

The accelerated appeal came before Lord Justices Bramwell, Baggallay and Lush on 30 March and generated great interest. It was understood that this hearing would decide finally whether Bradlaugh could lawfully affirm. The public area of the Court of Appeal was crowded, with standing room only. Aveling was there to report the case, and Labouchere, always fascinated by Bradlaugh's forensic skills, also attended. Aveling described Sir Hardinge Giffard in well-drawn terms: 'A short, condensed man, with a condensed face, who reasons closely according to his brief and his lights, speaks solidly, and on occasion not without a concentrated bitterness. But one ability he does not possess. It is his ability to keep his temper.' This reference to Giffard's temper arose from a dispute between him and Bradlaugh at the outset as to who should begin. Bradlaugh was the victor. Giffard could not conceal his distaste at losing this procedural point.

Bradlaugh had a new argument to put to the Court. He asserted that the Parliamentary Oaths Act 1866 did not provide for a common informer to bring the action for the penalty. The penalty went to the Crown so only the Crown could sue for it. This was a substantial point but the Court decided against him though not without hesitation. Lord Justice Bramwell, the presiding judge, said that it seemed to him that the penalty was one which could be sued for by a common informer 'but I have not a confident opinion about this question.' On the issue as to whether Bradlaugh was entitled to affirm, Bramwell said, 'I think it is about as plain a case as ever came before a court of justice.' Whilst Baggalay and Lush complimented Bradlaugh on 'his very able argument' they agreed with Bramwell 'that the Evidence Further Amendment Act 1869 did not permit the defendant to make the affirmation and he therefore incurred the penalty.'

This was a judgment on preliminary legal issues and there remained matters of fact to be determined. So the execution of the judgment as to costs was delayed until the final trial. But the decision as to whether Bradlaugh could affirm was clear – he could not. As a matter of law Bradlaugh's seat was vacated, as the statute said 'in the same manner as if he were dead'. There was to be a fresh election in Northampton.

Chapter Forty-eight

MATTERS MOVED FAST. THE COURT OF APPEAL gave its decision on 31 March. The next day in the House of Commons Labouchere successfully secured a writ for a new election in the borough of Northampton and polling day was fixed for 9 April. Bradlaugh spent all his time in the borough hard at work organising his supporters, posting his election bills and speaking every night at election meetings. He wrote a message to his supporters: 'It must be remembered that, although my seat has been vacated because I have not taken the oath, I was prevented from taking that oath by formal resolution proposed by Sir Hardinge Giffard, the very conservative counsel who has prosecuted me for not doing that which he actually moved in the House I should not be allowed to do.'

Labouchere proved a solid rock of support. He visited Northampton at the outset of the campaign to supply a powerful speech at a meeting in the Town Hall on behalf of his colleague. He spoke of a conversation he had recently had with Gladstone: 'Men of Northampton, I come to you with a message from the Grand Old Man [Cheers!]. I told him of our errand here and he laid his hand on my shoulder, saying in his most solemn tone "Bring him back Henry, bring him back."' This affectionate reference to Gladstone as the Grand Old Man is usually attributed to this speech by Labouchere though others had used it before. It was not a label that Gladstone himself favoured since as a vigorous Prime Minister of seventy-two he did not regard himself as old. Undoubtedly Labouchere had exaggerated Gladstone's concern for Bradlaugh, though it was also certainly true that Gladstone, despite his detestation of atheism, had developed a respect for the intelligence,

185

industry and integrity of his Liberal colleague during the few months he had occupied his seat.

The bye-election campaign was not only short, it was sharp and shrill. Interest in it extended well beyond the boundaries of the borough. The national press followed it closely and the general opinion was that Bradlaugh was unlikely to win. He had though one piece of good fortune. No reputable Conservative was willing to contest the seat. Four days before the poll, Edward Corbett was nominated as Conservative candidate. He was a young man with little to commend him other than a father and grandfather who had been Conservative MPs. He had little experience of political campaigns and was a poor platform speaker.

A serious problem for Bradlaugh emerged by way of a scurrilous pamphlet written by Henry Varley, known as the butcher from Notting Hill. He had been a prosperous butcher, was now retired, and was devoting himself to evangelical Christianity and pamphleteering. He was deeply hostile to Bradlaugh. On 29 March he published 'An Address to the Electors of Northampton' in which, among many other contentious comments, he wrote: 'In your town Mr Bradlaugh has disseminated doctrines insulting to God, and degrading in the highest degree to men and women.' Worse was to come. A few days later he circulated 'An Appeal to the Men of England' which he said was for private reading only. He sent a copy to every elector in Northampton and, after the election, to every member of Parliament. This second pamphlet opened strongly: 'Ours is a war in defence of honour and national right, and I send a clarion blast against Charles Bradlaugh, the champion advocate of iniquity and lawlessness.' There followed a compilation of quotations from Bradlaugh's debates and discussions, all inimical to religion, together with references to that 'indecent, lewd, filthy and obscene Fruits of Philosophy'. This pamphlet was difficult to deal with. Much of it consisted of Bradlaugh's words, wrenched from their context, and the rest of it was half truths and falsehoods. Henry Varley would undoubtedly have welcomed a libel action but Bradlaugh had the caution not to bring one. He never hesitated in the right circumstances to sue for defamation and usually won. He recognised that in this case an action would be difficult, time-consuming and expensive. So Annie Besant answered the pamphlet in a series of articles, 'Henry Varley Exposed', in the *National Reformer*.

On the eve of poll Corbett's supporters went round the constituency writing DEAD in large letters on each of Bradlaugh's posters. This shocked everyone until it was realised that it was no more than a cheap election ploy. But it displayed the acrimony of the campaign. Bradlaugh generated hostility amongst his opponents and they were willing to adopt trickery and chicanery to beat him. Nevertheless he won. The result announced by the Returning Officer was: Bradlaugh 3,437; and Corbett 3,305. A majority of 675 at the General Election had been reduced to 132. A substantial number of Liberals willing to vote for Labouchere and Bradlaugh as a team were not willing to plump for Bradlaugh alone. But he was immensely relieved that his core supporters had remained steadfast. He commented in the *National Reformer*: 'The election just ended has been the most bitter I have fought, and some of my foes have been more foul than ever I had thought possible.'

The next assembly of Parliament was delayed until 26 April to accommodate the funeral of Disraeli who had died on 19 April. This gave all the various parties time to consider their response to the Northampton bye-election. Bradlaugh was clear; he intended to present himself in order to take and subscribe the oath. The court had decided that there was no legal impediment to him doing this. He viewed his re-election as a new beginning that cancelled all proceedings and resolutions which had gone before. Of course he knew that some freethinkers, Holyoake prominent among them, thought he was wrong to swear the oath, but Bradlaugh's prime concern was to do his duty to his constituents and he knew that his course of conduct had been consistent throughout.

Gladstone took a legal view of the matter; since Bradlaugh was legally entitled to take the oath he should not be stopped from doing so by decision of the House. If Brand had been a strong Speaker he would now have advised that he would accept no interference with the oath taking. But he was not forceful enough to adopt this course.

He had in mind the Resolution of 22 June and regarded this as still operative. As for Northcote, it took him time to make up his mind. He would have preferred the decision to be made by Gladstone or by Brand. Fearful of his backbenchers, and especially of the aggressive Fourth Party, he took the easy way out. On the day before Parliament re-assembled he wrote a brief but courteous note to Bradlaugh informing him that he felt bound to object to his taking the oath 'in the absence of any statement on your part which might remove the difficulty felt by a considerable number of members'. All was set for another confrontation.

Chapter Forty-nine

ON 26 APRIL THERE WERE MASSIVE crowds outside the House of Commons cheering Bradlaugh as he entered. The public galleries were overflowing. Annie Besant had found a place in the Ladies Gallery and Aveling in the Speaker's Gallery, both expecting the occasion to be one worth reporting. After prayers Bradlaugh, with Labouchere at his side, advanced to the Table intent on taking the oath. As Bradlaugh was about to be sworn, Sir Stafford Northcote rose but the Speaker forestalled him:

> The Member for Northampton, having been introduced, has come to the Table to take the oath. He is prepared to comply with every provision of the Statutes in order to take his seat. Undoubtedly, a proceeding so regular and formal ought to be continued without interruption; but having regard to former Resolutions of the House, and to Reports of its Committees, I cannot withhold from the House an opportunity of expressing its judgment in the new conditions under which the oath is now proposed to be taken.

Speaker Brand was once again passing the responsibility to the House of Commons.

Bradlaugh immediately requested that he be allowed to address the House before any vote be taken. Northcote moved that 'Mr Bradlaugh be not permitted to go through the form of repeating the words of the oath prescribed by the Statutes' but was anxious to say as little as possible. He simply re-iterated the usual Tory view that 'it had clearly been shown that Mr Bradlaugh did not regard the oath as binding on his conscience.'

It was John Bright who most effectively defended Bradlaugh. With constant interruption from the Conservative benches, he emphasised that Bradlaugh had never intruded his opinions on the House. He accused the Conservatives of intolerance and enraged them by quoting Thomas Moore to great effect: 'Bigotry may swell / The sail he sets for Heaven with blasts from Hell.'

It was agreed without a division that Bradlaugh should speak to the House and he took up his position at the Bar. He first answered Northcote's objection: 'I would go through no form unless it were fully and thoroughly binding upon me as to what it expressed or promised.' Then he dealt with his election for Northampton: 'The constituency has judged me; it has elected me. The right of the constituency to return me is an unimpeachable right. I know some gentlemen make light of constituencies; yet without the constituencies you are nothing. It is from them you derive your whole and sole authority.' He referred obliquely to Newdegate: 'I have been plunged in litigation fostered by men who had not the courage to put themselves forward.' He referred finally to public opinion: 'You think I am an obnoxious man, and that I have no one on my side. If that be so then more reason that this House, grand in the strength of its centuries of liberty, should have now that generosity in dealing with one who tomorrow may be faced with a struggle for public opinion against it.' As Bradlaugh spoke the House had at first been deadly silent, observing the rule that a speaker at the Bar be not interrupted. But as he continued and spoke with passion, there was restlessness on the benches, murmurs of approval and cries of dissent. When he referred to Newdegate's litigation he received loud cheers. And there were cheers as he ended, the government front bench joining in the acclaim whist the Conservatives remained silent.

Bradlaugh was followed by Gladstone who spoke more favourably than before of his colleague; 'In my opinion there is very great force in the appeal just made by the Member for Northampton. Now Mr Bradlaugh is on trial before this House, but the House also, permit me to say with great respect, is also upon its trial.' He ended by quoting Bradlaugh's own words: 'If you are unable to fix on me a legal disqualification you must show, and as yet you have made no effort to show, that you have a right to inflict upon me a disqualification which is less than legal.' The final speech was by Sir Hardinge Giffard in which he clearly expressed the essence of the Conservative position: 'It is not an oath unless there is the existence of belief.' 'Mr Bradlaugh says a promise is binding on his conscience. But he has never said it is binding on his conscience as an oath. On the contrary, he proclaims that it is not binding on his conscience as an oath.'

When the vote came Northcote obtained his motion by 208 votes to 175. The House of Commons had again resolved to exclude Bradlaugh. Many Irish members had voted with the Conservatives and there were significant Liberal abstentions. As was now usual, Northcote asked Gladstone for his counsel, and Gladstone repeated that he did not propose to take the matter out of the hands of the majority.

Bradlaugh responded immediately to the vote by coming to the Table again. The Speaker asked him to withdraw. Bradlaugh declared in ringing tones: 'The Resolution of this House is against the law, and I respectfully refuse to withdraw.' Northcote, conscious of his previous experience, was unwilling to move that Bradlaugh be taken into custody. So an extraordinary performance resulted, with the Serjeant-at-Arms removing Bradlaugh to the Bar, only for Bradlaugh to return to the Table, and this sequence repeated time and again. This play of dramatic futility was ended when, with good sense, a member moved the adjournment, agreed to without hesitation. This was the only means by which the House could extricate itself from the undignified predicament in which it had been landed by its own decision.

This adjournment was not the end of the matter, for on the next day, after prayers, Bradlaugh again presented himself at the Table. Labouchere then asked the Government to resolve the difficulty by introducing an Affirmation Bill. Gladstone, speaking in a particularly prolix style, indicated that he might introduce such a Bill if it were not opposed. Northcote, in an equally prolix response, explained he was unable to agree to anything in the nature of a bargain. He was well aware that his followers, and the Fourth Party especially, would do anything to defeat an Affirmation Bill. So eventually after a fruitless debate Bradlaugh withdrew to await the intention of the Government.

Gladstone could not afford to introduce a Bill which by sustained opposition would consume valuable parliamentary time. His priority that session was to enact an Irish Land Bill, against Conservative resistance, to limit the riotous upheavals in Ireland generated by the difficulties of tenant farmers. The Bill was aimed at providing the so-called three Fs demanded by the Irish Land League: fixity of tenure; fair rents; and freedom to sell land leases. The Fourth Party were well aware of Gladstone's difficulty and were willing to use the Bradlaugh issue to disrupt Government business. Lord Randolph Churchill, the Fourth Party strategist, asked Members 'to resist the imperious and arbitrary behests of the prime Minister and to give no facilities for placing in the House of Commons brazen atheism and rampant disloyalty.'

On 10 May Bradlaugh presented himself once more at the Table and again the Speaker made the usual statement and instruction to withdraw. But for Northcote this was now insufficient. If Bradlaugh resumed his usual seat, below the gangway and just outside the Bar, he could at any moment proceed to the Table and interrupt proceedings. So Northcote moved: 'that the Serjeant-at-Arms do remove Mr Bradlaugh from the House until he shall engage not further to disrupt proceedings.' Gladstone, while not willing to move the motion himself, agreed to support it and ask his supporters to do the same. Bradlaugh therefore found himself excluded not just from the Chamber but from every part of the House. Keen himself to see the Irish Land Bill enacted, Bradlaugh decided for the time being to keep away and await the Government's decision on an Affirmation Bill. He gave an undertaking to Captain Gossett that he would not attempt to enter the House without giving due notice.

Chapter Fifty

WHILE WAITING FOR THE GOVERNMENT'S DECISION on an Affirmation Bill, Bradlaugh travelled the country speaking at crowded meetings and getting resolutions passed to support him in his parliamentary struggle. In the *National Reformer* he wrote a leading article 'Appeal to the People' in which he called on 'the people from whom alone Parliament derives its power.' He explained that 'the Conservatives really wish, under cover of my case, to jeopardise the Irish Land Bill and to delay the business of the country. I ask the people to speak out clearly, distinctly, thoroughly and at once on this issue.'

He visited Northampton to organise a meeting to clarify his conduct and to condemn Lord Randolph Churchill and his Fourth Party colleagues for formally opposing Gladstone's wish to amend the Oaths Act. He expressed with his usual passion his determination to persist to the end in his fight. 'If health and life hold, I will win. In this struggle someone must recede, someone must bend, someone must break. This I do pledge myself, that if health do keep and life do hold I will never give way.'

The lawsuit in the name of Clarke was proceeding from one interlocutory hearing to another and taking up much time and incurring much expense. This was indeed its purpose: to propel Bradlaugh into bankruptcy so putting an end to his parliamentary career. But Bradlaugh was fighting every inch of the way, winning some procedural battles and losing others. In the course of this process he pursued a technical legal point. The vote in the House for which he was being sued was cast on 2 July and the writ was served on him that same day. This haste on Newdegate's part was driven by his concern that a friendly party might get in before him with a pre-emptive action. Bradlaugh's case was that the writ of summons, by a legal fiction, had to be referred back to the earliest moment of the day. The writ was, on this supposition, issued before the vote was taken and hence the statement of claim was bad.

This ingenious argument was heard in the Queen's Bench Division on 20 and 21 June before Mr Justice Denman and Mr Justice Watkin Williams. As usual Bradlaugh appeared on his own behalf and Clarke was represented by Sir Hardinge Giffard and Mr Kydd. This was another occasion for Bradlaugh to display his skills as an advocate. His research was exemplary and the judges allowed a side-table for the plethora of law books he brought with him. Altogether he cited in detail twelve leading cases. A distinguished jurist of the day said of his thorough research, 'There is little gleaning to be done after Bradlaugh.' His style of speaking in Court was markedly different from that which he employed on the platform. He spoke with the same authority, but had the advocate's ability to insinuate, to imply and to conciliate. He had a remarkable reverential regard for judges, always giving them sincere respect and even flattering them in subtle and astute ways without losing any of his own masterfulness.

His assertion in this case was that the issuing of a writ was a judicial act and as such must be considered done at the first moment after midnight of the day before. The Court did not recognise fractions of a day and therefore the writ was effectively issued before the vote which gave rise to the cause of action. This was a well-contrived argument and Denman acknowledged that, in several of the cases Bradlaugh cited, strong consequences followed from the doctrine that judicial acts are referred back to the beginning of the day. But the judges found that the doctrine did not apply to the Clarke case. 'A fiction of law exists,' said Denman, 'for the purpose of doing justice and not to defeat justice.' Watkin Williams agreed: 'I do not think there is any authority which compels us to violate the rules of commonsense.' Bradlaugh's comment to his friends was, 'It may be in accord with commonsense, but it is not in accord with common law.'

So Bradlaugh had lost his argument that by presumption the writ had been issued before his vote had been cast. His next task was to argue, this time before a jury, that as a matter of fact the writ had actually been issued before he recorded his first vote in the House.

PLATE 2

Preliminary sketch in chalk and pencil of Bradlaugh
by Sickert (1890).

PLATE 3

Oil Painting of Bradlaugh by Sickert (1890).

PLATE 4

Pen and ink portrait by Sickert published in
the *Whirlwind* (1890).

Chapter Fifty-one

THE JURY TRIAL TOOK PLACE IN the Queen's Bench Division at Westminster Hall before Mr Justice Grove and a special jury beginning on 19 July and continuing for three days. This was the occasion Bradlaugh had been waiting for: the opportunity to cross-examine Newdegate and those assisting him. The nominal plaintiff Clarke was nowhere to be seen. He was a common informer but uncommonly absent from the action conducted in his name. He was represented as usual by Sir Hardinge Giffard and Mr Kydd, whilst Bradlaugh appeared in person.

The public areas of the Court overflowed, largely with Bradlaugh's supporters. Aveling was there, this time in the guise of a court reporter, preparing a graphic account for the *National Reformer*. Labouchere attended the trial, keen to see the contest between Bradlaugh and Newdegate especially when the dispute concerned parliamentary business. George Foote sat beside Bradlaugh for most of the hearing, helping him with his piles of books and documents, and acting as note-taker. The rift between these two which had lasted for three years was now over. They were well reconciled, the younger man willing to be led by the leader of the freethought movement Aveling in his article referred to the colourless eyes of Giffard, which indicated his clear head and cold heart, the thick bulbous lips of Kydd and the horizontal mouth of Newdegate suggesting the slit of a post box. Newdegate, dressed all in black as usual, gave his evidence in sepulchral tones, a voice, Aveling said, that would have made him a fortune as an undertaker.

The purpose of the trial, and the verdict to be rendered was simple. Bradlaugh had voted for the first time in the House of Commons on the afternoon 2 July 1880 after a debate on a new

parliamentary election for the borough of Tewkesbury. The plaintiff
was suing for £500 and the case turned on which came first, the
issue of the writ in the action or Bradlaugh's vote. If the writ had
been issued before the vote it was invalid. Newdegate's evidence
was that he voted in the first division of the day and observed
Bradlaugh coming through the tellers and drew this to the attention
of the clerk of the House, saying, 'this may become the subject
of inquiry'. At the close of the division Newdegate took a cab to
the offices of his solicitor William Stewart in Gray's Inn Square.
Stewart instructed his clerk, his namesake James Stewart, to go
to the Writ Office to get the writ stamped and issued before that
office closed at four o'clock. Stewart junior then went to the House
with Newdegate and served the writ on Bradlaugh at seven o'clock
as he left the House.

The Bradlaugh cross-examined Newdegate for several hours. He took
him painstakingly through the thirty or so items of business that
had occurred between prayers at 2.20 p.m. and the Tewkesbury
division. Bradlaugh was precise, particular and persistent. As the
cross-examination progressed, Newdegate became more and more
confused. It was a hot and humid day and he sweated profusely.
His recollections were vague, his replies meandering He could not
match with his answers the meticulous rigour of the questions.
He occasionally attempted to refer to papers in his pocket but was
instantly reproved, sometimes by Bradlaugh and sometimes by
the judge. The general effect of this cross-examination was to show
that the vote on the division took place not before 4.15 p.m. though
Newdegate denied this.

The most impressive and important phase of cross-examination
was when Bradlaugh asked Newdegate about his financial support
for Clarke:

Bradlaugh: Have you found any funds for Mr Clarke in this matter?
Newdegate: I have told Mr Clarke that this trial seemed likely to
                run on and involve considerable expense and that I
                would support him.
Bradlaugh: Have you found any funds for Mr Clarke in this matter?
Newdegate: I have given an assurance of money.

Bradlaugh: Have you found any funds for Mr Clarke in this matter?

Newdegate: I have endeavoured to procure him support.

Bradlaugh: Have you found any funds for Mr Clarke in this matter?

Newdegate: I mean money.

Bradlaugh: And so do I. [Laughter]

The Judge: The question is have you found him money already or have you promised him money?

Newdegate: I have found him money and I have promised him money.

Bradlaugh: How much have you found him?

Newdegate: In actual money about £200.

Bradlaugh: How much money have you promised him?

Newdegate: I promised him general support in money if the expenses exceeded his means.

Bradlaugh: Was that promise oral?

Newdegate: Oh, I promised in writing.

Bradlaugh: What date is the writing?

Newdegate: I cannot exactly remember.

Bradlaugh: Have you got it with you?

Newdegate: No, I think it is in the keeping of Mr Stewart.

Bradlaugh: Do you produce it?

Sir Hardinge
Giffard: We have got no notice to produce.

Bradlaugh: I never heard of it before.

Bradlaugh: On what day did you give the writing to Mr Clarke?

Newdegate: The document will show that.

Bradlaugh: Did Mr Clarke apply for it?

Newdegate: Not personally.

Bradlaugh: Have you indemnified Mr Clarke against any costs?

Newdegate: The document will show.

The Judge: Perhaps the document may be sent for.

Sir Hardinge
Giffard: I will adopt your Lordship's suggestion.

The document when produced was revealed to be a formal bond of indemnity to the common informer. The Clerk of the Court read the document which provided in part:

> Now I, Charles Newdigate Newdegate, of Arbury, in the County
> of Warwick, Esq., MP, declare myself firmly bound to the said
> Henry Lewis Clarke, his executors, administrators or assigns,
> to pay any sum or sums, which the said Henry Lewis Clarke
> has incurred or will incur in costs and expenses in or about the
> prosecution of the said action, or otherwise relating thereto.
> For which several payments I hereby find myself my executors
> and administrators by those presents.
>
> Dated 14 July 1880. C.N.N.

When the reading of this document was complete, Bradlaugh
quietly turned to Foote and said: 'I have him.'

The next most important witness was James Stewart, the clerk
who took the writ to the Office for issuing. By persistent cross-
examination Bradlaugh established that Stewart's rough diary
suggested the writ was dealt with the day before the vote and that
the time of issue was nearer 3.30 p.m. than 4.00 p.m. Any reader
of the transcript of the trial would be satisfied that Bradlaugh voted
after the issue of the writ. The judge's summing up was on the
whole favourable to Bradlaugh and the jury were locked up to
consider their verdict at 2.38 p.m.

While the jury were out there was a small incident which
illustrated Bradlaugh's character. Foote had recently prepared an
article for the *National Reformer* and knowing Foote was short of
money, Bradlaugh offered him a guinea for it. Thereupon Bradlaugh
discreetly wrapped two half guineas in paper and passed them under
the table to Foote so no one would notice. This generous act, and
the delicacy with which it was performed, when Bradlaugh was
in a state of suspense, was remembered by Foote many years later.

At 3.23 p.m. the jury intimated that they were not likely to
reach a unanimous verdict. Bradlaugh said he would accept a verdict
of the majority but Kydd declined. Asked to confer again, the jury
at 4.20 p.m. brought in a unanimous verdict in favour of Clarke.
Bradlaugh indicated immediately that he would appeal for a new
trial on the grounds that the verdict was against the weight of
the evidence.

The verdict went against Bradlaugh but he had extracted the
vital information that the action by the informer had been

maintained by Newdegate. Bradlaugh was never quite so effective before a jury as he was before a bench of judges. Perhaps his persistent and pertinacious manner, which was successful in extracting information from witnesses, had irritated the jury. It is more likely that a special jury, drawn from bankers, merchants and esquires, would never have allowed themselves to bring in a verdict in favour of a notorious atheist and republican. Bradlaugh had lost and his supporters outside knew it. But that did not stop them cheering wildly as he left Westminster Hall.

Chapter Fifty-two

ON 10 JUNE BRADLAUGH HAD WRITTEN to Gladstone to ask to see him on the matter of the proposed Affirmation Bill. Gladstone's reply of the same day was distinctly cautious: 'On reflection I am of opinion that it will be better if our communications are carried on in writing on this subject. I am sure it is expedient that there be no room for misrepresentation as to what may pass between us.' So Bradlaugh wrote a long letter, setting out his case, and ending with the question: 'Does the Government intend at any time this session, and if yes, when, to take a vote on the question of the introduction of an Affirmation Bill?' Gladstone was in no hurry to reply. For him there were more important issues at stake. But on 2 July he wrote to advise that the Irish Land Bill must take precedence. And on 4 July he made a statement to the House that 'we have no intention of proceeding this session with a Bill in respect of Parliamentary Oaths'. (Cheers from the Conservative benches.) The threatened opposition from the Fourth Party had achieved its purpose.

Bradlaugh had been thwarted and he decided on vigorous action. He wrote a formal letter to the Speaker asserting that the Resolution of the House on 10 May to exclude him was illegal and that to exclude him by force was also illegal. He followed this up on 14 July with a lengthy engrossed statement which he sent to the Speaker, the Clerk, the Serjeant-at-Arms, the deputy Serjeant-at-Arms, the House messengers and the police. After rehearsing the history of his attempt to take his seat he declared:

> And further take notice that it is my intention according to law
> and in compliance with the Standing Orders of the House on

or before the 3rd of August 1881 to again present myself at the
Table of the House for the purpose of complying with the law
and taking my seat and that if you or any or every of you shall
in any way by force interfere with or hinder me or endeavour
to prevent me from entering the House of Commons you will
be acting illegally and in breach of the Peace and in defiance
of the Electors of this Kingdom and of the laws and customs
of Parliament.

He had chosen 3 August as the crucial date because by then the
debates on the Irish Land Bill would be complete.

Throughout June and July Bradlaugh conducted a speaking tour
of the Kingdom in order to garner support. Despite the difficult
litigation of those months he spoke from platform after platform
in the North of England, in Scotland, and especially in
Northampton. These speeches were not directed to atheism or
republicanism, they were to Liberal and Radical clubs rather than
the secularist societies. His concern was the constitutional issues
which accompanied his difficulties in taking his seat. This
constitutional theme he enriched with oratory as good as he had
ever produced. He was speaking for the little man against the
oppressive forces of the establishment, using his own struggle to
illustrate the importance of law and justice as against the encrusted
privileges of the few. There was nothing of socialism in his speeches
for he was unsympathetic to any form of collectivism. His
passionate oratory was on the theme of justice for the individual.

One of his best meetings was in Edinburgh where he spoke
at the Music Hall to an audience of well over 2,000. The chairman
was a brilliant journalist, John McKinnon Robertson, twenty-five
years old but nonetheless a leading Scottish freethinker. Like
Bradlaugh, Robertson had left school at thirteen and educated
himself by constant reading and writing, and was leader writer
on the *Edinburgh Evening News*. He reported that the audience at
the meeting were not natural supporters of Bradlaugh and many
of them resented his views. But once Bradlaugh had demolished
the initial opposition with well directed repartee, he gained the
undivided attention of the audience which rose to cheer him with
repeated acclamation at the end. In his usual way Bradlaugh sought

a vote of confidence and there were no more than a dozen dissentients.

As Bradlaugh toured the country with his message it was remarkable that many newspapers published articles in his favour. The *Birmingham Daily Mail* recognised the principle at stake: 'The question at issue is the right of a constituency to choose its own representative, and that question cannot be ignored because other representatives choose to impose an inquisitorial test as to his religious belief or unbelief.' The *Newcastle Weekly Chronicle* was even more pointed: 'The House of Commons, at the instance of Sir Stafford Northcote, has expelled one of its duly elected members. Yet the right and title of the expelled member are as clear and unchallenged as the right and title of Sir Stafford Northcote himself.'

This provincial speaking tour culminated in a mass meeting in Trafalgar Square on 2 August, the eve of Bradlaugh's planned penetration of the House. The crowd began to build up at 3.00 p.m. and by 8.00 p.m. between 15,000 and 20,000 supporters had assembled, the largest meeting held in the Square up to that date. A platform was erected at the base of Nelson's column facing the National Gallery. Five hundred stewards controlled the crowd and protected the platform by linking arms to form a barrier. Annie Besant was present on that platform standing dramatically between two of the lions. Three hundred Northampton supporters came by special train and were met by Labouchere and escorted to the Square. Rosettes of mauve, green and white were worn by many. One supporter from Hastings attracted much attention by displaying these colours in a bunch of artificial flowers pinned to the high crown of a broad-brimmed grey hat. It was a joyous and yet orderly occasion.

At 7.40 p.m. the chairman of the meeting began reading a list of over fifty places in England and Scotland from where supporters had come. Bradlaugh's speech was brief. He reported that he had heard it said that such a meeting was a menace to the House of Commons: 'But this is a meeting to claim that the law be carried out and the House of Commons, which is the guardian of the law, should not feel menaced because the people assemble to record a protest in favour of observance of the law.' His final plea was that those who had come to hear him should disperse in a quiet and orderly manner.

The size of this meeting and the dimensions of his support had exceeded Bradlaugh's expectations. He was profoundly concerned that the demonstration the next day should be peaceful. His last words that evening to Annie Besant were: 'The people know you better than they know anyone, save myself; whatever happens, mind *whatever* happens, let them do no violence; I trust to you to keep them quiet.'

Chapter Fifty-three

AT 11.00 THE FOLLOWING MORNING EDWARD Aveling arrived at Circus Road to travel with Bradlaugh to the House of Commons. He found him in a serious and solemn mood. He also found him splendidly attired in his parliamentary dress, wearing a new black frock coat and a new black silk top hat. Outside the house a hansom cab was waiting with a horse bedecked in the Northampton colours. An admirer of Bradlaugh's, a radical supporter who was also a cab driver, was devoting himself and his cab to Bradlaugh for the day.

As they drove to Parliament many pedestrians waved them on their way and some hastened to follow them, but it was at Great George Street, at the entrance to Parliament Square that they became aware of the mass of supporters, many with petitions to deliver to their members, that were waiting for them. The Inspector of Police was there leading a force of more than a hundred to control the crowd. He advised Aveling to stay behind and escorted Bradlaugh to the Members Lobby where groups of MPs were clustered gossiping together. Bradlaugh stood alone in the middle of the Lobby facing the Chamber door. Annie Besant, Alice and Hypatia had travelled separately to Westminster Hall. Using large scrolled petitions as their entry ticket they passed through the Hall to the public entrance where Annie stationed herself at the top of the steps leading into the House.

At the door of the Chamber, David Erskine, Deputy Serjeant-at-Arms, was standing with two doorkeepers and four messengers. These staff were not dressed like Bradlaugh in their best, but in their oldest uniforms, prepared for trouble. At ten minutes past twelve, prayers were over and the shout went up, 'The Speaker is in the Chair.'

Bradlaugh, advancing purposely to the Chamber door where Erskine stood in his way, spoke in a commanding voice: 'I am here in accordance with the orders of my constituents, the electors of Northampton; any person who lays hands on me will do so at his peril.' Erskine replied that he had orders not to admit Bradlaugh. 'Those orders are illegal,' declared Bradlaugh, whereupon he stepped forward brushing Erskine aside. This was the signal for the messengers to act, and act forcibly. They grabbed Bradlaugh by his coat, by his throat and by his arms. Bradlaugh fought back, grasping one messenger by his collar and refusing to let go. He stood like an oak rooted to the floor of the Lobby. The messengers were joined by six policemen. These ten, tugging Bradlaugh mainly by the arms, slowly dragged him from the Lobby, down the passage, and threw him into Palace Yard.

This violent treatment of one of their number was watched by several MPs, one of them climbing a pillar to get a better and safer view. The most aggressive was Alderman Fowler, member for the City of London, and the most fanatical of Conservatives. He followed as Bradlaugh was pulled and pummelled into Palace Yard, shouting in his rough voice, 'Kick him out.' The sight of the burly Bradlaugh being manhandled was sickening, even to the police. One of them was heard to say, 'Of all I have seen, I never saw one man struggle with ten like that.' Bradlaugh staggered to a chair gasping for breath, his face deadly white and fixed in a fierce look of determination, his body bent and utterly exhausted. He fainted for a moment or two but recovered when a policeman brought a glass of water which partially revived him As for his dress, his frock coat was torn down one side, his collar and shirt dishevelled and his silk hat ruined. As he sat there, drained of all energy, Alderman Fowler watched from a distance, muttering and mocking.

Whilst Bradlaugh had been resisting in the Lobby, the massed crowd of supporters had become restless. When they heard the noise of conflict, the smashing of doors, the heavy trampling of feet, there was a wild rush to the public entrance, knocking the police to one side like ninepins. Annie, with presence of mind, flung herself between this tempestuous crowd and the police. She was mindful of Bradlaugh's words to her the night before. Planting her slender body at the top of the steps, spreading her arms wide, she used all her vocal power to persuade the militant crowd to back away. Annie's action prevented major violence. The crowd was wild with support for Bradlaugh. Without restraint that crowd might have forced their way into the Chamber, and thrown the Speaker, Lord Randolph Churchill and Sir Stafford Northcote out on to the streets.

One of those in the crowd watching these events with his companions was James Thomson. Now estranged from Bradlaugh, he was still fascinated by this close friend of so many years. He attempted to rush forward but was restrained by those with him.

Inside the House Labouchere was doing his best for Bradlaugh. He raised as a matter of privilege a motion to amend the Resolution of 10 May to provide that Bradlaugh, whilst not allowed to come within the Chamber, would be permitted to enter other parts of the House. The only telling support for this came from John Bright who, referring to the violent expulsion of Bradlaugh proceeding outside, said, 'No such scene has heretofore been recorded in the annals of the House.' Looking at the benches opposite and turning his attention also to members on his own side, including Gladstone, he added, 'Where are you leading us?' When Labouchere's motion was put to the House it was defeated by 191 votes to 7. By the time Bradlaugh heard this result he had recovered sufficiently to make his way through the cheering crowd of his defenders, find his cab and make his way home.

This had been another exercise in defeat for the junior member for Northampton. But at great cost to his health he had achieved something. He had demonstrated once again that the House would use force to prevent him from taking his seat. He had demonstrated to the majority in the House that they were evading their responsibility for the Resolutions they had passed. He had engineered a major incident to prove to Gladstone that an Arbitration Bill was necessary.

Chapter Fifty-four

THERE WAS NO EVENING MEETING PLANNED at the Hall of Science on 3 August but Bradlaugh's supporters wended their way there hoping to see him. When he arrived at eight o'clock the Hall was overflowing. His arms were swathed in bandages, his hands were swollen, and his face though resolute was deathly pale. The meeting was warmed up by speeches by George Foote, Aveling and Annie but the audience had really come to hear Bradlaugh. When he rose to speak there was loud and persistent cheering and the corrugated iron roof rattled in resonance. His voice was unusually feeble and he spoke only briefly, saying it was his duty to thank all those who had travelled hundreds of miles to Trafalgar Square the day before and to the House that day. He said: 'I am proud of you, very proud indeed. It is something for many thousands of men to wait as you did and then go home as orderly as you went.'

He added: 'There is absolutely no precedent for exclusion from the House of a man who has been duly returned, who is subject to no statutory qualification; there is absolutely no precedent for exclusion of such a man by brute force.' He asked all those present to exercise their right to see their MP and present a petition asking the House to rescind the resolutions of 26 April and 10 May. Victory for him would always mean recission of the resolutions that had excluded him. Here at that evening meeting, James Thomson was again present. He was anxious to speak to Alice and Hypatia, on the platform with their father, but again was restrained by his companions.

On Sunday evening Bradlaugh was too ill to give his usual lecture. The audience of 2,000 crammed into every space in the

Hall were disappointed not to see him, but Annie spoke on his behalf. She gave a speech rousing in its intensity:

> Mr Bradlaugh, [she said] bids me tell you that forbearance having been exhausted, consideration having been met with brutality, patience having been greeted with insult, he would no longer think as he had thought, of the dignity which the House was not careful to guard; that he would not only insist upon entering the House of Commons but would insist that every letter of the resolutions which have been passed in regard to him were expunged from the books of the House.

She ended on a militant note advising the audience that: 'They would do well to join the Volunteer Regiments and take advantage of the drilling and training. It was always well to know how to be able to guard themselves.' Two days later in the House of Commons a Conservative Member asked Gladstone about this speech of Annie's but his response was to dismiss it as something the Home Secretary could deal with adequately.

Bradlaugh was now seriously ill. The muscle sheaths in his arms were ruptured, his left arm was held in a sling, and he was suffering from a powerful attack of erysipelas. His doctor recommended a trip abroad but Bradlaugh, with litigation pending, could afford neither the time nor the expense. Instead he went with Annie and his daughters to the seaside, to Worthing in Sussex, where he slowly recuperated. It was two months before he was fit enough to resume his normal schedule of lectures.

The events of 3 August received much attention in the press, a great deal of it hostile to Bradlaugh, but many newspapers recognising the seriousness of the course the House had taken. The *Daily News* of London wrote of him in an editorial: 'We are by no means prepared to defend every step which he has taken, but this is perhaps scarcely the time to criticise his course minutely, and his own imprudence or inconsistency cannot in the least alter the fact that he has been treated with the greatest injustice and that he represents a principle of the highest political importance.' *The Times* of London wrote similarly: 'Mr Bradlaugh and his conduct, for which as a matter of taste and propriety we have not a word to say in defence, wholly disappear in the magnitude of the constitutional issue now raised. There is nothing less than a conflict between the House of Commons and the constituencies of the country.'

Certainly, members of the House of Commons were by a large majority deeply hostile to Bradlaugh's conduct. Many in his own party were unsympathetic, the Irish Home Rulers were against him, but the greatest hostility came from the Tories. Many of the Conservatives would do anything to ensure that he would never take his seat. In September 1881 a new opponent emerged from the Conservative benches, Sir Henry Tyler, a wealthy MP, director of many public companies and a man with influential friends. He had already used his influence to get Aveling dismissed from his lectureship at the London Hospital. He now took advantage of Bradlaugh's absence from the House to mount an attack on the classes held in the Hall of Science. He gave notice on 25 September that he intended to move a motion: 'That in the opinion of the House, the Hall of Science, Old Street, is by reason of its associations not a proper place and that Dr Edward Aveling, Mrs Besant, and the members of the Bradlaugh family, are not proper persons to be employed in the work of instruction in connection with the Science and Art Department of Her Majesty's Government.'

This direct attack on Bradlaugh's associates and his daughters had no merit because not one of them referred to atheism in the course of their teaching and the examination results achieved by the students were remarkably good. As a result of the attack, Annie decided to forgo any salary from her teaching so as not to prejudice the position of Bradlaugh's daughters. The Education Minister, Anthony Mundella, a Radical Liberal, held progressive views on education and praised the work done in these science classes. Tyler had little support from his Tory colleagues. Hostile to Bradlaugh as they were, for most of them it was a step too far.

In the autumn of 1881 Bradlaugh was heavily engaged in litigation. In September he brought a summons against Newdegate for maintaining Clarke in his action as a common informer but the magistrates dismissed it on the ground that the law was obsolete. In November his appeal was heard from the judgment of Justices Denman and Watkin Williams on the technical question whether a writ was void as being dated on the day that Bradlaugh voted. Here once again Sir Hardinge Giffard was Bradlaugh's opponent.

Despite generous comments made by the Lord Chief Justice as to the defendant's 'ingenious and able argument', the appeal went against him. In December Bradlaugh's application for a new trial on the point of fact as to whether Clarke's writ was issued before he voted, was heard by Justices Denman and Hawkins. Going carefully through the transcript of the original trial and hearing Bradlaugh's arguments, these judges were satisfied that a new trial was justified. That was a temporary victory because Newdegate and Clarke, after some hesitation, appealed against this decision and ten weeks later three Lords Justices, Brett, Cotton and Holker, reversed this judgment by ruling that no new trial could take place. This was the low point for Bradlaugh in the Clarke litigation. It looked likely that Newdegate would succeed in making him bankrupt.

Chapter Fifty-five

ANNIE BESANT AND AVELING HAD SUPPORTED Bradlaugh with great effect in his attempt to penetrate the House of Commons on 3 August. These three, the Trinity as they were known, worked well together. Recognising that she would never marry Bradlaugh, Annie had allowed herself to be fascinated by Aveling. He was a man who made a favourable first impression on most women and so it had been with her. For two years they had been constant companions, lecturing together, attending meetings together, studying together, teaching at the Hall of Science together.

Bradlaugh's daughters were aware of the close relationship between Annie and Aveling. Proudly protective of their father, these girls were acute observers and missed nothing. One August Annie and the two girls had gone on holiday to the Channel Islands to explore Jersey, Guernsey and Sark. A few days after their arrival, Annie casually suggested they go to the pier to watch the Southampton boat arrive. To the girls' astonishment, Aveling stepped off the boat to greet them. He stayed only a day or two, but this incident, and there were others, made the girls conscious of the close relationship between Annie and Aveling. They felt for their father who had to endure knowledge of this close friendship though it was likely that his concern was not for himself but to protect Annie from this notorious philanderer.

Despite her fascination with Aveling, Annie was also cautious. She gave Aveling a key to her house in Mortimer Crescent, so he could come and go at will. But it is unlikely that he had a key to her bedroom. Annie did not believe in sex outside marriage and though charmed by him she would have no intention of physical intimacy. Doubtless Aveling would at some stage have attempted seduction but Annie will have been deft enough to decline these advances and yet maintain a friendship.

Bradlaugh well knew of the unreliable character of Aveling, that he pursued young women students and continually borrowed money with no intention of repaying. He was concerned that Aveling might abuse the access he had to funds of the National Secular Society. Bradlaugh arranged that the premises of the Science Classes were leased jointly by himself and Aveling and that Aveling alone was responsible for the rent. These were sensible precautions, bearing in mind Aveling's shameless lack of financial probity.

The National Secular Society was rife with gossip about Aveling, his recklessness and his wrongdoings. One particular rumour came to Bradlaugh's ears – that Aveling, who passed himself off as a bachelor, was actually a married man. Bradlaugh confronted him directly with this allegation and as a result Aveling prepared a statement for Bradlaugh dated 26 January 1882 and entitled: 'Statement about my marriage and reasons for its failure'. In this document Aveling admitted his marriage ten years before to Isabel Campbell Frank. He asserted that he had been urged to marry by the Heads of the Women's Schools where he taught at the time. He said he and his wife had nothing in common. After the marriage she had taken to religion, filled their house with clergymen and had an adulterous affair with one of them. The letters she had written that condemned her had been in Aveling's possession but he returned them to her and promised never to speak of the matter. He had kept that promise until now. His wife had an income of her own and was better off than him so he was not supporting her. He ended the statement by adding that he was willing to answer questions, but only if they came in writing.

This statement was clearly calculated to win Bradlaugh's sympathy, but did nothing of the kind. It was miserably inadequate and could only ruin Aveling in Bradlaugh's eyes. Yet Bradlaugh had to be careful. He had supported Aveling in many ways, shared countless platforms with him, invited him to write regularly for the *National Reformer* and recommended him as a Vice-President of the National Secular Society. He explained his necessary caution in a letter at the time to Hypatia: 'I desire especially to avoid the semblance even of disagreement for it would be open to the enemy to say he quarrelled with Holyoake, with Foote, with Charles Watts and now with Aveling.' He might have added James Thomson to this list of names. Bradlaugh had a well deserved reputation for dealing ruthlessly with colleagues who crossed him; on this occasion he decided to handle Aveling with kid gloves.

Annie too was in no position to break with Aveling at this time. She had vouched for him, praised him in her speeches and writings, voted thanks to him at innumerable meetings. She, even more than Bradlaugh, had been beguiled, duped and deceived. She had her pride to consider. So for both Bradlaugh and Annie, this was not yet the time to drop Aveling.

Chapter Fifty-six

AT THE BEGINNING OF THE NEW parliamentary session on 7 February 1882, Bradlaugh again made his way through throngs of cheering supporters to the House of Commons. The resolution of April 26, that he be not allowed to take the oath, and the resolution of May 10, excluding him from the House altogether, applied only to that previous session so Bradlaugh was once more free to enter the House. The Cabinet expected that Northcote would again move that Bradlaugh be refused permission to swear the oath. They had laid their plans. Their tactic was to move as an amendment 'the previous question'. This was a procedural device, originated by the House itself, which took precedence over all other amendments and which if adopted would close further discussion without a vote on the main motion. The manoeuvre was favoured by Gladstone because it would allow Bradlaugh to take the oath subject to a decision of the Court. It was consistent with Gladstone's steadfast view that the House had no jurisdiction in the matter and that Bradlaugh's right to take the oath, like his right to affirm, should be a question for the courts of law.

Accordingly when Bradlaugh presented himself at the Table, he was intercepted by Northcote, who proposed his customary motion. The Government moved as an amendment the previous question. Bradlaugh asked to be heard and this was agreed. For the third time Bradlaugh stood at the Bar facing the Speaker and spoke to the assembled Commons.

There was laughter from the Opposition benches as he began but he quickly stifled this: 'I appeal to the House to give me a silent hearing. Judges do that. If you are unfit to be judges then do not judge.' [Hear, Hear!] He then dealt with some of the extraordinary statements that had been made about him. 'One noble Lord denounced me as a socialist. I do not happen to be one. I happen to think that socialists are the most unwise and illogical people you can meet. But the noble Lord knew that I ought to be something. [Laughter] I am a red rag to a Conservative bull, and it must rush at me and call me socialist.'

He dealt once again with Northcote's principal argument. 'It is said, "Our real objection is that you have declared that an oath is not binding on you." [A loud Hear, Hear from Alderman Fowler.]' At this Bradlaugh directed his penetrating eyes at Alderman Fowler and paused. 'The hon. Member whose voice I hear now I unfortunately heard on the 3rd of August and heard so I shall never forget it.' Bradlaugh then repeated the statement he had so often used: 'Any form I went through, any oath that I took, I shall regard as binding on my conscience in the fullest degree.' He ended his speech with a concession to the House in relation to any Affirmation Bill it might pass: 'Let the Bill pass without application to elections that have been held previously, and I will undertake not to claim my seat, and when the Bill has passed I will apply for the Chiltern Hundreds. If I am not fit for my constituents they shall dismiss me, but you [he looked steadily round the chamber] never shall. The grave alone shall make me yield.'

The previous question was defeated by 286 votes to 226 and Northcote's hostile motion agreed without a division. The majority included twenty-five Liberals and thirty-nine Irish Home Rulers. The Irish Catholics were now deeply antagonistic to him. Gladstone's tactic had failed and he wrote to Bradlaugh to inform him he could help no further. At least Bradlaugh had not been excluded from the House and was able to observe proceedings from his seat below the gangway and just beyond the Bar.

But Bradlaugh was preparing a dramatic development. Three weeks later Labouchere moved for a new writ for a bye-election in Northampton which he said he did with the agreement of Bradlaugh. There was a brief debate on this motion but it was soundly defeated by a massive majority of 289, only 18 Members voting in favour. As that majority was declared, Bradlaugh walked swiftly to the Table, took a copy of the New Testament from his pocket, read out the words of the oath from a piece of paper, kissed the New Testament, signed the paper and deposited the Testament and the paper on the Table. The House was paralysed and speechless. No one had anticipated that Bradlaugh might administer the oath to himself. The Speaker, slowly recovering composure, ordered Bradlaugh to withdraw. He did withdraw beyond the Bar and then re-entered to take a seat within the Chamber, announcing to the Speaker: 'I did obey your direction, Sir, and now having, in pursuance of the law, taken and subscribed the oath, I take my seat.'

The one member who immediately responded was Lord Randolph Churchill, incensed by what he had seen. Without hesitation he moved that Bradlaugh be expelled because 'his seat has been vacated in the words of the Statute "as if he were dead".' This was the occasion for a passionate speech by Churchill:

> Mr Bradlaugh has deliberately, with intention, and, I may almost say, of malice aforethought, offered a wanton insult to the House of Commons. This is not the first time he has insulted the House. Last session he endeavoured to force his way into the House by sheer muscular force. The Resolution of the House Mr Bradlaugh has deliberately contemned and in a manner perhaps the most insulting that could be imagined. He is an avowed atheist, advances to the Table and pulls out of his pocket a Testament.

At this point Lord Randolph Churchill pointed to the Table where everyone could see the New Testament. 'Or,' he said, 'what appears to be a Testament, for we have not the slightest guarantee that it is not "The Fruits of Philosophy". He has the insanity to imagine that such a course of conduct, such a pretence of complying with a most solemn and sacred form, is not the most deliberate insult which could be offered to the House.'

The debate was adjourned until the next day when Gladstone in a long bland speech repeated his view that the House was acting beyond its powers. He also reiterated his demand that the majority of the House, who had voted decisively against Bradlaugh should devise the means to effect their decision. But Churchill's passionate oratory of the day before proved persuasive and the motion to expel was passed by 291 voted to 83. Amongst those 83 was a vote by Bradlaugh. The tellers reported that he had voted in the Noes Lobby thereby providing grounds for a case.

That vote for expulsion, followed immediately by a vote for a new bye-election, was made on 22 February. The polling day in Northampton was eight days later on 2 March. Edmund Corbett was again selected for the Conservatives and he expected to win. The events of the last few months, coupled to a press generally hostile to Bradlaugh, encouraged him to anticipate success. The Conservatives had been wooing the new electors on the register. Corbett's campaign was largely focussed on Bradlaugh's religious views, rather than political issues. The Roman Catholics in Northampton, aided by a visit by Cardinal Manning, came out strongly for Corbett. But Bradlaugh's supporters remained faithful and Labouchere spent most of the week in Northampton working untiringly for his junior colleague. The result was: Bradlaugh 3796; Corbett 3688. By this small majority of 108 Bradlaugh was returned again, the third time in less than two years. Corbett was disgusted and left Northampton saying, 'I shan't come back to your dirty town again.'

Chapter Fifty-seven

TWO DAYS AFTER BEING RETURNED AGAIN at Northampton, Bradlaugh spent a few days at his favourite spot on the Lea at Broxbourne. Stealing a day with the fishing rod was his only means of refreshment. On arriving back at Circus Road in the evening, he opened a letter from Sir Stafford Northcote informing him of Northcote's intention to adopt the same course as previously, that is to object to his taking the oath. So on 6 March in the House Northcote again moved that Bradlaugh, if he presented himself, be not allowed to swear the oath.

A Liberal member, Mr Marjoribanks (later to become Lord Tweedmouth), intervened to move as an amendment a resolution that the law be changed so as to allow any elected member to make an affirmation, or swear an oath, at his choice. In speaking in favour of his amendment, Marjoribanks declared that he was one of the large sections of the House who regarded Bradlaugh's conduct, both inside and outside Parliament, with something like disgust and indignation. He went further and described Bradlaugh's recent self-administration of the oath as an unworthy manoeuvre. This led Labouchere to observe that he preferred the amendment of Marjoribanks to the reasons he gave for it.

There was a desultory debate on the amendment in which Labouchere undertook on behalf of his colleague that if it were carried, and implemented in a reasonable time, he would not present himself at the Table until a decision on a new Bill had been made. Gladstone supported the amendment but without committing the Government to a time table. When it came to a division the amendment was lost by 244 votes to 259, to the noisy delight of the Conservatives. Twelve Liberals as well as twenty-six Irish Home Rulers had voted with the opposition and thereby determined the result.

Bradlaugh's response to this further defeat was to postpone for the time being any attempt to take his seat. He concentrated on a campaign in the country, speaking at Liberal-held constituencies up and down the land. He recognised that the Government had no present inclination to assist him. He was discovering that Liberals in the constituencies were supporting him with more enthusiasm than Liberals in Parliament. But in any case his attention now had to turn to the common informer litigation in which he was immersed.

On 2 February Clarke's appeal against the earlier judgment that there be a new trial had been successful. Accordingly on 29 March in the Queen's Bench Division, before Mr Justice Grove and Baron Huddlestone, Sir Hardinge Giffard, with Mr Kydd at his side, moved for judgment against Bradlaugh for the statutory penalty of £500 for sitting and voting in the House without taking the oath, together with the costs of the action. It was clearly hoped by Newdegate that this judgment would render Bradlaugh bankrupt and thereby disqualify him from taking his seat. Bradlaugh conceded that he could not oppose judgment for the penalty, but resisted the motion as far as it claimed costs. He persuaded the judges that pending appeal to the House of Lords the £500 should be paid into Court rather into the pocket of Clarke and the Court further agreed that all questions of costs should await the final decision of the Lords. This was vital for Bradlaugh as he was desperately short of funds. He had to borrow the £500 having already found £200 for the purpose of appeal to the Lords and had to supply security for a further £500 in relation to that appeal. He was avoiding bankruptcy only by the slightest of margins. The costly litigation and the time it took up was preventing him from earning the money to pay for it. He appealed regularly for funds in the *National Reformer* which brought in small sums, but he was surviving mainly by support of his friends.

During the hearing on 29 March there was a significant exchange between Mr Justice Grove and Bradlaugh. Grove enquired whether there was to be an action against Newdegate for maintenance.

Bradlaugh explained that in the magistrates' court his summons had been dismissed on the ground that the law was obsolete. Mr Justice Grove: 'But it is by no means obsolete. I set aside an agreement for maintenance only a little while ago.' He was indicating the route that Bradlaugh should take.

Two deaths were announced in the *National Reformer* in May and June 1882. Ralph Waldo Emerson, who Bradlaugh had sat next to in Boston nine years before, died on 27 April. Bradlaugh wrote: 'Thirty years ago I knew his essay on "Self Reliance" almost by heart, and if its mere words are today less ready in my memory it is because at least I have tried to live the self reliance it taught.' On 3 June James Thomson died. The cause of death was certified as a ruptured blood vessel but in recent weeks he had been homeless and continuously drunk. The reference in the *National Reformer* to the death of this old friend of Bradlaugh and one time contributor to the journal was the briefest possible for they had not been on speaking terms for several years. In April 1874 Bradlaugh and Thomson had stood side by side in Highgate cemetery at the grave of Austin Holyoake. Thomson would have been dumbfounded if he had known that eight years later he would be buried in that same grave. But so it happened. Holyoake's widow had remarried and there was a vacant space in that grave. So Thomson's remains were laid next to Holyoake's at his funeral on 8 June.

For twelve months Sir Henry Tyler had continued to place on the Order Paper of the Commons his motion that Dr Aveling, Mrs Besant and Bradlaugh's daughters were not proper persons to teach courses in connection with the Kensington Science and Art Department. When he eventually raised the matter in the House he had little support even from his fellow Conservatives who, much as they detested Bradlaugh, detested even more an attack on him through his daughters. The Minister for Education, Mr Mundella, treated Tyler with officious coolness. He said that 'the Member should have used due diligence to have brought it before the House in less than twelve months. Was it serving the cause of charity and of true religion to attack in this way lady-like and well educated women and to attempt to associate the

Government with blasphemy?' But Tyler, like Newdegate, was vehemently hostile to Bradlaugh. He may not have been able to associate the Government with blasphemy but he could attempt another method of bringing Bradlaugh's parliamentary career to an end. In July 1882 Tyler took steps to prosecute him for blasphemy.

Chapter Fifty-eight

IN MAY 1881 GEORGE FOOTE HAD launched a weekly journal entitled the *Freethinker*. He did this with the support and encouragement of Bradlaugh and Annie Besant who for the first few months published it at their Freethought Publishing Company in Stonecutter Street. The journal was priced at one penny and proved an immediate success. It was designed to be aggressively anti-Christian and the first copy set out its aims: 'It will wage relentless war against superstition and against Christian superstition in particular. It will not scruple to employ any weapons of ridicule or sarcasm that may be borrowed from the armoury of common sense.'

The relationship between Bradlaugh and Foote had been uneasy for some years and between Foote and Annie rather worse than uneasy. Foote regarded her as too theatrical, as a drama queen, and viewed her attachment to atheism as superficial. These were penetrating observations. But in 1881 Foote was back as a Vice-President of the National Secular Society and contributor to the *National Reformer*. Bradlaugh was satisfied that the *Freethinker* would not compete with the *Reformer* which was a heavyweight journal increasingly concerned with philosophy and politics. There was room for a more light-hearted, racy, aggressive and popular journal. The *Reformer* was a broadsheet, the *Freethinker* a tabloid, and they could both survive.

George Foote was thirty-one when he launched the *Freethinker*, a handsome widower with a full curly beard and moustache. He was born to be a rebel. He had immense admiration for Bradlaugh but it was admiration tinged with resentment. He recognised Bradlaugh as the most powerful orator of his generation and as leader of the freethought movement, but Foote wanted to be a leader too. He probably saw the *Freethinker* as a tool for a decisive attempt to succeed Bradlaugh. Foote also had literary talents and the new journal provided him with an outlet for these. He wrote uncompromising prose and decided that his new journal would test the blasphemy laws to their limit.

A few months after the launch, Foote added a weekly series of Comic Bible Sketches which combined humour and mockery in such a way as to be downright offensive to religious minds of that period. Bradlaugh and Annie saw the danger immediately so in November 1881 they prudently ceased to publish the journal. They passed it to William Ramsey, their employee at Stonecutter Street, under an arrangement whereby Ramsey published it on his own account. What Sir Henry Tyler observed was that the journal was sold at Stonecutter Street and that it was written and produced by Bradlaugh's associates. Here was the chance to undermine Bradlaugh's parliamentary ambitions by prosecuting him for blasphemy. As a preliminary, Tyler's solicitors wrote to Bradlaugh on 8 July 1882 asking if he would sell them a copy of the *Freethinker*. Bradlaugh did not fall into that trap. He replied with a printed catalogue of his publications of which the *Freethinker* did not form part. Three days later prosecution for blasphemy was begun against Foote and Ramsay. After evidence had been given the prosecuting counsel, Mr Moloney, applied successfully to join Bradlaugh as defendant.

Foote was probably pleased to be indicted. The *Freethinker* published its next issue with the bold statement: PROSECUTED FOR BLASPHEMY. And the editorial summed it up: 'We are in for it at last.' For Bradlaugh, however, this was a serious matter. He wrote in the *National Reformer*: 'Not a solitary particle of evidence has been tendered to connect me personally with the paper nor to show that I have any interest in it. The attempt is solely to make me technically liable for the acts of others.'

Committal proceedings were held in the Mansion House before the Lord Mayor later in July. The allegedly blasphemous documents were issues of the *Freethinker* published in May. The proceedings were a remarkable demonstration of Bradlaugh's grasp of legal procedures. As in the Knowlton case, Bradlaugh wanted to transfer the prosecution, by writ of certiorari, from the Old Bailey (where he told Foote, 'I am bound to get twelve months') to the Court of Queen's Bench. He also wanted to be tried separately from his fellow defendants. This was vital in order for him to call Foote and Ramsey as witnesses on his behalf.

Bradlaugh was also concerned to determine the precise offence for which he was being prosecuted. There was a common law offence of blasphemous libel which derived from a decision of Sir Matthew Hale in 1676 in the case of *Rex v. Taylor*. Here Sir Matthew had declared that 'Christianity being part and parcel of the laws of England, therefore to reproach the Christian religion is to speak in subversion of the law.' It was by no means clear what was meant by the assertion that Christianity was part of the law nor why that law should not be reproached like any other law but it was on this base that the common law offence rested. There was also a statutory offence of blasphemy governed by the Blasphemy Act 1697 whose short title was: 'An Act for the more effective suppression of Blasphemy and Profaneness'. The Act applied only to those educated as Christians and Bradlaugh, at one time a Sunday school teacher, certainly came within its purview. The offence under this Act was to deny any one of the persons in the Holy Trinity to be God or deny the Christian religion to be of divine origin. The Act provided an increasing scale of punishments. A second conviction, apart from a long prison sentence, would prevent the offender from suing in the Courts or bearing any office which would include being a Member of Parliament.

It was clear why Sir Henry Tyler was determined to prosecute Bradlaugh and equally clear why Bradlaugh wished to know which of the alternative legal routes the prosecution would take. The remarkable fact was that Bradlaugh was breaching the strict terms of the 1697 Act in virtually every issue of the *National Reformer* and in every speech on religion which he gave. Even more extraordinary is that there is no record of anyone ever being prosecuted under that Act. Its presence on the Statute Book was intimidation enough. The Act was not wholly repealed until the

Criminal Law Act of 1967. The Lord Mayor declined to decide by which legal route Bradlaugh was being prosecuted but it emerged eventually that it was the common law offence. On 21 July Bradlaugh was committed for trial.

Bradlaugh's object was to delay the trial for as long as possible and he achieved delay by employing every legal stratagem he knew. On 29 July, before Mr Justice Stephens, a sympathetic judge, he obtained the writ of certiorari, despite the opposition of Mr Maloney, so transferring the trial to the Queen's Bench Court. He then moved to quash the indictment on the ground that the fiat of the public prosecutor, which had to be obtained by Sir Henry Tyler, was bad as being too general. He lost this point though the judge said that he argued the question with 'great power and learning'. He then moved to have two counts struck out of the indictment and this was successful. The matter was important because these counts were ones in which the *Freethinker* bore the imprint of the Freethought Publishing Company. The indictment was eventually included in the list of Crown Cases Reserved for trial in April 1883. Bradlaugh had achieved the delay he sought.

Chapter Fifty-nine

OF THE 103 IRISH MPS WHO were elected to Parliament in 1880, 53 of them were Roman Catholics and they had played a major part, even a decisive part, in the divisions which had excluded Bradlaugh from taking his seat. At first they had supported him, for example in the debate which led to the establishment of the Second Select Committee, but thereafter most of them voted with the Conservatives. This was a blow to Bradlaugh who, because of his army service in Ireland, had great sympathies for the Irish cause. But he understood the power of religion over politics.

A particular influence on the Roman Catholic vote was Cardinal Manning, the leader of the Church in England. In 1880 Edward Henry Manning was seventy-two years old, a former close friend of Gladstone, and wielded enormous influence. He had a strong interest in politics, his father having been an MP. He was a dominant personality with a liking for power. The Cardinal was regularly to be seen in the gallery of the House of Commons and in the Lobby exercising his influence among his Roman followers.

As a young man Henry Edward Manning had been ordained as a priest in the Church of England. His promotion had been rapid. Appointed a curate in the parish of Lavington and Graffham he soon became its Rector. Subsequently he was appointed Archdeacon of Chichester and was known there for his high Anglican approach to his clerical duties. In 1851 he underwent a conversion and was received into the Roman Catholic Church and, his wife having died many years before, he was soon afterwards ordained a priest. Again his rise in the hierarchy was rapid, possibly because he spent so much time in Rome, and within fourteen years he was Archbishop of Westminster, the head of the Church in

England, and ten years later Pope Pius IX elevated him to wear the red hat of a Cardinal. It has been noted many times that a convert to a faith is often more zealous and fervent than one born to it. So it was with Manning. He was an extreme member of the ultramondane wing of the Church – that is the group that took an exaggerated view of papal authority and discipline. He was, it might be said, more Catholic than the Pope and was an ardent supporter of the doctrine of infallibility. Because of this he was not without adversaries in Rome. He played a major part in the Vatican Council of 1870 and was known by his opponents as the 'Diablo del Concilio'.

With this background it is no surprise that Manning possessed and displayed a profound dislike of Bradlaugh and all that he represented. The man of faith was hugely hostile to the man of reason. He believed, like the jurist Matthew Hale, that 'the Gospel is part and parcel of the law of England'. He determined to exercise all his influence to oppose Bradlaugh's attempt to take his parliamentary seat. In August 1880, a few months after Bradlaugh's election, Manning had written an article in the monthly review, the *Nineteenth Century* entitled 'An Englishman's Protest' in which he referred to the Blasphemy and Profaneness Act 1697 reminding his readers that it still stood on the Statute Book. This Act he said, somewhat imprecisely, provided that undermining 'the principle of moral obligation is punishable by forfeiture of all places of trust'. Bradlaugh made no reply.

Soon after Bradlaugh was elected for a third time, Manning wrote a second article in the *Nineteenth Century* again with the title 'An Englishman's Protest'. Here Manning explained in detail why Bradlaugh should not be permitted to take his parliamentary seat. He denied bigotry but was especially concerned at Bradlaugh's qualification to take the oath. 'Where,' he wrote, 'is the bigotry of refusing to allow a man who publicly denies the existence of God and the sanctity of the oath to kiss the word of God, as the law of England explicitly holds it to be, and to make an oath which he believes not merely form but a farce.' Again, Bradlaugh made no reply.

Manning wrote a third article in the *Nineteenth Century* in

September 1882. entitled 'Parliamentary Oaths' in which he stressed the significance of the oath and especially the words 'So help me God'. He wrote: 'We have never yet betrayed the foundation of all morality, personal, private, domestic, public, by effacing the name of God from our laws; and that because the man who has ceased to believe and therefore to live in subjection to God and this law places himself outside the society of man.' In Manning's view Bradlaugh, despite his election three times for Parliament, was outside the society of men. This time Bradlaugh did reply. He was angered and incensed. James Knowles, editor of the *Nineteenth Century*, denied him space to respond despite the Review proclaiming itself as 'absolutely impartial'. So at the end of 1882 Bradlaugh published a tract, in the form of an open letter to the Cardinal, which he entitled 'A Cardinal's Broken Oath'. It was the most powerful polemic he had written.

He began:

> Three times your Eminence has – through the pages of the Nineteenth Century – personally and publicly interfered and used the weight of your ecclesiastical position against me in the Parliamentary struggle in which I am engaged, although you are neither voter in the borough for which I am returned to sit, nor even co-citizen in the State to which I belong. Your personal position is that of a law breaker, one who has deserted his sworn allegiance and thus forfeited his citizenship, one who is tolerated by English forbearance, but is liable to indictment for misdemeanour as 'member of the Society of the Church of Rome'.

He continued:

> But who are you, Henry Edward Manning, that you should throw stones at me, and should parade your desire to protect the House of Commons from contamination? Is it the oath alone which stirs you? Your tenderness in swearing comes very late in life. When you took orders as a deacon of the English church, in presence of your bishop, you swore 'So help me, God', that you did from your 'heart abhor, detest and abjure' and, with your hand on the 'holy gospels', you declared 'that no foreign prince, prelate, state or potentate hath, or ought to have, any jurisdiction,

power, superiority, pre-eminence, or authority ecclesiastical or spiritual, within this realm.' You may now well write of men 'whom no oath can bind'.

Manning had referred to the Blasphemy and Profaneness Act 1697 and Bradlaugh was equally capable of citing legislation. He referred to an 1829 Act which, whilst providing relief for Roman Catholics also provided that any person admitted to an Order of the Roman Catholic Church be taken to be guilty of a misdemeanour and ordered to be banished from the United Kingdom.

> In this country by the Act of George IV cap. 7, you are criminally indictable Cardinal Archbishop of Westminster. You only reside here without police challenge by the merciful forbearance of the community. Was the Rector of Lavington and Graffham covetous of an archbishopric that he broke his oath? Was the Archdeacon of Chichester ambitious of the Cardinal's hat that he became so readily forsworn?

Bradlaugh ended:

> You who have derived profit, pride and pomp from your false swearing – you who sign yourself 'Henry Edward Cardinal-Archbishop' by favour of the very authority you abjured in the name of God – it is in the highest degree indecent and indecorous for you to parade yourself as a defender of the sanctity of the oath. As a prince-prelate of the Church of Rome you have no right to meddle with the question of the English Parliamentary oath.

This powerful and penetrating tract, no more than six pages, was translated into Italian by a member of the Roman Church who had no sympathy for Manning and it was circulated among the hierarchy in Rome. If Manning had aspirations to become Pope, and he might well have had for his ambition was seemingly unlimited, that tract damaged his prospects. He wrote no more articles about the Parliamentary oath, in the *Nineteenth Century* or elsewhere, and never again attacked Bradlaugh in public. But in private he remained assiduous in urging that Bradlaugh not be permitted to take his seat and did what he could to thwart the passage of an Affirmation Bill.

Chapter Sixty

WHEN BRADLAUGH WAS INDICTED FOR BLASPHEMY it was clear to him and Annie that the *Freethinker* could no longer be published from their premises. So Ramsey proposed to leave 28 Stonecutter Street and take the journal with him. But Annie had a better idea. This was an opportunity for the Freethought Publishing Company to move to larger premises. So Ramsey stayed where he was and Annie and Bradlaugh took an expensive lease on part of a building at 63 Fleet Street on the corner of Bouverie Street. This was a good location with freethought connections, for Richard Carlile had for many years operated his printing business directly opposite at 62 Fleet Street.

Bradlaugh had grave doubts about moving because the new premises were expensive. He was heavily in debt and was reluctant to take on further financial burdens. But Annie was persuasive, so they made the move. With Ramsey no longer their employee, Annie and Alice, the elder daughter, managed the publishing side of the business with the assistance of the more experienced Bradlaugh. Annie had her office in the building and there spent her working hours as writer, editor and publisher.

It was at these premises that Annie, with Bradlaugh's support, started a monthly magazine which she called *Our Corner*. The magazine had sixty-four pages, was priced at 6d and the first issue appeared in January 1883. It was intended for a general readership and was comprehensively subtitled: 'A Monthly Magazine for Fiction, Poetry, Politics, Science, Art and Literature'. There was a Political Corner which Bradlaugh contributed. Annie wrote a Science Corner, and Aveling an Arts Corner. There were corners for gardening, chess and for young folk. A puzzle corner was entitled: 'Nuts for Sharp Little Teeth to Crack'. A work of fiction was serialised in the magazine. A significant contributor was John Robertson, the freethinker from Edinburgh who Annie had discovered on one of her trips to Scotland. He had a brilliant mind and could write with learning on almost any subject. There were other contributors, distinguished and not so distinguished. Annie paid well and used the magazine to support talented young writers. It was Annie's hard work which made all this possible. Apart from co-editing the *National Reformer* and writing her regular Daybreak article, she was giving a multiplicity of lectures and earning substantial sums from her booklets such as 'The Law of Population'. She had none of the expenses that Bradlaugh incurred from his parliamentary work, nursing his constituency, and constant litigation.

It was in 1883 that Annie decided to move from Oatlands in Mortimer Crescent to a larger house. One day she took Alice and Hypatia to view a house in Avenue Road, the premier thoroughfare in St John's Wood. The girls were astonished to see such a large house for Annie, her housekeeper and her companion. Annie confided to the girls that she had allotted rooms for their father and themselves. Alice and Hypatia froze. They said little except to suggest that the house did not commend itself to them. It was apparent that Annie retained a hope that she and Bradlaugh might yet live together but the girls knew full well that their father had given up the possibility. His rooms at 20 Circus Road, unsatisfactory though they were, remained his residence. Deeply fond as he was of Annie, all thoughts of sharing a home with her had gone. He would not imperil his parliamentary career. The girls understood their father better than Annie.

Soon after, Annie took another house, which might better be described as a mansion, at 19 Avenue Road. This had a large garden and here she could keep her birds, her dogs and her ponies. Here she could entertain guests and organise meetings. Here she had ample accommodation for friends and colleagues. Here she could satisfy her liking for lavish living.

Chapter Sixty-one

THE FIRST FEW MONTHS OF 1883 were an immensely busy time for Bradlaugh. He was heavily engaged in the Clarke case and in addition had to deal with his own prosecution for blasphemy whilst assisting Foote and fellow members of the National Secular Society with a second blasphemy prosecution. In January he announced in the *National Reformer* that he had to refuse all the many invitations to lecture in the provinces because he would have to remain in London to deal with the matters arriving daily which demanded his personal attention.

The prosecution for blasphemy begun by Sir Henry Tyler in July 1882 was being successfully delayed by the many procedural matters that Bradlaugh was raising. Despite the pending trial, Foote was determined that the *Freethinker* should continue its aggressive mockery of Christianity. At the end of 1882 he published a bumper Christmas number which included a comic strip ridiculing Christ and a cartoon depicting 'Moses getting a Back View' of God wearing tattered clothes with the caption, taken from Exodus 33:23, 'and thou shall see my back parts'. Foote himself described this Christmas issue as a 'very warm publication' and 'well calculated to arouse the slumbering blasphemy law'. He knew he was inviting prosecution again. And so it was, because Sir Henry Tyler initiated a second prosecution, though this time it was conducted by the City of London as prosecutor. Bradlaugh was not included because the *Freethinker* was not published from his new address.

The defendants were Foote as editor and owner of the *Freethinker*, Ramsey as publisher, and Kemp their shop assistant. Committal proceedings were held on 2 February. Foote attempted to emulate Bradlaugh by conducting his own defence and by applying for a writ of certiorari to transfer this trial to the Queen's Bench but Sir Hardinge Giffard opposed the application and it was refused. Though Foote was a practical and persuasive speaker, he had none of the legal skills of Bradlaugh. The three defendants were remanded on bail to appear at the Old Bailey on the 1 March.

In the meantime Parliament reassembled on 15 February for its new session. The first business in the Commons was the reading by the Speaker of a letter from Bradlaugh in which he announced his intention to present himself at the Table again and to do all those things that were lawfully required for him to take his seat. The Government had of course anticipated such action and in the absence of Gladstone the Leader of the House declared its resolve to introduce legislation that would allow Members to affirm. The next day the Attorney-General sought leave to introduce a Bill to amend the Parliamentary Oaths Act 1866 so as to afford an opportunity to those desiring to make an affirmation instead of taking an oath to adopt that course.

A brief debate followed in which Sir Henry Drummond Wolff, speaking from the bench occupied by the Fourth Party, made a sardonic speech announcing that he would not oppose the introduction of a Bill for he was pleased that the Government instead of attempting to force Bradlaugh on the House were at last facing up to public opinion and the opinion of Members. He noted that Gladstone was staying in Cannes, no doubt he opined in order to avoid the debate. Sir Stafford Northcote, not wanting to be outdone by the Fourth Party, also supported the introduction of a Bill and gave notice that he would lead the Conservatives to oppose it on second reading. The first reading of the Bill was agreed by a majority of 131 votes. Bradlaugh was satisfied for the time being.

On 1 March, Foote, Ramsey and Kemp appeared before Mr Justice North and a jury at the Old Bailey. Sir Hardinge Giffard was prosecuting counsel and opened the case by asserting his view that Christianity was part of the common law of England and hence the defendants were not entitled to outrage the feelings of the public by scandalous ridicule of their religion. The trial was remarkable for the extraordinary prejudice against the defendants displayed by Mr Justice North whom Annie Besant described as 'a bigot of the sternest type'. The judge continually interrupted the speeches of Foote and Ramsey and refused to hear as irrelevant the references that Foote wished to cite. Despite the manifest partiality of the judge, the jury after retiring for two hours were unable to reach a verdict.

The judge thereupon decided to hear the case again four days later with a different jury. Foote applied for bail to be renewed but the judge refused him in a peremptory and insulting manner. This was an outstandingly unjust refusal, giving little opportunity for the defendants, confined separately in Newgate gaol, to prepare for the new trial. The second jury was compliant with the judge's views and, without withdrawing to consider their verdict, found the defendants guilty. Mr Justice North sentenced Foote to twelve months imprisonment, Ramsey to nine months, and Kemp to three months, to be served in Holloway gaol. At these sentences there was much hissing in the Court and cries of 'Judge Jeffreys'. Foote spoke above the commotion to address the judge: 'My Lord, I thank you; it is worthy of your creed.'

Many of those who detested the style and content of the *Freethinker* were nonetheless shocked by the severity of the sentences. Misgivings about the judge were expressed in many newspapers. Members of the National Secular Society rallied round the three defendants and Annie started a Prisoners' Aid Fund through the columns of the *National Reformer*. Aveling, who was on good terms with Foote, accepted with enthusiasm the editorship of the *Freethinker* while Foote was incarcerated.

Bradlaugh normally held the judges in high regard but he had nothing but contempt for the manner in which Mr Justice North had conducted this trial. He addressed a public letter to the judge deploring his manipulation of the proceedings. He wrote: 'That you should have held the defendants in custody after the jury had disagreed, and when you had determined to again try them four days later, was mischievously and wantonly cruel... . If you had been prosecutor instead of impartial judge, you could hardly have done more to embarrass their defence than by sending them to this sudden and close confinement.' This open letter, received with approval by many responsible persons, including judges, may well have helped Bradlaugh five weeks later when he faced his own trial for blasphemy.

Chapter Sixty-two

THE END OF THE PROSECUTION OF Foote, Ramsey and Kemp, coincided with the beginning of the last lap in the lengthy proceedings in the case of Clarke against Bradlaugh. The hearing brought in the House of Lords by Bradlaugh as appellant was held on 5 and 6 March. As was standard, Bradlaugh appeared in person and was opposed by Sir Hardinge Giffard and Mr Kydd. This was a vital hearing. So far all judgments had gone against Bradlaugh. If he lost in the Lords he would have to pay the £500 penalty and the much greater sums incurred by himself and Clarke in costs. Bankruptcy would follow and he would then be disqualified from taking his parliamentary seat.

The appeal was heard by the Earl of Selborne, the Lord Chancellor, and Lords Blackburn, Watson, Fitzgerald and Denman. The appearance of Lord Denman on the Bench was most unusual because he was an hereditary peer and not a Law Lord. Bradlaugh had done his research thoroughly and as usual the table before him was piled high with law books, each citation carefully marked. Here, before the highest tribunal, he was at his best. He had a rapport with the most senior judges. They respected his knowledge of the law and the courteous, deferential, even if persistent manner in which he presented his case. For a radical politician he had a remarkable regard for them.

The single point at issue was whether Clarke, a common informer, was entitled to sue. It was admitted that on 2 July 1880 Bradlaugh had sat and voted without taking the oath prescribed by the Parliamentary Oaths Act 1866. Whether Clarke could sue depended upon the interpretation of that Act, which provided that the penalty of £500 was 'to be recovered by action in one of Her

Majesty's Supreme Courts at Westminster'. The question was, is this an action which a common informer can bring or is it one to be brought by the Crown? Sir Hardinge Giffard's argument was brief. The word 'action', he said, included a suit by a common informer but whether it could also be brought by the Crown is doubtful. Bradlaugh's argument was that a penalty imposed by Statute belongs to the Crown unless given in precise terms to an individual. He cited a line of cases to show that if the method of recovery was in doubt then the Crown alone could sue. After further argument, the Lords reserved their opinion.

Three days later, on 9 March, Bradlaugh's counter-attack, his action against Newdegate for maintenance, was heard in the Assize Court by the Chief Justice, Lord Coleridge. On this occasion Bradlaugh was represented by counsel, F. O. Crump and Dr W. A. Hunter, though Bradlaugh did most of the research and appeared as a witness. Hunter was from Aberdeen, a member of the English Bar, and had been Professor of Jurisprudence at University College, London. His politics were distinctly radical and he was known to be sympathetic to Bradlaugh's views on religion. Newdegate was represented as usual by Giffard and Kydd. Again the facts were not in dispute. By cross-examination of Newdegate at first instance, Bradlaugh had established that he had supplied Clarke with a bond to indemnify him against all expenses and costs he might incur in the action. Coleridge conducted the case with the utmost care for he had been advised that both sides would appeal if the judgment went against them. But it was clear that he was unsympathetic to the defence put forward by Giffard. Crump's argument was that without the bond Clarke would not have brought the case. By indemnifying Clarke, Newdegate had committed the tort of improperly upholding the action. Newdegate was aware that the action might result in Bradlaugh's bankruptcy and this secondary object was the main motive in the mind of Newdegate. Sir Hardinge Giffard's argument for the defence was again brief and when the case was adjourned until 17 March he left the matter to be dealt with by Mr Kydd. Lord Coleridge was aware that the House of Lords would shortly deliver its opinion on the main case and so he reserved judgment until that was known.

The House of Lords delivered its opinion on 9th April. The Lord Chancellor in a long and lucid opinion statement concluded that no part of the language of the Parliamentary Oaths Act afforded grounds for implying an intention by Parliament that a common informer, as well as the Crown, had a right of action for the penalty. That penalty was due to the Crown and not to an informer. Moreover he added that Bradlaugh had sat and voted from 2 July 1880 to 20 March 1881. The cumulative penalty (estimated at up to £350,000) was an enormous sum and Parliament would surely have hesitated to place it in the power of a common informer to receive this. The Lord Chancellor's opinion was therefore in favour of dismissing Clarke's action and that he pay the costs of the appeal.

Lord Blackburn gave a dissenting opinion. He was known as a hesitant judge and he hesitated in this matter, recognising, as he said, that the case was one where opinions might differ. Lords Watson and Fitzgerald delivered opinions agreeing with the Lord Chancellor. Then Lord Denman decided to take part. It was unheard of for lay peers to vote on appeals and this was the last occasion on which it happened. The unconventional peer cast his vote with Lord Blackburn but it was of no effect since the majority was with the Lord Chancellor.

This vital victory for Bradlaugh was won by thorough research and persuasive advocacy over almost three years. But the costs he would recover were small. He could survive financially only if he also won the action for maintenance.

Chapter Sixty-three

AS SOON AS HE HAD SUCCESSFULLY cleared the hurdle of the Clarke trial Bradlaugh was faced with a further hazard. On 10 April, the day after the House of Lords handed down its opinion, Bradlaugh and his co-defendants Foote and Ramsay were tried for blasphemy arising from the articles published in the *Freethinker* between March and June 1881. The trial was conducted by the Lord Chief Justice, Lord Coleridge and a special jury, in the splendid new Royal Courts of Justice in the Strand, opened only a few months before. Bradlaugh was representing himself whilst Foote and Ramsay, brought up from Holloway gaol for the trial, had counsel to advise them. Sir Hardinge Giffard was counsel for the Crown and with him Mr Moloney.

The Court was crowded with lawyers fascinated by the case and the public gallery was full of the defendants' friends. Bradlaugh had Foote on one side and Annie Besant on the other and in front of them the usual pile of law books. Before the special jury was sworn, Bradlaugh applied to be tried first and separately. This was to enable him to call his co-defendants as witnesses. As might be expected, Giffard vigorously opposed this application but Lord Coleridge granted it. Giffard had to accept the decision but did so with bad grace and much muttering. Here was the first sign that in this trial, as distinct from the one conducted by Mr Justice North, the prosecution was not to have it all its own way. The Crown case was that the Freethought Publishing Company had been the original promoter of the *Freethinker*, but the change in ownership in November 1881 was a pretext and that Bradlaugh remained the real publisher. Bradlaugh's defence was that during the period April to May 1882 he had nothing to with the *Freethinker* because his company had ceased to publish it in November 1881. He did not write for it, he did not edit it, he did not even see it before publication. His sympathy for the *Freethinker* was clear but he firmly denied responsibility for it.

Bradlaugh's defence required proof by witnesses and the most persuasive of these was Annie. She gave clear and precise testimony that it was she who had urged that she and Bradlaugh cease publication of what had become an illustrated journal. She insisted that from November 1881 the Freethought Publishing Company had no responsibility for the *Freethinker*. Annie stood up well to cross-examination, she was used to it. Her frankness discomfited Sir Hardinge Giffard and he could not shake her.

During the trial it was revealed by Bradlaugh's persistent questioning that the prosecution had gone behind his back to inspect, without any notice, his account at his bank, a few doors from his residence – the prosecution had been engaged in an illegal fishing expedition. The most damaging disclosure was that one of those inspecting the account was Mr Moloney, junior counsel. A gasp of surprise went round the Court at this revelation and Coleridge himself exhibited displeasure that a member of the Bar had stooped to examine Bradlaugh's bank accounts.

Just before adjournment for lunch on the second day, Bradlaugh intimated to Coleridge that he intended to call Foote and Ramsay as witnesses. Coleridge said quietly, but with clear meaning, 'Do you think it necessary?' Bradlaugh was faced with a difficult choice. If he called Foote and Ramsay they might decline to give evidence to avoid incriminating themselves; or they might save the case for him but at their expense. Over lunch, Bradlaugh, influenced by Coleridge's brief question, decided not to call them. Coleridge was evidently displeased when Giffard protested that this denied him an opportunity for cross-examination and he would therefore be asking the jury to draw certain conclusions. So Bradlaugh did call his co-defendants, just for the purpose of cross-examination. Foote and Ramsay gave no help to Giffard. They managed to tread without mishap the delicate path of avoiding harm to Bradlaugh or to themselves.

In a lengthy and lucid summing up, Coleridge denied that

Christianity was part and parcel of the law of the land or that to assail the truth of Christianity was to break the law. He adopted a liberal definition of blasphemy laid down by Starkie, a legal scholar: 'Blasphemy consists in the wilful intention to insult and mislead others by means of licentious and contumelious abuse applied to sacred objects.' On this basis the truth of Christianity may be denied in a decent way and with regard to the feelings of others. Coleridge went on to explain that the essential question for the jury was whether Bradlaugh was in any way responsible for the issues of the *Freethinker* alleged to be blasphemous. 'If he has not been proven to be responsible for the publication, better – a thousand times better that he should be acquitted than that the faintest or slightest disturbance of justice or distortion of the law should be made for the sake of a cause, however good.'

The jury was out for just over an hour. Bradlaugh knew that his parliamentary career lay in their hands. As they returned he stood rigidly to attention but his whole body relaxed as he heard the verdict of 'Not Guilty'. There were tears in his eyes as Foote squeezed his hand – a silent understanding between these two men. A sudden outburst of cheering from the public gallery was suitably checked by the Lord Chief Justice: 'This is not a place of entertainment but a Court of Justice.' All those cheering were doing so because they felt that Coleridge's Court had that day done justice.

Two days after the end of that blasphemy trial, Lord Coleridge read his written judgment in the Newdegate maintenance case. Coleridge knew of course that the House of Lords had dismissed Clarke's action with costs on the ground that 'he had not any right or interest in the penalty he sued for'. If Clarke had no right or interest it followed that Newdegate had none. After analysing the precedents, he concluded 'that Mr Bradlaugh is entitled to an indemnity for every loss which Mr Newdegate's maintenance has caused him and if that cannot be agreed between the parties it must go to an official referee'.

Newdegate, no doubt on the best advice, decided not to appeal. The costs and damages he had to pay were heavy. Though a landowner he was not as wealthy as he appeared to be and there were plentiful rumours that he was financially embarrassed by the several thousand pounds he had to pay and had to sell the timber on his land. He grumbled at Bradlaugh from time to time in Parliament but gave him no more serious trouble. Nevertheless Bradlaugh's total costs were not fully met either by the House of Lord's judgment or the maintenance claim. He had escaped bankruptcy but was still in debt.

The day after the maintenance judgment was delivered, Coleridge with a new jury resumed the blasphemy trial with Foote and Ramsay as defendants. Bradlaugh was in Court the whole time to give support to the accused. This trial was remarkably different from the one before Mr Justice North which had sent them to Holloway gaol. Coleridge was courteous as North had been obnoxious. Foote was allowed without interruption to make the citations from approved writers which North had denied him. The jury deliberated for several hours but were unable to reach a verdict. Since Foote and Ramsey were already incarcerated in Holloway for a similar offence the prosecution sought the leave of the Attorney-General to enter a *nolle prosequi*, that is to abandon the prosecution.

In most of the legal battles which Bradlaugh fought in the first four months of 1883, Sir Hardinge Giffard had been his adversary. Giffard was the leading lawyer of the day yet Bradlaugh had proved more than a match for him. These victories flowed from Bradlaugh's thoroughness combined with a profound practical understanding of the law. He had mastered the substantive civil and criminal law, he had proved an effective pleader, he was a skilful cross-examiner, able to elicit vital evidence from a witness, and he was able to address a jury with deftness and authority. He never missed a point and was persistent in presenting his case without prompting the hostility of the senior judges who treated him with respect. His greatest legal skill was his mastery of procedure. English common law is founded on procedure and he understood this.

It was said frequently of Bradlaugh that his legal abilities were so evident that he would have made a great silk. But this is to misunderstand him. As a young man he had attempted to become a lawyer but in the 1880s it was his parliamentary career, rather than thoughts of a practice at the Bar, which motivated him. He was not the man to speak to another's brief. For him mastery of the law was a protection and a tool to enable him to survive and succeed in his greater purpose of generating and implementing radical political ideas.

Chapter Sixty-four

THE SECOND READING OF THE AFFIRMATION Bill began on 23 April. Much concern had been expressed in the country about legislation that for the first time would admit an avowed atheist to take a seat in the House of Commons. The Conservatives made desperate efforts to arouse feelings against the Bill. Whilst non-conformists and congregationalists gave weak support to the Bill, it was vigorously opposed by the English and Irish Bishops, and so by their clergy who in their turn had a powerful influence on their parishioners. Cardinal Manning played a major part in alarming public opinion, though he was careful to do it from behind the scenes. In the 1880s signed petitions presented to Parliament were a common method of attempting to influence legislators by gauging public opinion. Manning was influential in garnering petitions against the Bill which eventually came to 700,000. Bradlaugh through the National Secular Society also gathered petitions but these amounted to no more than 175,000. This ratio of four to one may have overestimated the hostility of the public but there could be no doubt that press and public alike were ill-disposed to the proposed legislation.

The Bill had been drafted in February whilst Gladstone had been recuperating in Cannes, so he took no part in its formulation. It amended s.4 of the Parliamentary Oaths Act 1866 to allow those who wished to make a solemn affirmation in preference to taking the oath to do so. There had always been a sprinkling of unacknowledged atheists in the House of Commons who had quietly taken the oath. They sat in Parliament *de facto*; this Bill would allow them to sit there *de jure*. Gladstone decided that the Bill was sufficiently important that he should put the whips on, but he did not make it a matter of confidence. This was not an issue which Gladstone would wish to take to the country.

Many members intended to speak in the debate not simply because of their own views but because of the concern of their constituents. The debate extended over five days and on one of these it took precedence over all other business. Bradlaugh was present the whole time, sitting in his seat under the gallery and beyond the bar, able to see and hear all the proceedings. The first speaker was the Attorney-General, Sir Henry James, who supplied a detailed historical account of the development of the Parliamentary oath and expressed his view that a constituency should be free to elect any member they chose and Parliament should then allow him to take his seat An early speaker from the opposition benches was Sir Hardinge Giffard. Having been recently worsted by Bradlaugh in the courts he was now intent on keeping him out of the House. It was a fallacy, he said, to suppose that the mere kissing of the book and repeating certain words constituted taking the oath when those words 'are to me sounds conveying no clear and definite meaning'. The Bill he asserted was confined to one person and should be entitled: 'A Bill to enable Mr Bradlaugh to take his seat'. The Lord Chief Justice had expressed his view that Christianity was not part of the common law of England. Giffard would have none of it and repeated his opinion that Christianity was part and parcel of the common law. He ended grandly, 'Were they going to allow a person who had railed against religion, the common law of the land, to become one of the makers of the law, because they would admit no enquiry into his religious beliefs?'

It was on the second evening that Gladstone delivered a speech that had been carefully crafted. It was said of Gladstone that he could do excellently things that he hated to do. To be associated, even indirectly, with Bradlaugh was anathema to him. To have an atheist as a political colleague was deeply distasteful. But as he did the research for his speech, as he studied the practices of other legislatures, he came to see the question as one of principle, of justice, and could speak in favour of the Bill with conviction and certainty. He began by asserting that there was no legislative power whatever that prevented atheists duly elected from sitting in the House. As to public opinion he argued that the dignity of the House and the interest of the country demanded that the painful controversy be brought to a close. In dealing with the preponderance of petitions against the Bill he said:

> Do you suppose we do not feel pain? Do you suppose that we are unaware how difficult – how all but impracticable – it has become to do what we believe to be strict justice? But the difficulty is the measure of the duty and the honour; and just as if we were in the jury box and a person stood before us on a criminal charge, we will put a strong hand of self-restraint upon ourselves, and we will take care that full justice – nothing more and nothing less – shall be awarded to every citizen of England.

He then dealt with what he saw as the crucial issue. 'The business of every man in controversy is to try to find out what is the main and governing contention of his adversaries. As I read it, the governing contention is this – that the main question for the State is not what religion a man professes, but whether he professes some religion or none.' He referred to the speech of Sir Hardinge Giffard who had said that there should be some form of belief and some recognition of the supernatural. But Gladstone said, as confidently as he supported the Bill, he did it on the ground that this argument was a hollow and false one. He said of the opposition: 'They tell us that you may go any length you please in the denial of religion, provided you do not reject the name of the Deity. They tear religion in shreds, and they set aside one particular shred of it, with which nothing will induce them to part.' By making this point so clearly and eloquently Gladstone inverted the argument the Opposition had made. 'I am not willing, Sir, that Christianity, if appeal is made to us as a Christian legislature, should stand in any rank lower than that which is indispensable.' So it was Gladstone's Christian belief that persuaded him to support the Bill: 'The true and wise course is not to deal out religious liberty by halves, by quarters and by fractions, but to deal with it entire, and to leave no distinctions between man and man on the ground of religious differences.'

He then quoted from memory six lines, noble and majestic lines he called them, from the Latin poet Lucretius. He translated the essence of these as 'Divinity exists in remote inaccessible recesses of which we know nothing; but with us it has no dealing, with us it has no relation.' As Gladstone spoke these Latin words, in his beautifully modulated voice, Members of the House were visibly moved, by the learning of the Prime Minister as much as by the meaning of the words. He finished by saying:

> I have no fear of atheism in this House. Truth is the expression of the Divine mind; and however little or feeble our vision may be able to discern the means by which God will provide for its preservation, we may leave the matter in his hands and we may be quite sure that a firm and courageous application of every principle of justice and of equity is the best method we can adopt for the preservation and influence of truth.

Gladstone's speech deeply affected the whole House, even those members opposed to him. The Chamber had been full to overflowing whilst he spoke but there was an immediate exodus after he had finished as though members wished to leave the debate in order to discuss and better contemplate what they had heard. The speeches that followed varied from the mediocre to the banal until Lord Randolph rose to move successfully that the debate be adjourned early until the following Monday so as to give the House time for reflection.

Chapter Sixty-five

ON MONDAY EVENING WHEN THE DEBATE was resumed it was clear that Lord Randolph Churchill, the opening speaker, had done much reflection and much research over the weekend. It was his practice when preparing a speech to confine himself to his study and not emerge until he had a 'red hot' draft. He always memorised his speeches and this gave them an air of spontaneity. He was a slight man, with a penetrating voice and a pronounced lisp. His speeches were imbued with audacity, vigorous language and striking metaphors. Whereas Gladstone as a speaker was erudite and emollient, Churchill was forceful, and aggressive with a touch of vulgarity.

He began by asserting that there was no possibility of compromise between Government and Opposition: 'They had all gone too far to recede from the positions they had taken up.' He observed that in the 'wonderful oration of the Prime Minister he did not once dwell upon the rights of Northampton or of Mr Bradlaugh. He did not mention these because in the matter which the House was considering Parliament recognised no rights but its own.' The position was, he said, that the constituencies might elect whomsoever they pleased, and Parliament might admit or reject those who were chosen.

He continued: 'Was it expedient to alter the laws of England for one man – representing, as far as they knew, only himself.' Then he made a severe attack on those who supported atheism: 'Let them consider for a moment who were the classes outside who were opposed to the representatives of atheism. They were the religious, the law abiding and the industrious. Who were the personal supporters of atheism outside the House? For the most part they were the residuum, the rabble and the scum of the population; the bulk of them were persons to whom all restraint, religious, moral, or legal was odious and intolerable.' Bradlaugh, listening to this speech from his seat under the gallery, was never to forget that Lord Randolph Churchill had described his supporters as 'the rabble and the scum'.

Churchill then dealt with the judgment of Lord Coleridge in the recent blasphemy case. 'From the days of King Alfred to the days of Queen Victoria, by the common law of England, open and notorious atheists were absolutely incapable of discharging any public duty, or filling any position of confidence and trust.' He said that he knew this had recently been denied by Lord Coleridge: 'but Lord Coleridge was obtaining an unfortunate celebrity for allowing his political opinions to be incidentally set forth from the judicial bench; and though Lord Coleridge might be a distinguished judge, no one had ever yet claimed for him that he was a great lawyer. His law might be dismissed without further notice.' This was a remarkable attack by a member of Parliament on an eminent Lord Chief Justice.

The speech resounded with lively comment and memorable phrases, honed by Churchill over the weekend. Referring to his attack on Bradlaugh he said: 'if they tell me that my argument was an argument *ad hominem*, my reply is that their legislation was legislation *ad hominem*'. A speech like this was designed to end on a strong note:

> It was of course possible – he trusted it was not probable – that in this matter the Opposition might be ultimately be defeated; but should that be so, and should the time arrive, as in that case it most certainly would, when *The Fruits of Philosophy* should become the Bible of the people and when the age of so-called 'Reason' should have supplanted the age of Christian morality, it should then be recognised by a suffering posterity that these great principles were not so sacrificed, and that their great cause was not lost, except after the bitterest conflict which could be recorded on the annals of a Parliament or in the history of a people.

Churchill's speech had been completely different from Gladstone's but of the same high intensity. Where Gladstone had reasoned carefully and exhibited tolerance, Churchill had been combatant and compelling. Political opportunist that he was, Churchill had seized the chance of dominating the House. This one speech marked him out as a future Cabinet Minister and one of the leaders of his party. Labouchere followed him and in a lengthy speech praised him with faint damnation. 'I am willing to admit that the speech of the noble Lord was the ablest which had been achieved from his side of the House, for more wretched debating than was exhibited by the Opposition I have never heard in my life.' Speeches that followed lived up to Labouchere's criticism though there were flashes of imagination from a few members.

Charles Newdigate Newdegate, speaking on the last day, criticised the Lord Chancellor who he pointed out had drafted the Parliamentary Oaths Act when he had been Attorney-General. He also joined in criticism of Lord Coleridge who had described his conduct as legally discreditable. In a rambling speech Newdegate complained that it was the Government, and not him, who should have brought the action against Bradlaugh. The final speech for the Opposition was an uncomfortable one by Sir Stafford Northcote. He showed that he did not have Gladstone's capacity for doing well a task which he disliked. His main concern was to show why, having agreed that the Bradlaugh issue be resolved by an Affirmation Bill he was now going to vote against it.

When the question was put late at night on 3 May the Bill was defeated by 292 votes to 289. The Opposition was jubilant and there were frenzied shouts of delight from their benches with waving of arms and flashing of handkerchiefs. The failure was a blow for Gladstone and the worst discomfiture of his second administration. His Ministry had been defeated and deflated. He had hoped to put an end to the Bradlaugh controversy but it was now certain to give him further trouble. Lord Randolph Churchill was triumphant and regarded by his party as their champion. Conservatives had voted against the Bill to a man. Despite being whipped, nine Liberals voted with the Opposition and several abstained. The Irish Nationalists also claimed the victory since 45 had voted with the Opposition. Their cry was: 'The Irish have beaten Bradlaugh.'

But Bradlaugh was not beaten. The Affirmation Bill having failed he was ready yet again to present himself at the Table in order to take and subscribe the oath of allegiance.

Chapter Sixty-six

THE NEXT MORNING BRADLAUGH ROSE EARLY to deliver a letter to the Speaker. He asked the Speaker to call him that day to the Table to take the oath and failing that he sought leave to be heard once more at the Bar. When the House assembled, Speaker Brand, hesitant as ever, left the decision to members. Northcote moved his usual motion that Bradlaugh be not permitted to go through the form of taking the oath but he raised no objection to Bradlaugh addressing the House.

So Bradlaugh stood for the fourth time at the Bar surveying both sides of the House with his penetrating eyes. He had grown stouter with the years. Bulky and resolute, he spoke without notes with vigour and confidence. He first dismissed the suggestion, made by Newdegate, that he was a candidate of the Government put forward by the Government. 'I have never had, directly or indirectly, the smallest aid or assistance from either the present Prime Minister or from any member of the Liberal party in any of the elections I have fought.' He emphasised that there was no declaration of atheism involved in what was said at the Table and no member had a right to examine his opinions [Loud cheers from the Liberal benches]. 'Under great temptation I have refrained from saying one word which could wound the feelings of the most religious.' He dealt firmly with the view that he was against marriage and in favour of socialism. 'Members who have said that I attacked marriage and the family, cannot have read what I have said on the subject for I have never in my life attacked either. Members who charge me with socialism and communism are ignorant of the whole history of my life and the whole political strife in which I have been engaged.' [Hear, Hear.]

Bradlaugh then maintained his view that the House had no right to stand between him and his seat and challenged it to declare his seat vacant at once so he might again let the people of Northampton decide at the ballot box. In his peroration he referred to the speech of Lord Randolph Churchill:

> I heard a strange phrase from the noble lord, that both sides had gone too far to recede. The House honours me too much in putting me on one side and itself on the other. The House, being strong, should be generous. The strong can recede, the generous can give; but the constituents have a right to more than generosity – they have a right to justice. The law gives me my seat. In the name of the law I ask for it.

As Bradlaugh returned to his regular place, under the gallery but outside the Chamber, Labouchere moved the previous question, a tactic approved by Gladstone, which would have removed any obstacle to Bradlaugh coming to the Table and taking the oath. In the brief debate that followed, Newdegate made a fanciful point that if Labouchere's motion were carried Bradlaugh might come to the House late at night when it was nearly empty and unable to defend its dignity by excluding him. In the division that followed, Labouchere's motion was defeated by a majority of 106 and Northcote's motion approved. Once again the House had defeated Bradlaugh.

Whenever he faced such a setback, Bradlaugh's response was to tour the country using his oratory to gather support. In the next few weeks he visited many provincial cities, especially in the North of England, and spoke to over 300,000 people in all obtaining almost unanimous assent. His audiences consisted not only of secularists and freethinkers but of Liberals generally. The view in the country and in the press was slowly moving in his favour. His persistence in claiming his seat was generating admiration. There was still plenty of hostility, mainly from Conservatives and the professional classes, but there was an undoubted shift in opinion.

This provincial tour was completed by a mass assembly in Trafalgar Square on 6 August. But the most interesting meeting was held two weeks before in St James's Hall, Piccadilly. The hall was densely packed and dressed overall with flowers in mauve, green and white. Thousands of people were unable to gain admission and just stood outside waiting to greet Bradlaugh as he left. Labouchere was the chairman with Bradlaugh on one side and Alice, Hypatia, Annie and Aveling on the other. Labouchere's message was that in attacking Bradlaugh and Northampton the House of Commons had attacked every constituency and every man. 'The House of Commons was using its privilege not to defend the liberties of the country against the inroads of monarchs but to oppose the constitutional rights of the people of England.' Bradlaugh made plain to his supporters that he would engage this fight to the end. The end was not merely the taking of his seat in the House. 'How will the struggle end?' he asked. 'It will end when in my seat in the House I move that these resolutions that have excluded me be expunged from the pages of the journal of the House.'

In the meantime Bradlaugh had decided on a new plan of action. He would endeavour once more to take his seat and if the Serjeant-at-Arms, Captain Gossett, indicated that he would exclude him by force he would bring an action against him. In this way the Courts would be bound to decide whether or not his exclusion was lawful. Accordingly on 6 July Bradlaugh wrote an open letter to Gladstone announcing that he would at an early date take his seat for the borough of Northampton. 'In doing this I shall claim to disregard the Order of the House made this session. I cannot and must not passively permit my constituents to be robbed of the voice and vote to which they have a constitutional right.' On 9 July Northcote swallowed the bait and moved: 'That the Serjeant-at-Arms do exclude Mr Bradlaugh from the House until he shall engage not further to disturb the proceedings of the House', a motion passed by a majority of 167.

By an exchange of correspondence with Captain Gossett, Bradlaugh obtained confirmation from him that it would be his duty, in obedience to the Order of the House, to exclude Bradlaugh from the House until otherwise instructed by the Speaker. Bradlaugh established that the requirement that 'he engage not further to disturb the proceedings of the House' meant that he should not attempt to take the oath. This confirmation by the Speaker was necessary because six months before Bradlaugh had unsuccessfully brought an action against Erskine, Gossett's deputy, for damages for the assault made on him as he attempted to enter the Commons on 3 August 1881. The action against Gossett was better formulated to test whether the House had power lawfully to exclude him.

Bradlaugh commenced the action in the Queen's Bench Division on 19 July and on the following day the matter was debated briefly in the House. Sir John Gorst argued that the Court had no jurisdiction to hear the case. Sir Hardinge Giffard contended that to allow an officer to appear in the proceedings was tantamount to the surrender of the privileges of the House. Nonetheless the House authorised Captain Gossett to appear and plead in the action. One Conservative Member suggested that Giffard should act as counsel for Gossett but the House finally appointed the Attorney-General to represent it. The stage was set for a determination of the extent of the lawful powers of the House of Commons.

Chapter Sixty-seven

THE HEARING IN *BRADLAUGH V. GOSSETT* began in the Queen's Bench Division on 7 December 1883. A month before that Bradlaugh had applied for the case to be tried by a full Court on the ground that it dealt with a fundamental issue of Parliamentary privilege. The Attorney-General was against him on this but the Court agreed. So the case was heard by Lord Coleridge, the Lord Chief Justice, Mr Justice Stephens and Mr Justice Matthew. The Attorney-General appeared with two juniors whilst Bradlaugh represented himself. The case being on demurrer to Bradlaugh's Statement of Claim it consisted only of legal argument which fell mostly to Bradlaugh.

Bradlaugh's claim was that as an elected member of Parliament he was obliged by a statute of the reign of Richard II to take his seat on pain of a fine or imprisonment. He maintained that the Order of the House of 9 July 1883 which excluded him 'until he shall engage not further to disturb the proceedings' went beyond the jurisdiction of the House and was therefore void and of no effect. He further sought an injunction to restrain the Serjeant-at-Arms from acting on the Order.

He argued that once an MP had been duly elected no one could lawfully hinder him from taking his seat. The duty of the House was to see the oath taken whilst it was sitting and with the Speaker in the Chair. Bradlaugh then cleverly cited the recent action of *Clarke v. Bradlaugh* to support his argument. In that action Clarke had charged him with not having taken the oath as prescribed by the Parliamentary Oaths Act 1866. Bradlaugh had argued that a resolution of the House had forbidden him from doing so but that argument had failed. It thus appeared that a resolution of the House did not over-rule the statute and by necessary implication the statute was pre-eminent and the Commons had to give effect to it. This was an ingenious argument but the Court was not persuaded.

A significant point emerged from the trial in an exchange between Bradlaugh and Stephens J. The judge agreed with Bradlaugh that the 1866 Act said nothing about administering the oath and therefore any member might take and subscribe it himself by an act of self-administration, provided the Speaker was in the Chair.

The judges put to Bradlaugh that there was an essential distinction between two situations. The first was where there was an action between party and party in which the legality of a resolution of the House rose incidentally. Here the Court may over-rule the resolution if it was necessary to do justice between the parties. The second situation was where the matter related purely to the internal procedure of the House and here the judges suggested the Court had no jurisdiction. Despite his thorough search of the case law, Bradlaugh found no precedent directly on point and his arguments proved unconvincing. By the end of the hearing it was apparent that Bradlaugh was likely to lose the case. But Lord Coleridge said that in deference to the importance of the matter the Court would take time to hand down its judgment and put its reasons in writing.

The unanimous judgment was delivered by the Lord Chief Justice on 9 February 1884. He paid the usual tribute to Bradlaugh for arguing his case 'with abundant learning and ability'. But he ruled that where an Order of the House was made for the purpose of determining its own internal procedures it was not susceptible to being over-ruled by the Courts. 'What is said or done within the walls of Parliament cannot be inquired into in a court of law. The jurisdiction of the Houses over their own members, their right to impose discipline within their walls, is absolute.' Lord Coleridge added, no doubt prompted by some sympathy for Bradlaugh, 'If injustice has been done it is injustice for which the Courts of law offer no remedy.' The decision was clear and unassailable. The House of Commons might be restrained in the case of an illegal Order affecting a stranger, but not where the illegal Order was against one of its own members. The case of *Bradlaugh v. Gossett* remains the authority determining the powers of Parliament in respect of its own members.

On 11 February, two days after the judgment and with Mr Justice Stephens remarks about self-administration in mind, Bradlaugh advanced to the Table, read the words of the oath from a paper in his hand, kissed a book which he had brought with him, signed the paper and left it on the Table. There was uproar. The Speaker called on Bradlaugh to withdraw, and he did withdraw but to a seat within the Chamber. Northcote moved belatedly his usual motion that Bradlaugh be not permitted to go through the form of taking the oath.

Gladstone immediately appreciated the situation and said he would prefer Bradlaugh to sit and vote in the House. It would then be the duty of the Government to raise in the Courts the question whether Bradlaugh had incurred a penalty. Labouchere in a most remarkable speech argued that Bradlaugh's self-administration of the oath was lawful. He added: 'I confess that, for my part, I regard the words of the oath as an utterly unmeaning form. To me they are just the same superstitious incantation as the trash of any Mumbo-Jumbo among African savages.' The House was astonished and stilled by what they were hearing. The stillness derived from their appreciation that though they had excluded Bradlaugh, who had never in the House attacked the form of the oath, it would make no sense to attack Labouchere who knew and would be willing to publish the names of other atheists who had sworn the oath of allegiance.

The debate grew more confused. Speaker Brand was asked to prevent Bradlaugh from voting on Northcote's motion but he said he had not the power. Eventually when Northcote's motion was put, Bradlaugh voted with the Noes. He voted again on a motion that his vote be disallowed and voted a third time on Northcote's further motion that he be excluded from the precincts of the House. So that afternoon Bradlaugh exercised his vote on three occasions. The following day Labouchere moved that a new writ be issued for a bye-election in Northampton. Lord Randolph Churchill opposed this, preferring that Bradlaugh be declared incapable in perpetuity of sitting in the House. Ultimately the House saw sense, and a writ for a new election was agreed.

Bradlaugh then began his seventh election fight in Northampton and the third since he won in 1880. There was a new Conservative candidate, Mr H. C. Richards, a London barrister. In a short and strenuous campaign there was the usual canvassing, statements to the press, and of course the speeches, until the poll on 19 February. Bradlaugh obtained 4,032 votes and Richards 3,644. The majority of 368 was more than in the previous bye-election suggesting that Bradlaugh had now touched bottom in Northampton and would improve his position. It appeared he could rely on his constituents remaining steadfast.

Chapter Sixty-eight

THE SEEDS OF SOCIALISM IN BRITAIN were planted by Robert Owen in the early 1800s and by Karl Marx fifty years later but did not sprout until after the death of Marx in 1883. The man responsible for this germination was Henry Mayer Hyndman who had been a student and friend of Marx though estranged from him three years before his death. In June 1881 Hyndman in collaboration with William Morris, the wealthy poet and artist, founded the Democratic Federation (later to be re-named as the Social Democratic Federation) whose purpose was to propagate socialism in Britain even if necessary by revolution. The Fabian Society whose members were in favour of nurturing socialism by a subtle and evolutionary process was founded in 1884.

Bradlaugh was well aware of these growing shoots of the socialist movement for many secularists, rebels by nature, were attracted to it. Bradlaugh was profoundly opposed to socialism in all its aspects. He was a freethinker and his unfettered thought told him that individualism, not socialism, was the way forward. In February 1884 he delivered the first of four lectures in the Hall of Science in which he defined and confuted socialism as it was developing in France, Italy, Russia and England. He explained that he supported social reform, his political life was devoted to it, but was opposed to socialism. He always set his face against revolution of any kind. 'Revolution,' said Bradlaugh, 'breaks yesterday but does not build today.'

On 19 January 1884 Hyndman and Morris published the first issue of a new journal, entitled *Justice: The Organ of Social Democracy*, which was founded to advance the cause of organised socialism in Britain. The journal commended Bradlaugh's struggle to take his parliamentary seat, stating in its third issue: 'We admire the courage with which one man coolly confronts six hundred and we most heartily wish him all success in the unequal contest.' But this was as far as support for Bradlaugh went; the journal was belligerently opposed to his attacks on socialism.

The March issue of Justice reported that arrangements had been completed for a debate between Bradlaugh and Hyndman on the question: 'Will Socialism Benefit the English People?' There had been some difficulty making these arrangements because Hyndman wanted the cost to be shared by the SDF and the National Secular Society whereas Bradlaugh insisted that every debate should pay its way. This preliminary skirmish was won by Bradlaugh and it was agreed that the debate take place in St James's Hall on 17 April with 300 seats priced at 2/6d each, 600 at 1/- and the remainder free. The Chairman was to be Professor Edward Beesly, a popular figure, who was Professor of History at University College, London.

Bradlaugh and Hyndman were contrasting figures. The older by nine years, Bradlaugh had left school at twelve and had struggled his whole life to pay his way. Hyndman was the son of wealthy parents and had been expensively educated, first by private tutors and then at Trinity College, Cambridge. He was tall, handsome and invariably dressed in a black frock coat, top hat and gloves. Whilst his creed was one of altruism and brotherly love, he earned his ample living and financed his socialist agitation by successful speculation in stocks and shares. As so often happens, it was the wealthy man who was dedicated to the destruction of capitalism and the poorer man who opposed any form of socialism.

On the evening of the debate, St James's Hall was completely full. The audience was an intelligent one, eager to see the clash of these two forceful figures. It included many who, fifteen years later, were active in the formation of the Labour Party. John Burns was there, as was Keir Hardie and Herbert Burrows. George Bernard Shaw, always fascinated by Bradlaugh and by now a socialist, was there in the audience. The platform was dominated by the officers of the SDF and Bradlaugh was alone there with no room for his supporters. Annie Besant, used to the high table, was disappointed not to be on the platform and sat with Alice and Hypatia at one side of the Hall where they had a good view.

Hyndman began the debate with a vague explanation of the meaning of socialism which was, he said, 'an endeavour to substitute for the anarchical struggle or fight for existence an organised co-operation for existence'. He then added, always rising on his toes to make a point: 'It is a distinct historical theory which accounts for the progress of man in society by his command over the forces of nature, the power which he has of creating wealth.' His view of wealth creation was taken straight from Marx. It was the working man on starvation wages who generated surplus value, which is divided up by the idle, non-producing class. Consequently, 'the workers must control the system of exchange in the interest of the whole community'. He was in no doubt that revolution may be necessary: 'We do preach discontent and we mean to preach discontent; and we mean if we can to stir up actual conflict.'

When Bradlaugh spoke he went straight to the point. 'We both recognise many social evils. He wants the State to remedy them, I want the individual to remedy them.' He then observed that Hyndman had not provided an adequate definition of socialism: 'I urge the importance of exact definitions.' And then gave his own definition: 'I say that socialism denies all individual property, and affirms that society organised as the State should own all wealth, direct all labour, and compel the equal distribution of the produce.' Bradlaugh criticised those who supported socialism without giving details. 'Dare you try to organise society without discussing details? It is the details of life which make up life.' Bradlaugh then asserted that property owners in England were in the enormous majority. 'All savings in the Savings Bank, the Co-operative Store, the Building Society, the Friendly Society and the Assurance Society are property; and I will show you that there are millions of working men who are in that condition.' He emphasised the importance of individual action. 'I urge that the only sufficient inducement to progress in society is by individual effort, spurred to action by the hope of private gain; it is the individual motive which prompts and spurs the individual to action.'

This approach reduced Hyndman to a nonplus. When he spoke again he said: 'Mr Chairman, I must confess when I entered the Hall I did not expect that I had to explain all the details of bottle-washers, cooks and cabmen in the remote future. I must honestly say that it never entered my mind that my opponent would adopt that line of argument.'

Bradlaugh's response was crushing: 'It is no use appealing in vague phrases to the future. Take the broom and sweep one street clean by individual effort, and do not blow bubbles in the air.' He added: 'Why do you jeer at the bottle-washer? Surely the bottle-washer is as good as the prince. I belong to the bottle-washers and I wish to know how our bottles are to be washed.'

Hyndman once again: 'I say what we look to is a thoroughly organised England wherein each man will work for all, where there will be a free exchange of the fruits of labour without any profit.'

Bradlaugh had the final word: 'My definition of socialism has not been touched, nor even objected to; yet if it be the true definition, it is fatal to the whole of the argument that has been put to us.'

This debate exhibited Bradlaugh at the height of his oratorical powers. His eloquence stemmed not from rhetoric alone but rhetoric allied to logic – the art of reasoning, of defining, of drawing distinctions between concepts. This was the ability that made him effective in the courts. On the public platform he was able to add the ingredient of emotion and the faculty for repartee. One of those attending the debate referred to the way in which Bradlaugh's ripostes 'squelched' the adverse remarks and criticisms hurled at him.

Hyndman commented on Bradlaugh: 'He was an individualist of individualists. Every man must make his own way with his own right arm. That the weakest go to the wall was beneficial for the race: that he, Bradlaugh would survive in this competition as one of the fittest he had no doubt.' Certainly in this debate Bradlaugh had proved the fitter. The *Western Daily Mercury* reported the next day: 'Mr Bradlaugh simply pulverised Mr Hyndman last night. Few men would have had any chance with so ready and practised a debater as the secularist leader.' The *St James's Gazette* wrote: 'Mr

Bradlaugh defending common sense and private property and private effort is a pleasanter spectacle than the same person defying the House of Commons.'

Interest in the debate lingered on for many months. The Freethought Publishing Company sold over 5,000 transcripts and then had to print more. There was no doubt that Bradlaugh had won the battle of the evening in St James's Hall. But as time passed it became apparent that he had lost the war. Bradlaugh had supplied Hyndman with an audience he could never otherwise have achieved. Several of those who had attended to cheer Bradlaugh pondered over the months on what Hyndman had said and became born-again socialists. The debate also had a significant effect on the long-term influence of Bradlaugh. Conservatives in particular, who identified him solely as an atheist and republican, were impressed to hear him speak so forcefully against socialism. For Bradlaugh the tide was beginning to turn.

Chapter Sixty-nine

WHEN ON 11 FEBRUARY IN THE House of Commons Bradlaugh had administered the oath to himself and then voted in three divisions he knew that Gladstone had decided to bring an action for a penalty of £500 for each of those votes. The basis of the action was breach of the provisions of the Parliamentary Oaths Act 1866. The case of *Clarke v. Bradlaugh* had determined that a private person could not bring the action so it was brought by the Attorney-General on behalf of the Crown. Newdigate Newdegate had at last got his way.

The hearing in *Attorney-General v. Bradlaugh* began in the High Court on 13 June 1884. Because of the constitutional importance of the case the trial was held 'at bar', that is before three judges and a special jury. The judges were Lord Coleridge the Lord Chief Justice, Baron Huddlestone and Mr Justice Grove, all well known to Bradlaugh. The importance of the case was also demonstrated by the fact that Bradlaugh, who represented himself, was opposed by the Attorney-General, the Solicitor-General, Sir Hardinge Giffard and two junior counsel. The best lawyers in the country, from both Liberal and Conservative benches, were employed against this one man.

In his long opening speech the Attorney-General surveyed the events leading up to the trial including Bradlaugh's letter to *The Times* of 21 May 1880 and the report of the second Select Committee. In essence there were two decisions for the judges: (1) Did Bradlaugh take the oath in accordance with the provisions of the 1866 Act? and (2) Was he a person capable of taking an oath in the sense in which the Act used that word? On the first question the jury had to decide whether it was right that Bradlaugh

269

could administer the oath to himself and whether he did it before a full House with the Speaker sitting in the Chair. As to the second question, it was for the jury to consider Bradlaugh's state of mind; was he on 11 February a person on whom the oath was binding on his honour and conscience as an oath in the fullest sense of that word?

The Attorney-General called seven witnesses, most of them clerical officers in the House of Commons. The principal Crown witness was Sir Thomas Erskine, Clerk to the House, and by diligent cross-examination Bradlaugh was able to extract from him the helpful admission that the usual way in which the oath was administered was a matter of custom rather than a matter of law. Bradlaugh called only Labouchere who quietly described what had occurred in the House as he had observed it: that Bradlaugh had not hurried his act of swearing and that the Speaker was sitting in the Chair at the time.

It was puzzling that the Crown chose not to call Speaker Brand to testify, even though he was the person who knew best what had happened on that day. At the end of February Brand had retired as Speaker and gone to the Lords as the first Viscount Hampden. The House had elected in his place Sir Arthur Wellesley Peel, the youngest son of Sir Robert Peel the former Conservative Prime Minister. Perhaps the Attorney-General preferred not to call a member of the House of Lords to assist with this question for the House of Commons.

A significant uncertainty in the trial was whether an offence under the Act was a criminal or a civil matter. The Crown argued that it was a criminal proceeding whilst Bradlaugh contended it was a civil process. The distinction was important. Bradlaugh decided not to go into the witness box himself because he would have been asked the one question he wished to avoid: was he on 11 February a person who believed in a Supreme Being? The Crown did not call Bradlaugh because they held it was a criminal prosecution and in 1884 a defendant in a criminal trial could not testify on his own behalf. The crown was also aware that if it was a criminal process then Bradlaugh, under the law as it then was, would have no right of appeal.

After a two-week adjournment, Lord Coleridge delivered his summing up on 30 June and it was clearly not in Bradlaugh's favour. There were eight questions of fact for the jury to determine and they retired for three hours to reach their conclusion. They accepted Labouchere's evidence as to what had happened in the House and that the Speaker had been in the Chair when the oath was administered. But they decided that on 11 February the defendant had no belief in a Supreme Being and had not taken the oath as an oath. Consequently the judges found for the Crown.

Bradlaugh sought a new trial on the ground that the verdict was against the evidence. He had to wait until December for the same Court to refuse him a new trial. But he was granted leave to take the case to the Court of Appeal when on 28 January 1885 it was heard before Lord Justice Brett, Master of the Rolls, and Lord Justices Cotton and Lindley. The Master of the Rolls, known for his common sense rather than legal profundity, delivered a long and detailed judgment. He agreed with Bradlaugh that an offence under the Act was a civil matter even though providing for a penalty. On the main question, whether Bradlaugh was a person who could properly have taken the oath, he relied on the verdict of the jury. The crucial matter was Bradlaugh's state of mind when he administered the oath. The jury had found that the oath had not been binding as an oath. Accordingly the penalties had been incurred and judgment given for the Crown.

Bradlaugh was not willing to stop there. He asked the Master of the Rolls to stay execution and give leave to appeal to the House of Lords on the basis that the case raised a question of grave constitutional import. The Attorney-General raised no objection so in these circumstances the Appeal Court ordered both a stay of execution and leave to appeal further. That saved Bradlaugh immediate payment of £1,500 in penalties and payment of the Crown's heavy costs, payments which would have ruined him. Lord Justice Cotton asked Bradlaugh if he would undertake to proceed forthwith in prosecuting the appeal. 'Hardly "forthwith" my Lord,' replied Bradlaugh. For him delay was essential and he intended to postpone appeal to the Lords for as long as the law allowed.

Chapter Seventy

ON 30 JANUARY 1884 BRADLAUGH MADE his last will and testament, describing himself as lecturer and journalist. What his will demonstrated was how little he had to bequeath and his great affection for Annie Besant. He appointed Alice and Hypatia as executors and willed them his realty and personalty. But he had no realty and his personalty consisted of his few sticks of furniture and his cherished library of 10,000 books. Annie was co-proprietor of the Freethought Publishing Company and referring to this in his will he wrote: 'I fear the liabilities will be greater than the assets.' He concluded: 'I have nothing to leave to the true good woman who has so stood side by side with me and bore calumny and slander for my sake save my tenderest love and most earnest hope.'

Annie was in fact far better off than Bradlaugh. She lived in an imposing house in the best part of St John's Wood with a housekeeper and a companion. Apart from her income as co-editor of the *National Reformer* she earned substantial sums as a lecturer and received healthy royalties from her pamphlets. She was widely acknowledged to be the best woman platform speaker of her generation and was much in demand. Unlike Bradlaugh she had none of the expenses of parliamentary campaigns and law suits.

Early in 1884 Bradlaugh was faced with further expense. The building at 63 Fleet Street was to be sold unless the Freethought Publishing Company was willing to lease the whole building. Reluctantly, but persuaded by Annie, Bradlaugh took on an eighteen-year lease. In order to meet their capital expenditure the partners issued debentures to the value of £5,000 secured on the lease, the stock-in-trade and the copyrights. The debentures paid five per cent per annum and were taken up largely by friends and supporters. The quarterly payments were an added burden for the hard-pressed Bradlaugh.

There was, however, a significant advantage. Bradlaugh now had room to establish his own printing works on the additional floors of 63 Fleet Street. This operation was put in the charge of Arthur Bonner who had just become engaged to marry Hypatia. This young man, three years younger than his fiancée, came from a religious family and his father had been a clergyman. Arthur had broken away from this pious background to become a member of the National Secular Society. Hypatia had taught him mathematics in her classes at the Hall of Science and they had enjoyed each other's company in the students' association. Bradlaugh had a high regard for Arthur who had largely educated himself and welcomed him as a valuable member of the family.

Edward Aveling had been giving Annie and Bradlaugh a great deal of trouble and it was in 1884 that this 'trinity in unity' came to an end. Since 1882 Aveling had been spending much of his time in the British Museum Library engaged in research for his articles. Karl Marx who died in 1883 had worked most days in the Library and it had become a meeting ground for young socialists. A main attraction for Aveling at the Library was Eleanor Marx, the youngest and favourite daughter of Karl Marx who Marx always called by the affectionate name of' 'Tussy'. As well as losing her father Eleanor had recently lost her mother and a sister. There was an emotional vacuum to be filled and Aveling made sure he was the one to fill it.

Eleanor was an intelligent young woman, five years younger than Aveling and, influenced by her father, was devoting her life to left-wing politics. She had black eyes and black curly hair flowing in all dimensions. She was full of life and attractive but with a complexion that suggested she relied too much on stimulants. She let herself down by dressing in a slovenly though picturesque way. There was a natural affinity between her and Aveling; they were both brilliant and at the same time emotionally unsettled. They had a common love of the theatre and drama played a large part in their lives. Eleanor had a beautiful voice, wonderfully modulated, which was a good match for Aveling's magnificently resonant vocalisation. Annie Besant, an occasional visitor to the British Museum, knew and disliked the younger woman, a disaffection that was inevitably reciprocated.

It was most probably Aveling's passion for Eleanor that turned him into a socialist. He and Eleanor joined Hyndman's Social Democratic Federation and became members of the governing committee. Hyndman was delighted to receive into his fold such a prominent colleague of Bradlaugh. Aveling gave a series of lectures on socialism beginning at Ball's Pond and had the temerity to give one of the lectures at the Hall of Science. Hyndman's journal noted that 'it is very remarkable that a declared socialist should have been so warmly received.' Neither Annie nor Bradlaugh attended the lecture.

On one of these occasions Aveling stated that he was a socialist first and an atheist afterwards. This was nonsense and Annie pounced on it. In her Daybreak column she wrote:

> I am sure that Dr Aveling never said anything so untrue. It is less than five years since Dr Aveling joined the freethought party...All his work was carried on with me. During all this time he never uttered a word on socialism, nor studied it in any way... . He had not a single socialist book in his library which was entirely literary and scientific... . In fact he never touched socialism in any way or knew anything about it until in 1882 he took to reading in the British Museum, and unfortunately fell into the company of some of the Bohemian socialists, male and female, who flourish there.

The term female Bohemian socialist was an apt coded description of Eleanor Marx.

Bradlaugh was of course keenly concerned that Aveling was giving up secularism for socialism, but it was his financial indiscretions, exacerbated by his relationship with Eleanor, that troubled him most. Aveling had been lent substantial sums by the Freethought Publishing Company and he had borrowed money from many members of the National Secular Society as well as from anyone else he considered to be a likely prospect, be they rich or poor. Complaints about Aveling were growing and his ruthless indifference to paying off any of his debts was damaging the Freethought Movement.

The tipping point, the act that determined Bradlaugh to deal with him at last, was a letter which Aveling sent to Bradlaugh on 29 July. The letter came from the Nelson Inn near Winterworth in Derbyshire to which Aveling had eloped with Eleanor. He addressed it to Bradlaugh as 'President of a Society of which I am Vice-President'.

In that letter Aveling wrote:

> I feel that I ought to tell you of the important step I have just taken. I have decided to live as man and wife with Miss Marx. You know that we cannot live thus legally but I hope we shall do so morally and be able to know the true nature of a union that is only a mutual pledge from one human being to another. You will let me know if this step long considered and taken with a full sense of its serious nature will make any difference to my official position. Faithfully yours, Edward Aveling.

In his cold formal reply of the following day, Bradlaugh advised Aveling that he had been elected Vice-President of the National Secular Society by the Conference and his letter should therefore be addressed to the Secretary, Robert Forder, for communication to the Executive. Bradlaugh's letter ended ominously: 'In such case you must remember that other questions of conduct would probably arise.'

Chapter Seventy-one

FOR SEVERAL YEARS BRADLAUGH HAD SHOWN remarkable forbearance towards Aveling but now his patience was exhausted. He acted with his usual ruthlessness with colleagues who seriously crossed him. On 9 August he wrote to Aveling in Derbyshire to ask for repayment of the sums he was owed: 'I shall be obliged by your making me forthwith some definite proposal for the liquidation of the large amount you owe to the Freethought Publishing Company. I do not care how small the instalments are so long as they are specific and frequent, but they must be secured by judgment.' To reinforce this demand Bradlaugh's solicitors served a writ on Aveling.

Two days later Bradlaugh wrote again to Aveling telling him that he could no longer use a room at 63 Fleet Street: 'I hereby determine any tenancy at will or on sufferance, if any, between yourself and myself and Mrs Besant.' By then Aveling had heard from the secretary of the National Secular Society that Bradlaugh was to recommend his expulsion at the next meeting of the Executive. He replied to Bradlaugh to say that he had no doubt the resolution would be carried and added: 'But if there is to be war between us, it will be war a outrance. And in that no one will be saved. Nor will the battle be confined to the N.S.S. as far as I am concerned.'

Bradlaugh's response was clear: 'I am in receipt of your threat which is as absurd as it is despicable. I will be at your disposition here any morning you may fix before 11 to state in the presence of any friend you may bring the matters of dishonesty on your part which it will be my duty to lay before the Executive.' Bradlaugh had already prepared notes summarising the accusations he was to place before the Executive. These included such items as: how Bradlaugh had lent £75 to pay Aveling's rent when he feared being distrained; how he had procured Aveling's release from Holloway gaol when committed as a fraudulent debtor; how he had paid money Aveling had borrowed from a servant whilst staying as a guest in a house in Ireland; how he had redeemed books and scientific apparatus that Aveling had pawned; and how he had paid sums in respect of many of Aveling's dishonoured cheques. It was a damning list and extended in Bradlaugh's handwriting to twenty-seven pages.

Aveling did appear one morning – alone – at 20 Circus Road to hear Bradlaugh's statement and admitted its substantial accuracy. He realised the game was up. Before the next Executive meeting Aveling wrote to the Secretary of the NSS. to tender his resignation, adding: 'My reason for doing so is that I am indebted in certain sums to members of that body for moneys lent. As it is not possible for me to discharge at once and completely all these obligations, I prefer to withdraw from the Society.' Aveling agreed to pay Bradlaugh at the rate of 30/- a week, or more if he could manage it, and did so erratically over the next four years. The debt was never completely extinguished.

Annie had also written to Aveling to terminate their friendship. His reply in the circumstances was pitiful. He explained that his work would be 'outside the Freethought movement until *you* ask me to return. I grieve you will not see me. But I will be true.' There was one more matter for Bradlaugh to attend to. When Aveling and Eleanor returned to London from Derbyshire, where Aveling had failed to pay his bill at the inn, Bradlaugh turned up one morning at 12 Fitzroy Street where they were lodging. He arrived by cab and peremptorily demanded the return of letters that Annie had written to Aveling. The mission was successful. This was the final severance of this secular trinity.

In that summer of 1884, Annie and Bradlaugh had their first extended holiday together. They travelled to Portincaple a small village on Loch Long, thirty miles north-east of Glasgow. There they stayed in the cottage of Finlay McNab, a fisherman and his wife. They were well chaperoned, for apart from the Mcnabs they were accompanied by John Lees and his daughter. John Lees was an Edinburgh business-man, a manufacturer of rope and twine, and a friend of Bradlaugh's. He was a Vice-President of the NSS. and Chairman of the Edinburgh Secular Society. It was a pleasant holiday, thoroughly relaxing for Bradlaugh. Every day McNab rowed him up and down the loch, having lunch at Ardintenny, and towards evening they would arrive back at the cottage with the catch of the day. For a couple of weeks Annie and Bradlaugh were living under the same roof, with Annie playing the part of housekeeper. This was the only time that the two of them could enjoy some semblance of domestic life.

In October Annie went back to Scotland, this time to bring back to London John Robertson, a new protégé to replace Aveling. Robertson was a first-rate capture. Born on the Isle of Arran, he had moved to the mainland at the age of thirteen when his formal education stopped. Like Bradlaugh he subsequently educated himself, and so well that in 1878, when he was twenty-two, he succeeded William Archer as leader writer on the *Edinburgh Evening News*. In that same year he heard Bradlaugh speak in Edinburgh. As he put it, that lecture crystallised his transition to atheism. He joined the Edinburgh Secular Society and assisted John Lees to run that organisation. He was a handsome young man tall, spare and always well-dressed. He had caught the eye of Annie on her trips to Edinburgh and she had already invited him to write occasional articles for the *National Reformer* and for *Our Corner*.

On 3 October there Annie organised a farewell party in Edinburgh for Robertson. She presided proudly at the top table with Robertson on her right and John Lees and his daughter on her left. The testimonial given to Robertson was a beautiful inkstand, a golden pen and a pack of stationery. The message was clear: Robertson was to replace Aveling as a leading writer for the *National Reformer*.

Chapter Seventy-two

WHEN ROBERTSON ARRIVED IN LONDON HE immediately put his testimonial pen to good use. Annie and Bradlaugh appointed him assistant editor of the *National Reformer* and he proved able to write on almost any subject. He composed many articles on freethought topics and also on politics, international affairs, on drama and the arts. He served also as court reporter. Bradlaugh gave him advice: 'Never think you know all about your subjects: always rethink them; always restudy them; always test your positions and your arguments.' Just as Thomas Allsop, Bradlaugh's mentor of his younger days, taught Bradlaugh to be thorough, so he was passing on this message to Robertson.

Annie was delighted with her protégé, nine years her junior. She invited him to live in her house in Avenue Road, making sure he was available for discussion. Much of their exchange was on socialism, for Robertson was a socialist. He had been at the Hyndman debate and though he admired Bradlaugh's pre-eminence as a speaker, he was persuaded by Hyndman's arguments. But Robertson was a different type of socialist from Hyndman. He eschewed Marxism and revolution. He was a scholarly intellectual socialist who regarded the State as a means of redistributing wealth and as agent for gradual social reform.

In the months since that Hyndman debate Annie had also been pondering on the arguments she had heard. Brilliant as she recognised Bradlaugh's debating triumph, the more she considered Hyndman's ideas the more she liked them. She was getting tired of secularism. To her it was becoming materialistic, grey, unexciting. She missed the idea of 'social brotherhood'. She felt the lack of opportunities that being a vicar's wife had given her, for helping mankind, of ministering to the poor. Secularism for her was ceasing to be dramatic and she lived on drama. Her slow but steady conversion to socialism was under way, encouraged by constant conversation with Robertson.

There was another young man, the same age as Robertson, who helped to persuade her that the future rested with socialism. This was George Bernard Shaw, an early member of the Fabian Society, and admirer of both Bradlaugh and Annie. He had attended the Knowlton trial, been at the Hyndman debate, and occasionally attended the Sunday lectures at the Hall of Science. An aspiring orator himself, he delighted in platform speeches. He recognised Bradlaugh as a hero, a giant who dominated everything around him. And he was thrilled by Annie's contralto voice and its immense persuasive power. When Annie first met Shaw in the middle of 1884 she misunderstood his levity for laziness and described him as a loafer. She soon realised her mistake and that he chose to conceal his industry with humour and light-heartedness, so two weeks later apologised in her weekly column. In fact these two had much in common. They were both Anglo-Irish, had both lost their fathers at an early age, and both lived for the spoken word.

Annie's carefully calculated commitment to socialism took place in January 1885. She made it known that she was going to attend a lecture on socialism that Shaw was giving to the London Dialectical Society. It was expected that at the end of Shaw's speech, Annie in a few well-chosen sentences would demolish him. But to the great surprise of Shaw, she kept her silence until another member of the audience attacked Shaw, and then she demolished the attacker. Annie had her reasons. At the end of the meeting she asked Shaw to nominate her as a member of the Fabian Society. That evening she invited Shaw to dinner and within ten days they were playing piano duets together. By April she had begun publication of Shaw's second novel, *The Irrational Knot*, in *Our Corner*.

Annie's choice of the Fabian Society for her espousal of socialism was inevitable. She had so damned Hyndman in the pages of the *National Reformer* that joining the Social Democratic Federation was unthinkable. She might have been tempted to join William

Morris in his Socialist League, which had broken away from the SDF, but Aveling and Eleanor had followed Morris into that organisation. So she plumped for the Fabians. It suited her well as a middle-class society of gentlemen and gentlewomen committed to a gradualist approach to social changes. And the Fabians presented her with opportunities. She brought to the Society an impressive reputation as a platform orator. For the time being Annie kept her membership of the Fabians from Bradlaugh. She hesitated for several months before disclosing beyond doubt that she was a socialist convert. She was unwilling to put to the test the strong affection between her and Bradlaugh by taking a public position which differed so much from his. Her alliance with the socialists was eventually revealed to the public by *Justice* in July 1885 much to the satisfaction of Hyndman who regarded her conversion as one of his triumphs.

Hypatia and Arthur Bonner were married at the Marylebone Register Office on 18 June 1885 with Arthur's brother, Bradlaugh and Alice as the witnesses. Hypatia did not want Annie at the wedding but Bradlaugh appealed to his daughter to include her as she expressed a strong wish to be present at the family occasion. Hypatia agreed at last but commented: 'It is always what she wishes, not what others wish.' The young married couple moved to modest accommodation in Tufnell Park, North London, more than three miles from Circus Road. It was left largely to Alice to look after her father.

One of those who early noticed Annie's move to socialism was William Platt Ball, an exponent of teetotalism, of freethought, and especially of individualism. He was a colleague of Foote's at the *Freethinker* and shared Foote's unsympathetic view of Annie. Ball detected 'socialism in disguise' in one of Annie's articles in the *National Reformer* in late 1884. He subsequently published a pamphlet on 'Mrs Besant's Socialism' in which he accused Annie of working hard to bring radicals and freethinkers into the socialist fold. He emphasised that socialism is not a mere extension or derivative of the word 'social'. He claimed that individualism was the true source and guarantee of social union and progress. His most damaging criticism of Annie was a personal one: 'Mrs Besant's mind is like a milk jug; that which is poured into it is in turn poured out of it.' These were sentiments with which Foote undoubtedly agreed.

Whilst Bradlaugh was remarkably tolerant of Annie's move from secularism to socialism he was deeply disappointed. For the first time their views separated rather than united them. Annie continued to write her 'Daybreak' column and to be co-editor of the *National Reformer*. But the sparkle had gone from their friendship. Bradlaugh had lost confidence in Annie's judgment and thereafter ceased to consult her on his policies and his activities. For him the secularist movement had lost one of its leaders. It would never be glad confident morning again.

Chapter Seventy-three

IN JUNE 1885 GLADSTONE'S SECOND ADMINISTRATION ran into trouble. The opposition moved an amendment to the Liberal budget and the Government was defeated. This downfall was largely due to Lord Randolph Churchill who in the previous three years had come to national prominence by effective speeches up and down the country. Plotter that he was, he had persuaded the Irish nationalists that the Conservatives would govern Ireland without the coercive laws introduced by the Liberals. When the budget amendment was put to the vote, many Liberals were absent and the Irish, without warning, went into the opposition lobby. Gladstone's administration was beaten and the Grand Old Man resigned the next day.

In normal circumstances such a Government defeat would have prompted an immediate general election. But the previous year had seen the enactment of the third Reform Bill which extended the franchise. It took time for the new voters to be registered. And the Redistribution of Seats Act 1885 re-apportioned constituencies so as to make them more equal. Many boroughs were reduced to one member but Northampton was one that retained its two seats.

This electoral reorganisation meant that a general election was a few months away. So Gladstone's administration was replaced by a minority Conservative Government led by Lord Salisbury as Prime Minister. Sir Michael Hicks-Beach, said to be the most handsome man in the Commons, became Leader of the House and Chancellor of the Exchequer, whilst Northcote, on Churchill's insistence, went to the Lords as the first Earl Iddesleigh. Sir Hardinge Giffard, the bitter opponent of Bradlaugh in both the

House and the Courts, also went to the Lords as Lord Chancellor with the title of Baron Halsbury.

Members of the Fourth Party did especially well. Churchill, though he had held no office before, joined the Cabinet as Secretary of State for India, Sir John Gorst became Solicitor-General and A. J. Balfour became President of the Local Government Board. As for Sir Henry Drummond Wolff, his diplomatic skills were recognised by sending him on an expensive mission to Cairo and Constantinople for which he received a substantial salary. By these means the Fourth Party, which had achieved its purpose of invigorating the Conservative Party, was extinguished.

With this change of administration Bradlaugh considered himself free to attempt yet again to take his seat and so informed the Speaker. On 6 July, soon after prayers, he advanced to the Table ready to swear the oath and kiss the book. Hicks-Beach played the part that Northcote had played on so many occasions. He moved that Mr Bradlaugh be not permitted to go through the form of repeating the words of the oath and that the Serjeant-at-Arms exclude him from the precincts of the House. The Speaker, Arthur Wellesley Peel, elected to the Speakership only fifteen months before, had no choice but to accept the motion as being consistent with the decisions of the House in that Parliament.

Immediately, Charles Hopwood, a Liberal sympathetic to Bradlaugh and who had already attempted to bring in an affirmation measure, moved an amendment to the effect that legislation be introduced. In the ensuing debate Gladstone strongly supported the amendment, which was in his view required to meet the unsatisfied constitutional claim of the constituency. Hicks-Beach urged the House to adhere to its former decisions to exclude Bradlaugh and argued that the Northampton constitutional question should be left to the constituencies. When the amendment was put it was defeated by 263 votes to 219. The House was clearly determined to maintain its previous stand. Once more Bradlaugh had to retire defeated beyond the Bar.

The general election was called in November 1885. Bradlaugh was fully prepared to fight for his seat the eighth time and his election manifesto, published in the *National Reformer*, was consistent with all his previous addresses. His radical programme called for the extension of the franchise to all men – and to all women. He demanded the disestablishment and disendowment of the State Church. He sought the abolition of the hereditary privilege to legislate and the cessation of perpetual pensions. He argued for stringent economy on the part of the Government. Conscious of the growth of socialist ideas he advocated more strongly than before his individualist principles: 'Radicals should check and avoid the tendency to look to Government to provide food and work for the people. Government can do nothing of this kind except with means entrusted to it by the people. It has no purse save that the people fills; no property save that the people creates.'

Bradlaugh's popularity as a radical brought him an invitation to stand for election not only in Northampton but also in the newly created London constituency of East Finchley in which the Hall of Science was located. But Bradlaugh, wanting to supply Northampton with the loyalty that Northampton had given him, turned down this attractive offer. He was confident of winning Northampton again, so much so that he published no electoral bills relying on public meetings and his personal canvassing. The Conservatives were so doubtful of their prospects that they fielded only one candidate. They selected again Mr H. C. Richards, the young Barrister from London who spoke with an unimpressive lisp and was thoroughly outshone by his two experienced opponents.

The poll was held on 25 November and the voting results were: Labouchere, 4,845; Bradlaugh, 4,315; and Richards, 3,890. Bradlaugh had received more votes than ever before. Hicks-Beach had argued that the Northampton constitutional question be left to the constituencies and Northampton had given a resounding answer. The result for Bradlaugh was better than these figures suggest because the tendency in the country was for those Liberals who had voted against him in the House to do badly and several were defeated. A friend of Bradlaugh's, Dr W. A. Hunter an advanced radical, entered the House for the first time as Member for Aberdeen. Two of Bradlaugh's most hostile Conservative adversaries were defeated. Drummond Wolff was beaten at Portsmouth and, most satisfying of all, Charles Newdigate Newdegate was so certain that he would lose in Warwickshire that he withdrew halfway through the campaign.

Chapter Seventy-four

THE RESULT OF THE 1885 GENERAL Election was troublesome for both major parties. The Liberals had won 335 seats, the Conservatives 249 with the difference being made up by 86 Irish Nationalists. The Conservatives could continue to rule only with the Irish members, and the Liberals also required their support if they were to maintain a majority. So the Irish found themselves in a pivotal position. In these uncertain circumstances it was agreed between the parties that the Conservatives would continue their administration for the time being.

There was much gossip and speculation, in the press and in Parliament, as to what Bradlaugh would now do. Between the election and the opening of the new Parliament the Conservative ministers considered how they could best thwart any move Bradlaugh might make. In December Bradlaugh wrote to Hicks-Beach to ask what view the Government would take if a new Affirmation Bill were introduced. He received a non-committal reply. Behind the scenes Lord Randolph Churchill, in his wily way, was arguing that the better course was to allow an Affirmation Bill to be presented. This would quiet Bradlaugh for a while and Churchill was brashly confident that he could persuade the House to defeat the Bill just as he had done three years before.

At first Bradlaugh was undecided. He naturally wanted an Affirmation Bill but it would take time, might fail, and would certainly be a matter outside his control. Who could tell what this new Parliament might bring? So in the absence of a clear understanding with Hicks-Beach he decided to attempt once more to take his seat in the normal way with the other members. When the Conservatives learned this the party managers issued a four-line whip. They were determined to defeat him.

On 12 January Arthur Peel was re-elected Speaker by unanimous vote. The following day, the formal opening of Parliament, the Gentleman Usher of the Black Rod advanced towards the Speaker, bowed three times and announced that Her Majesty required the attendance of the Commons in the House of Lord's to hear Her Majesty's Commission. When the Commons Chamber had emptied the Serjeant-at-Arms and his assistants placed two tables on either side of the Chamber, each one holding ten Bibles with ten cards containing the words of the oath.

On his return from the Lords the Speaker entered the House in his formal robes and full-bottomed wig and went straight to take his seat in the Chair. Members filed in after him, filling the Chamber to overflowing and creating an expectant hush. Assisted by the Clerk, the Speaker took the oath and subscribed the Parliamentary roll. He then announced that he had received a letter from Sir Michael Hicks-Beach, Leader of the House, about the proceedings in relation to Mr Bradlaugh and read out part of it. The letter rehearsed the facts including the judgment of the Court of Appeal which held that Bradlaugh was incapable of taking the oath. It ended by emphasising that Bradlaugh should not be permitted to take the oath without the House expressing its opinion. The Leader of the House was thereby asking Speaker Peel to follow the practice set by Speaker Brand of referring the matter to the decision of the House.

Having read out the letter, the Speaker then said that, before the House was properly constituted by members coming to the Table to take their oaths, he thought it right that he should state his view, a view arrived at after full consideration. He noted that in the previous Parliament the decision had been made by the House, and the Speaker had not taken original and independent authority for himself. Then came his dramatic statement:

> We are assembled in a new Parliament. I know nothing of the Resolutions of the past. They have lapsed, they are void, they are of no effect in reference to this case. [Loud Opposition

cheers.] I have no authority, no right, original or delegated, to interfere between an honourable member and his taking of the oath...I have come clearly and without hesitation to the conclusion that it would neither be my duty to prohibit the honourable gentleman from coming nor to permit a motion to be made standing between him and his taking of the oath. The honourable member takes that oath under whatever risks may attach to him in a court of law. If a member comes to this Table and offers to take the oath, I know of no right whatever to intervene between him and the performance of a legal and statutable duty.

Hicks-Beach attempted to raise an objection but the Speaker was firm: 'I must remind the right hon. member that a debate cannot now be initiated.' Hicks-Beach rose again to object only to be silenced conclusively by the Speaker: 'The right hon. gentlemen is not allowed to make a speech and I must remind him that he has not himself yet taken the oath.' There were loud cheers and shouts of 'Hear, Hear' from the Opposition benches. The Conservatives were dismayed. Their four-line whip was to no effect. The Speaker had given what he termed a considered view but every member understood that it was a ruling that could not be gainsaid. Bradlaugh was permitted to take the oath – and he was to take it under a Conservative administration.

Members immediately scrambled to the two tables to read out the words of the oath and to kiss the Bibles. As they pressed slowly towards the Speaker's Chair, a card and a Bible were handed to Bradlaugh. He stood for a long time with both in his hands and then read out the words and kissed the book. The pressure was so great that half an hour elapsed before Bradlaugh reached the Clerk. He explained that he had already taken the oath but the Clerk asked him to read the words once more and again kiss the book. He then signed the roll and shook hands with the Speaker. There was no disturbance, no interference, no demonstration by the Members around him.

Almost six years after election to Parliament, Bradlaugh had at last taken the oath, and not once but twice. He owed that to the common sense and determination of Sir Arthur Wellesley Peel.

Two Select Committees, a multitude of debates, four speeches at the Bar, repeated bye-elections at Northampton and a failed Arbitration Bill had all been unnecessary given a Speaker with the practical wisdom and the firm independent resolve to insist that the matter was one for him and not for a vote by the Members.

After shaking the Speaker's hand, Bradlaugh went quietly to take his seat under the gangway, and this time he was within the Bar.

Chapter Seventy-five

DESPITE HAVING AT LAST TAKEN HIS SEAT, Bradlaugh was not yet home and dry. When in January 1885 the Court of Appeal had ruled against him in the suit brought by the Attorney-General he had been granted a stay of execution only on his undertaking to appeal to the House of Lords. He had been able to extend the time for bringing that appeal but it could not be put off much longer. He knew that he was likely to lose in the Lords and then the question of his seat in the House would begin all over again. Moreover he would be ruined by having to pay damages and the costs incurred by the Crown. It was with this uncertainty hanging over him that he began the new Parliamentary session.

The Conservative Government was fragile, existing only with the support of the Irish nationalists. But the Irish rapidly lost faith with the overtures Lord Randolph had made and realised that Gladstone would do more for them. So when an amendment was moved in the debate on the Royal Address the Irish voted with the Liberals. They thereby brought about Gladstone's third administration whose major theme was to be Home Rule for Ireland. Churchill's response was to say to the Irish: "We've done our best for you. Now we shall do our best against you."

Having waited so long to secure his seat, Bradlaugh was determined to make up for lost time. He was assiduous in attendance at the House. If not in the Chamber he could be found in the Library. He preferred the Chamber where he could follow the movement of debate and gauge the mood of the House. Often he would attend a committee meeting at 11.00 a.m. and remain in the House until 2.00 a.m. the next day. He made sure to become a master of parliamentary procedure. His speeches were prepared thoroughly, usually short, but always containing matters of substance. When he asked a question the responsible Minister knew that he had to supply a meticulous answer because Bradlaugh would have the facts at his fingertips. It soon became known that he was a member who did his homework.

Bradlaugh had an early success by moving a resolution requiring the Government to take immediate steps to collect and publish Labour statistics. His visit to Massachusetts in 1869 had taught him the importance of accurate data on employment as a basis for negotiations between employers and employees. This resolution was not a party matter and was carried unanimously. As a result the Board of Trade established a department to compile statistics that were made available to the public. Early in the session Bradlaugh , by means of questions to Ministers, was able to embarrass two of his opponents. He exposed the heavy cost of Sir Henry Drummond Wolff's ineffective diplomatic expedition to Cairo and that the mission had spent £3,000 on telegrams alone. He also revealed that the Rhymney Iron Company, based in Wales, had persistently breached the Truck Act 1831 and had been successfully prosecuted and heavily fined. The chairman of this company was Sir Henry Tyler, Conservative MP, who had been the originator of the prosecution of the *Freethinker* for blasphemy.

Bradlaugh raised the question of perpetual pensions at the first opportunity. He had aired this matter in the House in 1881, and since then many of those pensions, including the one enjoyed by the Churchill family, had been commuted on terms which Bradlaugh considered far too generous. He won a ballot for the opportunity to move that a Select Committee be appointed to consider this question but Gladstone was unwilling to give the matter preference. Nonetheless he obtained a pledge from the Government that there would be no more commutations until the question had been considered comprehensively by Parliament.

The primary concern of Gladstone's third administration was his attempt to enact an Irish Home Rule Bill which was introduced in April 1886. The Bill had two main objectives: agrarian reform; and the creation of an Irish legislature with limited powers. The first of these was long overdue and the second was highly controversial. There were many days and nights of debate characterised by high oratory and powerful argument. Bradlaugh played a full part in the debate and shortly before the decisive division he made a long speech and Gladstone delayed his dinner to hear this. Bradlaugh supported the Bill; he had long favoured limited independence for Ireland as long as it did not lead to the destruction of the Kingdom. But many Liberals opposed Gladstone's proposals, including such a long-standing Liberal as John Bright. This political fissure led to the formation of a substantial breakaway group calling themselves Liberal Unionists.

Gladstone's principal lieutenant in Irish matters was John Morley who had been appointed Irish Chief Secretary. He was a new MP elected for Newcastle in an 1883 bye-election. As well as being a politician he was a journalist and had been a distinguished, though somewhat cautious, editor of the *Pall Mall Gazette*. He was a freethinker with radical views and might have been expected to be a supporter of Bradlaugh. But Morley kept his distance. He had criticised Bradlaugh for being prepared to take the oath even though when elected himself he had sworn the oath without demur. Bradlaugh referred to him as 'one of my false friends' and the relationship between them was uneasy.

Dissension in the Liberal camp inevitably resulted in the loss of the Bill, which was defeated on its second reading. Gladstone's only recourse was to appeal to the country. The following general election, fought on the issue of Irish Home Rule, took place between 1 and 29 July. So for the ninth time Bradlaugh campaigned in Northampton. In addition to himself and Labouchere there was a new Conservative candidate, Hasting Lees, a barrister. A local retired shoe manufacturer, Richard Turner, stood as a Liberal Unionist and added excitement to the hustings. The results in Northampton were declared on 3 July and were: Labouchere, 4,570; Bradlaugh, 4,353; Turner, 3,850; and Lees, 3,456. The introduction of a Liberal Unionist had reduced Labouchere's votes whilst Bradlaugh's total was his highest ever.

As soon as Bradlaugh knew he had been returned he wrote to Gladstone to seek what was termed a *stet processus*, a permanent stay of further proceedings in the suit brought against him by the Attorney-General. In his letter to Gladstone he wrote: 'surely there can be no real objection now to a stay of proceedings by the Crown?' Gladstone referred the matter to Lord Herschell, the Lord Chancellor, who advised against a stay, and Gladstone in his reply to Bradlaugh courteously but firmly confirmed this decision. If Gladstone had so wished he could have brought an end to this litigation and thereby repaid Bradlaugh's loyal support inside and outside Parliament. But he chose not to. He had consistently taken the view that the House had no jurisdiction in regard to the oath and wanted the matter to be decided by the courts. For Bradlaugh, this decision was a bitter blow.

The election results in Northampton were a local triumph for the Liberals but in the country at large the outcome for Gladstone was disastrous. The electorate had spoken and shattered all prospects of Irish Home Rule. Churchill had told the Irish that 'we shall do our best against you' and had fully met that promise. As soon as the complete election results were known Gladstone resigned to make way for Lord Salisbury's Conservative administration. Churchill was the greatest winner. In 1885 he had ensured that Northcote would be replaced as leader of the House by Hicks-Beach and now a year later he succeeded Hicks-Beach as Chancellor of the Exchequer and Leader of the Commons. This was rapid advancement for a man of thirty-seven and followed from his popularity in the country, his brilliance as a speaker, and especially from his lack of scruple in party manoeuvre.

No one was more contemptuous of Churchill's accession to the Commons leadership than Bradlaugh. He wrote: 'The worst enemy of the Tory party could hardly have planned for a greater degradation than this leadership.' But in return for this contempt Churchill was remarkably placatory. When the new Parliament assembled in August, Churchill announced that Bradlaugh was to get his wish for a Select Committee on Perpetual Pensions. So Churchill, whose family had for many years benefited from such a pension, gave to Bradlaugh what Gladstone had denied him. More was to come. In September the Attorney-General, on Churchill's recommendation, entered the *stet processus* that was so vital to

Bradlaugh. Again the Conservative Government had granted what his own party had refused to give.

These two concessions by Churchill were undoubtedly intended as friendly overtures. Churchill did not want as Leader of the House the troubles that had beset Northcote and Hicks-Beach. In any case the Bradlaugh episode had now served Churchill's purpose and there was no further need for rancour, real or artificial. But there was a deeper reason for Churchill's new-found goodwill towards his old opponent. The Conservative party was beginning to recognise that Bradlaugh was not the political ogre they had supposed. He was undoubtedly an effective parliamentarian and the Conservatives were impressed by his opposition to socialism.

Churchill may have changed his attitude to Bradlaugh but these helpful acts did not extinguish Bradlaugh's contempt for Churchill. He could not forget the years of passionate hostility he had endured or that Churchill had called his supporters 'the mob, the scum and the dregs'. These bitter words had bitten deep. In October 1886 Bradlaugh published an open letter to Churchill in which he condemned him for his proposal to change the procedures of the House and for his ungenerous attitude to Gladstone. Referring to the English gentlemen and country squires who supported the Conservatives, Bradlaugh wrote: 'These belong to a class to which I, as well as yourself, are strangers – I from birth and you from habit.' And as to Gladstone, Bradlaugh wrote a stinging rebuke to the son of a Duke: 'You might have for a moment aped a leader's dignity. Noblesse oblige but no such obligation weighs on you.'

Nevertheless Bradlaugh was deeply relieved by the removal of a heavy burden. He wrote in the *National Reformer*: 'For the first time for many years I am glad to say that I am free from the worry and painstaking strain of litigation.' He revealed his weariness in his final sentence: 'I am quite tired of law which is costly in every way.'

Chapter Seventy-six

NOW THAT BRADLAUGH HAD TAKEN HIS parliamentary seat he had little time for social life. He had to earn his living and when he was not at the House he was giving lectures or sitting in his study preparing those lectures or writing a pamphlet or composing the weekly contribution to his journal. The six-year struggle had aged him. He had enjoyed little relaxation, just a snatched day fishing on the river Lea and the occasional few days at Loch Long. Fishing gave him rest but little exercise. He had put on weight and was now a massive man with a gait that was elephantine.

When Hypatia married Arthur Bonner in June 1885 they moved to rooms in St George's Avenue, Tufnell Park. Alice stayed at Circus Road to act as her father's secretary and organise his domestic arrangements. Hypatia soon became pregnant and, missing the proximity to her father, she accepted Annie Besant's offer of accommodation. They paid Annie thirty-five shillings a week for unfurnished rooms in that capacious house. One of the benefits of this move was the friendship that developed between Hypatia and another resident, John Robertson. The relationship between Hypatia and Annie was always distant but Hypatia found Robertson, that dour and blunt Scotsman, to be invariably sincere and sensitive. He gave her practical sympathy when her son Kenneth Bradlaugh Bonner, born on 3 April 1886, fell ill and died five months later. Bradlaugh was dispirited. He had lost his son and now his grandson.

The close relationship between Bradlaugh and Annie was profoundly affected by her increasing absorption in socialism. She introduced monthly socialist notes in *Our Corner* and she wrote articles for that journal on 'The Evolution of Society' in which she portrayed socialism as an inevitable evolutionary development, and on 'Why I am a Socialist'. She also introduced socialist ideas, obliquely if not directly, in her weekly columns in the *National Reformer*. 'Socialism,' she said, 'with its splendid ideal appealed to my heart, while the economic soundness of its basis convinced my head.'

Bradlaugh on the contrary was a consistent and vigorous anti-socialist. Speaking in a debate in the House in March 1886 he said, to much laughter: 'There were a few poets and a few idiots, and some to whom one could not apply as kindly words, who sought to make people believe that socialism was gaining ground in the country. It was not.' He apologised partially for these words in the *National Reformer* the following week but there was much speculation as to which category, poets, idiots, or others he placed Annie. In June 1886 Bradlaugh reviewed in the *National Reformer* a pamphlet by Annie on 'Modern Socialism'. He began by explaining: 'This notice is penned from a very anti-socialist viewpoint.' He then wrote: 'Mrs Besant states her case with great force and the want of clearness is due to the difficulty of the position she has undertaken to maintain.' There was certainly no want of clarity in his final sentence: 'All the faults are not on the side of capital; all the virtues are not on the side of the workers.'

Despite this difference, Bradlaugh and Annie contrived to continue working together. They met frequently and occasionally took the chair at each other's lectures. Whilst Bradlaugh was pitiless with male colleagues who disagreed with him, when he dealt with Annie, 'his brave and loyal co-worker', he was gentle and forbearing. What kept them together was an immense residual affection derived from the troubles and dangers they had jointly faced and the intellectual intimacy they had once known.

Through her socialist connections Annie was fast gaining other friends. She remained on good terms with Bernard Shaw and attended Fabian meetings with him. She also supported him by publishing, and paying generously for, his novels in *Our Corner*. But the initial magic of their connection had gone. Shaw was at a stage where he liked to play the field and Annie was only part of that feminine field. He was troubled by her gravity and she by his levity. Annie was always serious, Shaw rarely so. As the distance between them lengthened, Annie developed a much closer friendship with a more active socialist, Herbert Burrows.

Burrows was largely self-educated, a tall, well-made man with a moustache and a clean-shaven chin who was two years older than Annie. He was a teetotaller, a non-smoker, a vegetarian and a pacifist. As a member of the National Secular Society, he had known of Annie for years, but when they actually met as socialists a deep friendship resulted. As once with Aveling, Annie was now in the constant company of Burrows. He added to his socialism a keen interest in spiritualism and they attended séances together. This spiritual side to his socialism was in keeping with Annie's growing dislike of materialism and growing interest in the transcendental.

Burrows had helped Hyndman to form the Social Democratic Federation and was its treasurer. Under Burrows's influence Annie became reconciled to the militant SDF. Her susceptibility to Burrows' ideas went to confirm the remark by W. P. Ball that 'I have heard Mrs Besant described as being, like most women, at the mercy of her last male acquaintance for her views on economics'. Annie railed bitterly against this comment but it was true and the truth pained her. It was not only Burrows's ideas that she adopted. He dressed casually, as socialists did, wearing a tweed suit and a strawberry coloured tie. Annie changed her style of clothes. From the dark dresses with high-bosomed waists and long skirts that she had worn when accompanying Bradlaugh, she was now to be seen in loose, shorter skirts, and heavy laced boots and always with something of red about her. She too was looking older. There were streaks of grey in her hair and she had developed a slight stoop. As might be expected there was deep hostility between Bradlaugh and Burrows. They were of quite different political and philosophical views. Hyndman had described Bradlaugh as 'the individualist of individualists' whereas Burrows was a collectivist from head to toe. Despite his appearance as a gentle dreamer, he had ample courage and regularly heckled Bradlaugh at his meetings. His view was that Bradlaugh had sold out his beliefs for his career in Parliament; Bradlaugh regarded the younger man as favouring violence and having no integrity.

The economic depression and wide spread unemployment in England in 1887 led the Social Democratic Federation to join with others in organising a series of protests in London against the policies of the Salisbury Government. By far the most significant demonstration was one, forbidden by the Commissioner of Police, held in Trafalgar Square on 13 November. Because of its violence it became known as Bloody Sunday. Annie with many other socialists, including Burrows, Shaw, William Morris and John Burns, played an active part leading a procession from Clerkenwell into the Square.

Bradlaugh was absent, lecturing that weekend in Hull. He could no doubt have cancelled this lecture as he had occasionally had cause to cancel others but he chose to stay away from what he understood would be a violent occasion. He detested violence and this demonstration generated violence indeed. As the processions reached the Square, squadrons of mounted police charged the crowd striking out with their truncheons and dispersing men and women like ninepins leaving scores of broken legs, broken arms and bloodied heads behind. The next day Annie was at Bow Street Magistrates' Court assisting those who had been arrested and endeavouring to secure their release. Another who assisted was W. T. Stead, the most famous journalist of the day. Annie and Stead knew each other by reputation. Now they met for the first time and there was instant rapport.

William Thomas Stead, two years younger than Annie, had come from the north of England in 1880 to serve as deputy to John Morley on the *Pall Mall Gazette*. Three years later when Morley became an MP he succeeded him as editor and transformed the journal. He introduced bold headlines, provocative leading articles, special interviews and galvanizing campaigns. Most sensational of all was his campaign against the abuse of young girls. This had led to his imprisonment for three years and, more importantly, to the enactment of the Criminal Law Amendment Act 1885, which raised the age of consent for women to sixteen years. Annie had undoubtedly secured a powerful new friend.

Annie's conversion to militant socialism was deeply troubling to many readers of the *National Reformer*. Something had to be done about this and it was done on 23 October 1887. The issue of the journal for that day carried Charles Bradlaugh's name alone as editor. Annie gave the reason in a notice inside:

> For a considerable time past, and lately in increasing number, complaints have reached me from various quarters of the inconvenience and uncertainty that result from the divided editorial policy on the question of socialism. When I became an editor of this paper I was not a socialist, although I regard socialism as the necessary and logical outcome of the radicalism which for so many years the *National Reformer* has fought, still, as in avowing myself a socialist I have taken a distinct step, the partial separation of my policy from that of my colleague has been of my own making and not of his, it is therefore for me to give way. I therefore resume my former position as contributor only thus clearing the *National Reformer* of all responsibility for the views I hold.

Bradlaugh's addition to this statement was emollient. 'I need hardly add how deeply I regret the necessity for Mrs Besant's resignation of the joint editorship of this journal...I agree with her that a journal must have a distinct editorial policy; and I think this distinctness the more necessary when, as in the present case, every contributor has the greatest freedom of expression.' Bradlaugh understood the necessity for Annie to yield up her co-editorship. He was determined that his journal should not embrace socialism. Each of them had shown generosity in their own way. But their ways were now pointed in different directions.

Chapter Seventy-seven

ON 23 DECEMBER 1886 LORD RANDOLPH Churchill resigned as Leader of the House of Commons and Chancellor of the Exchequer. He was a Chancellor who never introduced a budget. The budget he had planned provided for a reduction in the Army Estimates and was opposed by W. H. Smith, the Minister of War, who was supported by Lord Salisbury. As a result of this dramatic event Smith succeeded as Leader of the House. Smith was an experienced businessman, patient and self-controlled. It was never likely that Churchill, impetuous, restless and arrogant, would have got the better of him.

Bradlaugh was concerned at having to face a new Leader who might be unfriendly. He knew that Smith had once contemplated taking holy orders, and that he made a point of excluding from his bookstalls any material he judged to be corrupting. This ban included the *National Reformer* which was never sold in any of Smith's stores. However, Smith turned out to be, if not friendly, certainly fair to Bradlaugh, and honoured Churchill's promise that a Select Committee on Perpetual Pensions be established. Smith went one better and appointed Bradlaugh to it. Here was the opportunity that Bradlaugh had wanted for years, a chance to investigate the whole questions of hereditary pensions and put an end to them.

In the Parliamentary session of 1887 Bradlaugh also pressed for a Royal Commission to inquire into Market Rights and Tolls. The imposition of high rents on market stallholders derived from charters granted by the Crown in feudal times. These heavy tolls increased the prices paid by the poor for their food. Bradlaugh was in favour of free markets but against the privileges, largely hereditary, of the market holders. In April 1887 Bradlaugh made one of his longer speeches in the House moving for a Royal Commission. He described some of the holders of the original charters as leeches sucking the vitality of the districts. The value of the wage to the labourer, he said, is not measured by its nominal amount but by what it will purchase in food and other necessaries. The purpose of a Royal Commission would be to decrease the cost of food. He was successful in persuading the Government to appoint a Commission though this time he was not made a member of it.

A little later in 1887 Bradlaugh introduced a Truck Amendment Bill. For many years he had been critical of the truck system by which employees, instead of being paid in coins of the realm, were given their wages partly in goods, groceries or other products of the employer. Sometimes they were paid in vouchers redeemable only at the employer's 'tommy shop'. There had been numerous attempts in the previous two hundred years to prevent these covert tricks of an employer, culminating in the Truck Act 1831. This Act had not proved effective and was constantly being breached, mainly because of the problem of its enforcement. Bradlaugh's Bill extended the prohibition on truck to all manual workers and most importantly entrusted administration of the Act to mining and factory inspectors. The Bill, amended in several particulars in its passage through Parliament, was eventually enacted as the Truck Amendment Act 1887.

These three campaigns, on perpetual pensions, on market rights and tolls, and on the truck system, had a common thread. They denied hereditary privileges and they protected individual rights. In the case of truck, for example, Bradlaugh asserted that employees should have freedom to spend their earnings in their own way and in the shops they selected. If they chose to spend them in a market they were not to be charged excessive prices because of some ancient grant that had no present meaning. There was no party interest in any of these campaigns; support came from all quarters of the House. This man who had been kept from his seat by his unpopular views was introducing reforming measures that attracted general assent.

Bradlaugh was also assiduous in raising in Parliament the problems of India. It had become a practice that a Liberal MP should specialise in Indian affairs and be recognised as 'Member for India'. John Bright had undertaken this task, followed by Henry Fawcett and when Fawcett died the mantle fell on Bradlaugh. It was a mantle he thoroughly earned. He had always been fascinated by India, by the size of the country, by the manner in which 250 million hindoos (as they were known) were ruled from a small country a third of the world distant. Bradlaugh was shocked to discover how little interest the House of Commons took in India and how when Indian matters were debated it was difficult to achieve a quorum of members to keep the debate alive.

Sir John Gorst, one of Bradlaugh's former opponents, had become Secretary of State for India and a new rapport developed between these two as Bradlaugh asked a whole series of questions obviously based on detailed research. Bradlaugh was well informed. He was friendly with William Digby, of the British Committee of the recently formed Indian National Congress. He met senior Indians visiting London and often took them to Northampton to speak to his constituents. Gorst recognised that the questions put to him and his officials were soundly based on accurate knowledge from reliable sources.

It was not merely matters of detail that concerned Bradlaugh. He was primarily interested in the larger picture of how India was governed by the British. In a sense India was a blank sheet, a country so much later in development than Britain that radical ideas might fruitfully be planted there. By 1887 Bradlaugh had given up all expectation that Britain would become a republic in the near future, but a Republic of India was a distinct possibility. He was of course in favour of Indian self-rule but recognised it was some way off. Meanwhile he argued for greater representation of Indians in the top levels of the administration and a reformed role for the Governor. At the same time he was wary of the premature introduction of democracy. He wanted an indigenous solution to Indian problems but he also wanted to avoid an institutional structure that was rigid and inflexible. He saw individual rights as the key, growth from the bottom up, rather than democratically entrenched privileges.

The Parliamentary session of 1887 had been fruitful for Bradlaugh. No backbencher had been busier. One or two newspapers referred to that parliamentary year as 'Bradlaugh's Session'. But he had made no progress on an Affirmation Bill to which in his list of legislative objectives he gave first place. For that he had to wait until 1888.

Chapter Seventy-eight

SINCE THE FAILURE OF THE AFFIRMATION Bill in 1883 there had been several attempts by Liberals to introduce new legislation. Charles Hopwood had tried twice but had lost his seat in 1885. Sir John Simon, a man of religion and yet sympathetic to Bradlaugh, had also made the endeavour but had achieved nothing. Bradlaugh had attempted to introduce a Bill in 1887 which, remarkably, Lord Randolph Churchill, in his new propitiatory mode, had supported in a letter to *The Times*. When that Bill came before the House late one night it was met by a Conservative filibuster and Bradlaugh had to give way. Nonetheless he drew from that debate hopeful signs that he might be able eventually to gain sufficient Conservative support to succeed.

At the beginning of the 1888 session Bradlaugh accordingly introduced a new private member's Bill, renamed as the Oaths Bill and supported by ten members including Sir John Simon and two Conservatives. The second reading was on 14 March and Bradlaugh's introductory speech was measured, moderate, almost conciliatory. He passed quickly over his own unsatisfactory experiences, explaining that it was no longer a matter for political bitterness, and simply said he would be glad if the House would permit him to do by law what it had been his desire to do eight years before. His Bill was designed to solve a problem which had beset the House for a long time.

The Bill consisted of two short clauses, the first providing 'that every person, upon objecting to being sworn, shall be permitted to make his solemn affirmation instead of taking an oath in all places and for all purposes where any oath is or shall be required by law.' Thus a person wishing to affirm would have to object to being sworn but need give no reason for his objection. The clause was comprehensive; it applied to witnesses, to jurors, to officials, to members of Parliament, Justices of the Peace, barristers, solicitors, police officers and those in the army and navy. The Bill extended to Scotland, bringing that jurisdiction into line with England. Particularly important was its application to witnesses, so that all competent evidence could be received by the courts.

In the short debate that followed, Bradlaugh received support from all parts of the House. Opposition to the Bill was led by Edwin de Lisle, a High Tory Catholic. It was de Lisle that raised a matter that troubled many Conservatives. They argued that permission to affirm ought not to be given to a Christian because he could have no conscientious objection to swearing an oath. He might, they said, choose to affirm in order to tell an untruth whilst not having the breach of an oath on his conscience. Many Conservatives urged an amendment to the Bill to meet this objection and Bradlaugh undertook to propose one at the Committee stage. With this assurance the second reading was agreed by 250 votes to 150, a majority which exceeded Bradlaugh's best hopes. Many Conservatives had voted in favour in addition to Liberals and Liberal Unionists. Both Gladstone and Churchill supported the Bill. These two, who had so passionately opposed each other in the 1883 debate, now voted in the same Lobby.

At the Committee stage in June Bradlaugh moved an amendment whereby a person choosing to affirm was required to state as the ground of his objection that he had no religious belief or that the taking of the oath was contrary to his religious belief. This amendment satisfied Conservative objections but to Bradlaugh's annoyance it met with strong opposition amongst a few of his own nearest supporters. Dr Hunter, a close associate, had already given notice of his objections. His argument was that the performance of a public duty (to swear or affirm) should not be the occasion of an inquisition into a person's religious views. In a forceful speech he said that he accepted Bradlaugh's original clause but could not accept it as amended. John Morley, revealing his opposition at the last moment, also spoke against the amendment. It meant, he said, that a man would have to assert before a judge and jury that he had no religious belief and this might damage his evidence. He regretted that a compromise had been made. Bradlaugh said in response, 'to protest against the Bill because you do not get it in your own form of words, in spite of the fact that the measure contains a good deal of the highest value, was not a philosophical kind of opposition.' Bradlaugh understood the necessity of a compromise in order to secure his Bill. His reference to philosophy was deliberate. In 1877 Morley, in his Essay on Compromise, had described with approval precisely the form of compromise that Bradlaugh was making. He defined a legitimate compromise as 'a rational acquiescence in the fact that the bulk of your contemporaries are not yet prepared to embrace the new idea'. Hunter and Morley voted against the amendment which the Committee approved by the slender margin of 172 votes to 166. When the Bill was read for the third time neither Hunter nor Morley supported it but the House was in favour by a majority of 87.

There was a final hurdle: the Bill had to win the approval of the Lords. The debate in that Chamber was on 27 November and the Bill was introduced by Earl Spencer supported by Lord Coleridge. It was widely supposed that the Church of England, the Lords Spiritual, would oppose the Bill. But not so. The Archbishop of Canterbury speaking for his Church, said that the Bill should be treated on its merits and he supported it. The one member of the Lords who gave strenuous opposition was Bradlaugh's opponent, the former Sir Hardinge Giffard, now again Lord Chancellor with the title of the Earl of Halsbury. Speaking for himself and not for the Government, he moved an amendment to provide that if a juror stated that he had no religious belief that statement should be good cause for a challenge. A person, said Halsbury, should have a right to have his case tried by a juror who was bound by the sanctity of the oath. This amendment was rejected and Halsbury did not vote against adoption of the Bill. The Oaths Bill was finally approved without a division on 3 December.

The newspapers the next day were full of Bradlaugh's success in securing at last the right to affirm. The most cogent comment was in the *Northern Echo* which after reference to an historic occasion wrote:

> Six years ago the Gladstone Government was labouring to remove a legal disability which obstructed the entry into Parliament of a duly elected representative. The Ministry manfully strove to pass a Bill which should permit a member to make affirmation if he objected to the taking of an oath. From every Tory platform in the country, and almost every pulpit in the Church of England, there arose the greatest confusion of clamour that ever assailed English statesmen. A few years have sped away. The men who made the fearful charges are in power. They permit Mr Bradlaugh to take his seat. He drafts a Bill which gives to every man in every relation in life on avowing that he objects to taking the oath, the right to make a simple affirmation. The people who professed to believe that the Fate of Nineveh would overwhelm us did we accept the Affirmation Bill have given Mr Bradlaugh every aid in passing his sweeping measure through the House of Commons. Last night the measure was pronounced by the Primate to be perfectly innocuous. Not one beat of alarm has come from the Bishops, not one objurgatory sermon about the connection between oaths and religion has been preached by the clergy during the passing of the Bill. Was the outcry insincere? If it was the present silence is dishonourable.

Chapter Seventy-nine

A BOOK WITH THE TITLE *LIFE of Charles Bradlaugh MP* was published in February 1888 by D. J. Gunn and Co. of 84 Fleet Street. The author was given as Charles R. McKay and the book was a substantial hardback of 480 pages priced at 10/6d. The work was highly defamatory of Bradlaugh, vilifying him directly and by innuendo almost from the first page to the last, and it came to be known in freethought circles as 'the libellous life'. Weary though Bradlaugh was with litigation it was necessary that he act quickly to prevent distribution.

The purpose of the book was undoubtedly to make money for its backers. It dealt with Bradlaugh from his earliest days until his entry into Parliament. Based on a plausible biographical structure, the book took every opportunity to present Bradlaugh in a false light and its malicious intention was plain to see. It attacked Bradlaugh's attitude to the Carlile family; it questioned his relationship with his wife; it commented unpleasantly on Annie Besant. The book rehearsed the publication of *The Fruits of Philosophy* and the Knowlton trial. It referred offensively to Bradlaugh's daughters, describing them as 'uppish'. One of the themes of the book was that Bradlaugh made an ostentatious show of poverty whilst covertly enriching himself from the publication of indecent literature.

The first task was to discover who was the source of the book. It was not his political opponents nor his religious adversaries. The three conspirators who together were responsible for the work were secularists who resented his dominant position in the freethought movement. The idea for the book had probably originated with McKay but he was not in fact the author. McKay was a protégé of William Stewart Ross, a secularist publisher who wrote under the nom-de-plume of 'Saladin'. He had written for the *National Reformer* in its early days and had developed a strong dislike for Bradlaugh and the National Secular Society. Ross was the brains behind the defamatory exercise. The author was William Harral Johnson who wrote secular material under the name 'Anthony Collins' and in 1858 had collaborated with Bradlaugh and John Watts in writing the series 'Half Hours with Freethinkers'. Johnson resented Bradlaugh's success, referring to him as the 'Atheistic Pope'. He gladly accepted £50 from Mckay to do the writing though he was given help from Ross who also arranged for the printing. The publisher's name, D. J. Gunn, was fictitious.

Bradlaugh's friend in Edinburgh, John Lees, discovered that the printer was John Colston and Bradlaugh sued him successfully in the Scottish Courts. He also obtained an interim injunction in England to restrain distribution until trial. The litigation proceeded slowly in 1888 and meanwhile the conspirators fell out with each other. In February 1889 Bradlaugh settled with McKay, who had by then been declared bankrupt, obtaining a formal expression of regret. That same month Bradlaugh settled with Ross on the basis that all copies possessed by Ross be destroyed, that £50 be paid to a charity nominated by Bradlaugh, and payment of full legal costs. Bradlaugh also sued successfully two newspapers which had published defamatory extracts.

The allegations in the book that Bradlaugh had made substantial sums of money were painfully false. In 1888 Bradlaugh's finances were in a serious condition. He still had debts of £3,000 from his parliamentary struggle and was finding it difficult to pay the interest on this sum. Subscriptions to the *National Reformer*, particularly from the north of England, were falling. The interest on the debentures taken out by him and Annie were proving a heavy burden. And his parliamentary work left him little time to earn his living. The summer of 1888 was a critical point. He could not afford to pay for a holiday, and more seriously was concerned that he might have to give up Parliament.

Fortunately, William Stead came to his aid. In August the *Pall Mall Gazette* sponsored an appeal to relieve Bradlaugh of his debts.

The appeal was taken up by the *Star* newspaper and two Northampton papers, the *Guardian* and the *Mercury*. The response was impressive, many hundreds contributing, including some MPs. There were small sums, as little as sixpence, and a few anonymous donations of as much as £100. Some debenture holders waived their right to their securities. Bradlaugh was both relieved and embarrassed. He wrote in the *National Reformer* that the fund should close on 26 September, his fifty-fifth birthday. The total sum collected was just under £2,500, not enough to extinguish all debts but enough for him to continue in Parliament. That summer he was after all able to enjoy four and a half days' fishing in Loch Long.

Despite these financial troubles Bradlaugh remained highly active in Parliament. The Select Committee on Perpetual Pensions reported in 1888 and it was apparent that Bradlaugh had exerted a major influence on its deliberations. The unanimous recommendation was that 'Pensions, allowances and payments ought not in future to be granted in perpetuity and all such grants be limited to the persons actually rendering the services'. It also recommended that 'all existing perpetual pensions, allowances and payments , and all hereditary offices be determined and abolished'.

Bradlaugh moved the adoption of this Report and his speech won general acceptance. He was concerned with two matters: the abolition of all hereditary financial privileges; and that this be done with a minimum cost to the public purse. Economy of public expenditure was a constant theme in his speeches, inside and outside Parliament. Bradlaugh's motion was seconded by Louis Jennings, a Conservative member who was a close ally of Lord Randolph Churchill. If anything, Jennings spoke in favour of the motion in stronger terms than Bradlaugh and carried with him a large number of his party. W. H. Smith also supported the Report on behalf of the Government and, with one minor amendment, it was carried without a division. Thus the surviving hereditary pensions were abolished, though it remained for Bradlaugh to urge that they be terminated on terms that represented a real saving to the nation.

It was Louis Jennings who brought about a reconciliation

between Bradlaugh and Churchill. Despite Bradlaugh's deep dislike of his opponent he was aware of the friendly overtures that Churchill was making. Moreover Bradlaugh, unlike most MPs, had some respect for Churchill's dramatic resignation as Chancellor based as it was on a wish to reduce the military estimates. As a backbencher, Churchill had been elected chairman of the Army and Navy Committee. Bradlaugh spoke to Jennings one afternoon, said he had been reading the proceedings of the Committee and thought Churchill was giving enormous service to it: 'He has done so much good that I must close up my account with him.' Jennings replied, 'There is no use in keeping it up, it looks like vindictiveness.' 'Yes,' said Bradlaugh, 'I will close the ledger.'

In November 1888 Alice, who was looking after her father at Circus Road, fell ill with typhoid fever which rapidly became complicated by meningitis. Hypatia moved her sister from the dust and noise of Circus Road to the quieter situation of 19 Avenue Road and employed a nurse to help care for her. Because of the meningitis Alice was never fully conscious and was frequently delirious. She disliked Annie Besant being in her sick room. One day, when she was near to death, she sat up in bed and screamed in a strange tone: 'There is someone in the room wishing me ill, someone who is watching, watching all the time.' It was Annie who was standing by the bed observing intently. Deeply interested in spiritualism at that time, Annie was evidently curious to observe that moment when the spirit leaves the body.

Alice died on 2 December. She was thirty-two years old, two years older than Hypatia. She was quieter than Hypatia, less confident but just as fiercely intelligent and a mainstay of the classes in the Hall of Science. She wrote with her sister a weekly Summary of News for the *National Reformer*. Her one publication was a pamphlet on mind/body unity published in 1884 with the title 'Mind Considered as a Bodily Function'. Her life was largely devoted to her father. Her final wish, to be cremated, was frustrated by building works at the Woking Crematorium so she was buried at Brookwood Cemetery instead. Bradlaugh wanted a quiet funeral for his quiet daughter and wrote in the *National Reformer*: 'Many friends have desired to attend the funeral. Any public funeral would be painful to me; and I trust to offend no-one in not acceding. The funeral, private and silent, will have taken place at Woking Cemetery. The funeral wreath and flowers sent are reverently laid on the grave.'

It was apparent to Hypatia that she and Arthur must now move to Circus Road to live with her father. Annie thought she had a better idea. Not as prosperous as she had been, for she had written no pamphlets in 1888, she wanted to rid herself of the lease of 19 Avenue Road. So she urged Bradlaugh to take over that lease and told him it was Hypatia's wish. Questioned by her father, Hypatia promptly and emphatically rejected the suggestion. She understood that the house in Avenue Road was too expensive and troublesome for her father, struggling with financial problems and grieving for his first born. Bradlaugh was relieved. He had no wish to move from Circus Road.

Chapter Eighty

DESPITE HIS CONTINUING FINANCIAL PROBLEMS, HIS sadness at the death of his elder daughter, and emerging signs of his own ill health, Bradlaugh faced the 1889 Parliamentary session with unflagging industry. He was not, however, as successful in 1889 as he had been the year before. One of the Bills he introduced was a measure to abolish the blasphemy laws. It had the long title: 'A Bill to Abolish Prosecutions for the Expression of Opinions on Matters of Religion'. It was drafted to put an end to criminal prosecutions for heresy, blasphemous libel, and common law blasphemy. If enacted the Bill would have repealed the law under which Bradlaugh had been prosecuted in 1883.

In the debate on second reading Bradlaugh made a moderate speech, simply and clearly setting out his reasons for the Bill. He was supported by Dr Hunter. The Bill was strongly opposed by the Conservatives and some sanctimonious Liberals. The most passionate opposition came from Sir Edward Clarke, Solicitor-General, who had replaced Sir Hardinge Giffard as Bradlaugh's most fervent opponent in the Commons. 'If this Bill were to pass,' said Clarke, 'people would be free to scatter broadcast the most scandalous and shocking suggestions with regard to sacred things of religion without being subject to any prosecution.' There was never hope that the Bill would succeed and it failed on second reading by a large majority.

In 1889 Bradlaugh again dealt with the matter of perpetual pensions. The Government had accepted that these pensions were to be terminated, but the Chancellor of the Exchequer had proposed that the rate of commutation be twenty-seven years purchase. For Bradlaugh this rate was outrageously high and he led the opposition to it. Gladstone made a long speech apparently in support of Bradlaugh but, as so often with the Grand Old Man, there was ambiguity in his views. Bradlaugh again lost this debate by a large majority. He was also unsuccessful in obtaining a Royal Commission to consider the grievances of the Indian native population. He urged that the time had come to advance self-government in India by ensuring that Indians of ability played a wider part in the administration of their country. He failed to get the Commission but was relentless in putting questions to Sir John Gorst. In that session he asked thirty-six detailed questions on Indian affairs and demonstrated that he knew as much about the Indian Budget as any member including the Secretary of State.

In the midst of all this activity Bradlaugh attached most importance to his attempt, in March 1889, to expunge from the journals of the House the Resolution of 22 June 1880 'that he be not permitted to take the oath or make the affirmation'. Ever since that Resolution, proposed by Sir Hardinge Giffard, had been approved by the House it had been Bradlaugh's intention to get it expunged. Now that he had been permitted to take the oath, and his Affirmation Bill had been enacted, he judged the time was right to move the expunction.

His speech in favour of his motion was calm and considered; he had no wish to reawaken the bitterness of his exclusion. He referred to precedents and in particular to the case of John Wilkes, the infamous champion of liberty, who had been expelled from the House of Commons as member for Middlesex in February 1769 on the ground that he was a person incapable of being a member of Parliament. This Resolution of expulsion had been expunged from the Records in May 1782 'as being subversive of the rights of the electors of the Kingdom'. These same words were used by Bradlaugh in his own motion and he asserted that he was asking the House to do no more than it had done 107 years before.

Bradlaugh's case was that nothing, other than the Standing Orders of the House, should become between a member and the performance of his duty. He asked for the Resolution to be expunged as a measure of justice to his constituents and to the electorate of the UK. If, he said, the Resolution remained on the

Journals of the House it would be a precedent for a state of things so dangerous that members in a minority at any time could not contemplate it with calmness. If the House could exclude one member it could exclude more. His final plea was: 'I trust that this House may feel it can accept the motion in the spirit in which I move it, without taunt or boasting, only entreating the High Court of Parliament to do itself the justice which none other has the power to do.'

Strong opposition came from the Conservative Government. Sir Michael Hicks-Beach distinguished Bradlaugh's motion from the Wilkes' case. The House had not only expelled Wilkes but debarred the electors from returning him again. The Resolution of 22 June 1880 did not touch the power of the Northampton electors to return Bradlaugh as many times as they wished. Sir Edward Clarke spoke for the Government and spoke with force: 'It is an idle thing to tear out of the history of the House of Commons one page. If this motion were carried it would not alter the fact that the House of Commons did, in 1880, take upon itself the right represented by the Resolution in question. I am against tampering with and falsifying the Records of the House.'

The main support for Bradlaugh came from Sir William Harcourt, Gladstone's deputy in the House. Like Gladstone he averred that in 1880 the House had acted beyond its jurisdiction. 'We do not want to falsify the Record, as has been suggested, but merely to point out that the House of Commons committed an illegal act and we do not desire that the precedent should remain.' When the motion was put to the vote it was soundly defeated. Bradlaugh told the House that though he had failed that night he would bring his motion again and again, session by session, for the sake of his electors.

Sir William Harcourt was the one member of the House who understood the special importance for Bradlaugh of having the record expunged. At the request of Gladstone, Harcourt had spoken to Bradlaugh to advise him that the Leader of the Liberal Party desired that he should be prepared to accept office in a forthcoming Liberal administration. Bradlaugh had told Harcourt that he deeply appreciated the kind suggestion but there was one absolute barrier against acceptance. This was a barrier that lay in Gladstone's power to remove. 'I will not,' said Bradlaugh, 'accept office and become a Minister of the Crown so long as the Resolution concerning my expulsion from the House remains on the Record.'

A few days later Harcourt spoke again to Bradlaugh to report that Gladstone saw no insuperable difficulty in giving the assurance that was required.

'You would, then, really take office, Mr Bradlaugh?'

'Yes, certainly,' Bradlaugh replied, 'I think I should be able to do some good and would be glad of the opportunity.' 'Besides,' he added, 'after all that has happened it would be particularly gratifying for me to hold office.'

Chapter Eighty-one

IN FEBRUARY 1889 WILLIAM STEAD GAVE Annie Besant two bulky volumes to read. 'Can you review these?' he asked her. 'My young men fight shy of them but you are quite mad enough to make something of them.' The two substantial quarto volumes, amounting to almost 1,500 pages, entitled *The Secret Doctrine* were written by Madame Helena Petrovna Blavatsky, the leader of the Theosophical Movement in Europe. Far from fighting shy of them, Annie took the two volumes home and devoted the next few days to their study. The work bowled her over. She was fascinated by the mysticism, the occultism, the symbolism and the psychic content of the volumes. She knew immediately, by a flood of illumination, that she had found something that she was yearning for. In those few days she became convinced of the truth of Theosophism.

Straightaway Annie asked Stead for a letter of introduction to Madame Blavatsky which he willingly gave for he was himself interested in spiritual matters. He was curious about Blavatsky and said that he was both delighted and repelled by her. Annie had shown the two volumes to Herbert Burrows who was also excited by them so together on 15 March they went to 17 Lansdowne Road, Notting Hill, to meet this exceptional woman. Madame Blavatsky already knew of Annie and was expecting her to visit. Her first words were, 'My dear Mrs Besant, I have so long wished to see you.' It was a brief meeting, with Annie overcome by the emotion of the moment. She and Burrows made their exit calmly but they walked back along Lansdowne Road in awe-struck silence.

Madame Blavatsky had been born in Russia in a family with

aristocratic connections. Married as a young woman she had divorced her husband. She had travelled widely in America and India before settling in London and this gave her a cosmopolitan air. By 1889 she was corpulent, confined to a wheelchair, and chain-smoked cigarettes which she rolled from Russian tobacco. The fog of the cigarette smoke amplified her inscrutable presence. Through this haze she emanated personal power. There was an implication of androgyny about her and she had the manners of a man. She was a bundle of contradictions, at once massive and sensitive, vulgar and intelligent.

Annie's review of the two volumes appeared in the *Pall Mall Gazette* on 25 April under the title, 'Among the Adepts, Madame Blavatsky and the Secret Doctrine'. It was a favourable review, interpreting occidental thought, and suggesting by implication that Theosophy embraced a higher truth. It was the *Gazette's* Practice not to publish the name of its reviewers and this suited Annie because she was not yet ready to declare to the world, and especially not to Bradlaugh, her new-found fascination. Soon after publication, Annie went back to Blavatsky seeking further information. Blavatsky advised her to read a damaging Report from the Society for Psychical Research and Annie spent a day examining this. She did not care what the Report said, she was not in the mood to believe anything which disparaged Madame Blavatsky. Her mind was made up. She went to the offices of the Theosophical Society, asked for an application form which she completed then and there to become a Fellow of the Theosophic Society. To her surprise she discovered Burrows had stolen a march and had already become a Fellow. Annie then hastened to tell Madame Blavatsky of her decision. This was a time for Blavatsky to speak softly: 'You are a noble woman. May Master bless you.'

Bradlaugh knew nothing of this development even though he saw Annie several times a week. He knew of her growing interest in spiritualism, of her attendance with Burrows at seances, of her growing dislike of what she regarded as materialism. But he learnt that she had joined the Theosophists from a newspaper comment. He felt it keenly that this 'true good woman who has so stood side by side with me' as he had written in his will, should show her dissatisfaction at the work they had done together. Hypatia was horrified and the relationship between her and Annie was never the same.

In the *National Reformer* of 23 June Annie wrote a second review of *The Secret Doctrine*, this time with her name at the end. This second review was naturally more favourable than the first, for she was now a Fellow of the Theosophist Society. She described the distinction between the East and the West. The West studied the material universe by way of the five senses assisted by scientific instruments. Whereas the East, she averred, had cultivated superior senses, mental and spiritual faculties which enabled investigation of a higher plane than the physical. This review generated a shower of complaints from regular readers of the *National Reformer*, objecting to this evidence of apostasy in their atheistic journal. Once again Bradlaugh had to act.

The following week under the heading 'Some Words of Explanation', Bradlaugh wrote that following the review of Blavatsky's book he had been asked for his opinion on Theosophy. As always, Bradlaugh defined any term he used. A Theosophist he said, means 'one who claims to have a knowledge of God, or of the laws of nature, by means of internal illumination'. He added: 'I very deeply regret that my colleague and co-worker has, with somewhat of suddenness, and without any interchange of ideas with myself, adopted as facts matters which seem to me as unreal as it is possible for any fiction to be. The editorial policy of this paper is unchanged and is directly antagonistic to all forms of Theosophy.' He concluded: 'I would have preferred on this subject to have held my peace, for the publicly disagreeing with Mrs Besant on her adoption of socialism has caused pain to both; but on reading her article and taking the public announcement of her having joined the Theosophical organisation, I owe it to those who look to me for guidance to say this with clearness.' In that same issue, Annie replied to this statement, lamely and unconvincingly, saying that it was not possible for her then to state fully her reasons for joining the Theosophical Society. The following week she announced her intention of writing a pamphlet giving the explanation that she felt was due to the party for which she had worked so long. Writing a pamphlet was her usual method of justifying a conversion. In 1877 she had written 'My Path to Atheism'; in 1886, 'Why I am a Socialist'; and later in 1889 she produced 'Why I became a Theosophist'.

George Foote was scathing about Annie's change of views and wrote a pamphlet: 'Mrs Besant's Theosophy'. He said of Annie, 'She seems to be very much at the mercy of her emotions and especially at the mercy of her latest friends. A powerful engine she runs on lines laid down for her.' His particular concern was her use of the *National Reformer* to propagate her new persuasion. 'Her procedure on her conversion to socialism was a warning. She used the Freethought platform, as I think, in an unjustifiable manner. She had not made it; none of us made it; it has been made by hundreds of workers through more than one generation. Yet Mrs Besant insisted on using it to the utmost for the ventilation of her new views on the principle I suppose that the end justifies the means.'

Despite these strong reactions to her change of mind, Annie continued to regard herself as a close colleague of Bradlaugh, insensitive to the distress caused by her growing intimacy with Madame Blavatsky. Hypatia understood that to hear of Annie's conversion indirectly, and to recognise her subservience to Blavatsky, was profoundly painful for her father. But he continued to speak no ill of her. She remained as co-proprietor of the *National Reformer* and a regular contributor of articles.

Chapter Eighty-two

IN ADDITIONAL TO HIS PARLIAMENTARY WORK, Bradlaugh was giving five lectures a week and was a tired man. He wrote in the *National Reformer* that: 'My only means of existence from day to day are the precarious produce of my tongue and pen.' He was endeavouring to use his tongue less and his pen more. Lecturing incurred the stress of travel and the strain of speaking in front of new audiences, and it was easier for him to write. Those lectures he did give tended to be on political rather than theological subjects, a tendency that George Foote constantly regretted. It was Foote's view, which he never hesitated to express, that Bradlaugh was wasting his time in Parliament instead of concentrating on leadership of the freethought movement.

Bradlaugh was therefore delighted to be commissioned by the *North American Review* to write a long essay on atheism and he chose as his title 'Humanity's Gain from Unbelief', which allowed him to revisit and refresh arguments that had concerned him all his life. The essay was a consistent development of a paper he had prepared twenty years before, 'Heresy: Its Utility and Morality', in which he had written: 'Belief too often means nothing more than the prostration of the intellect on the threshold of the unknown.' His new essay was published in the March 1889 issue of the *North American Review* and its theme was manifest in its first sentence: 'that the gradual and growing rejection of Christianity – like the rejection of faiths which preceded it – has in fact added, and will add, to man's happiness and well-being.' He recognised the persistent nature of religious faiths, which he expressed in the memorable epigram, 'None sees a religion die.' He went on to assert that progress is the outcome of scepticism rather than of belief. He gave as examples of the clear gain to humanity of unbelief the abolition of slavery, the rejection of witchcraft, the growth in astronomical knowledge, the repudiation of the divine right of kings and the abandonment of the persecution of Jews, Roman Catholics, and so-called infidels. His assertion was that unbelief, the critical and challenging spirit, was a vital contribution to the enterprise of human progress.

This essay proved to be a best-selling pamphlet and was reprinted in several journals in North America, Australia and India and was immediately published in England. Bradlaugh's aim was to stimulate discussion and this was certainly achieved. Consideration and analysis of the pamphlet was vigorous throughout England and especially in the North-East. The *Newcastle Daily Leader* and the *Newcastle Weekly Chronicle* generated discourse throughout North and South Shields. As a result the Rev. Marsden Gibson, a Newcastle clergyman, invited Bradlaugh to defend and justify the pamphlet in a debate which was held in the Central Hall, Newcastle, on two successive evenings in September 1889.

More than 1,400 people attended the debate on those two hot autumn evenings.

The essence of Bradlaugh's speech came from his pamphlet. Marsden Gibson responded well, giving his view that unbelief has achieved little. 'Look around and see what unbelief has done. What hospitals has unbelief founded, what buildings has it created, what Sunday schools has it taught? None.' Gibson could not resist a verbal sally on Bradlaugh personally who, he said, stood alone in his own secularist party. He could count eleven of Bradlaugh's apostles who had left him in recent years, including in the last few weeks the person of Mrs Besant who had set out on a welcome return journey. Bradlaugh's rejoinder was swift: 'I am not so sure that it is material we have to debate this evening whether I stand alone and eleven apostles have deserted me, but I remind the speaker that eleven apostles deserted his founder in the surest hour of his need.' [Laughter and Cheers.]

It was a delightful debate with plenty of healthy good-natured commotion from supporters of both speakers. Bradlaugh finished as usual with a rousing peroration: 'It is true that improvement has been made on every side, but in spite of religion and not because of it. Science has lit the world which the Churches kept in darkness. Humanity has gained from unbelief, if it was only that doubt has stirred the people to thinking, brought hearing to the deaf, and cleared the eyes to find the world's beauty, long creed-hidden.' He was glad to be back on a platform arguing for freethought. Foote commenting in the *Freethinker* wrote: 'Mr Bradlaugh in another anti-theological debate is a gratifying spectacle. It quite looks like old times again.'

Chapter Eighty-three

BRADLAUGH CAUGHT A SEVERE CHILL IN October 1889 after delivering a lecture in London. The chill developed into a high fever accompanied by congestion of the kidneys, a manifestation of the Bright's disease from which his mother had died. He was seriously ill. All his lectures were immediately cancelled, and he was confined to bed, a confinement which lasted twenty-three days. Bradlaugh recognised that the cause of his collapse was the physical and mental strain he had been under since 1880. His doctors advised him to see no person, read no letters, and transact no business. Hypatia looked after him with the aid of two nurses. No one except Hypatia, the doctors, and the nurses were allowed into his room, though Annie, with her usual insistence, visited for a few minutes each morning.

The decisive day was 22 October when, in his own words, he was as near death as a man could look and still live. He pulled through but recovery was slow. Not until 17 November could he leave his bed and walk a few times round his library. Apart from the fever and the inflammation of his kidneys, he had a severe pain in his left shin, a leg that had never completely healed from the violence of 3 August 1881. The progress of his illness was reported in the *National Reformer* and to his colleagues in Parliament and many people in the country were aware of it. Remarkably, a few churches offered up prayers for him which led to the rumour, quickly dispatched, that he was no longer an atheist.

When he had partially recovered, George Foote came to see him and was startled by his appearance. He looked much older, was pale and grey and apparently infirm. But his mind was clear. These two men, the leaders of the freethought movement, who had known many differences, shared an intimate moment. Bradlaugh pointed to his simple bed and said, 'When I lay there and all was black the thing that troubled me least was the convictions of my life.' Then, after a moment, and with a broken voice he added, 'The freethought party is a party I love.' With these few words Bradlaugh chose to reveal his soul to his freethought colleague.

The recipe for recuperation universally recommended for a desperately sick man in 1889 was a long sea voyage. By happy coincidence, Bradlaugh had been invited by the Indian National Congress to travel by sea to Bombay to attend as a distinguished visitor its fifth Annual Convention to be held between Christmas and the New Year. The Congress would pay all travel expenses but even so Bradlaugh had not the means to meet the heavy additional costs. A fellow Liberal MP, William McEwan, sent Bradlaugh a cheque for £200 to make the visit possible. McEwan was a wealthy brewer, who had built a fortune by selling McEwan's Export Ale to the British colonies. He was known for his philanthropy and was pleased to assist.

Bradlaugh's illness had convinced him that in future he had to restrict his multitude of activities. With great regret he decided he could no longer serve as President of the National Secular Society. The Society had been losing members, it needed reinvigoration, and required too much of Bradlaugh's time. Hypatia was reluctant to see her father give up the Presidency, which gave him an effective platform for his views. But Bradlaugh recognised the inevitable and before leaving for India issued a notice, repeated every week in the National Reformer, convening an extraordinary special meeting of members to be held on Sunday 16 February 1890 with the sole purpose of receiving Bradlaugh's resignation and appointing a new President to act until the next Annual Conference.

On 28 November, a bitterly cold day, Bradlaugh, drawn and pale, left Liverpool Street Station for the Albert Docks to join SS Ballaarat. He found he had his own stateroom, a luxury enjoyed by only a favoured few. The ship visited Gibraltar, Malta and then Brindisi where Sir William Wedderburn embarked having saved a week by travelling overland from London. Wedderburn was the fourth baronet, a former Indian civil servant who had retired early in 1887 after disagreement with his senior officials over his strong identification with Indian aspirations. He thereafter devoted his time to promoting political reform for India and was to preside over the 1889 Convention.

From Brindisi, the *Ballaarat* sailed to Port Said, through the Suez canal to Aden where Bradlaugh and Wedderburn transferred to the SS *Assam*, a smaller vessel that plied regularly between Aden and Bombay. At each of the ports he visited, Bradlaugh posted a letter, sometimes several letters, to Hypatia, mainly about his health. He was feeling fitter but his left leg was still painful and he had bouts of severe lumbago. These letters to his daughter were full of fatherly feeling; he knew that Hypatia was again pregnant. He liked to write to his daughters partly in French and he ended these letters with the affectionate, 'ton pere qui t'aime bien'.

The SS *Assam* arrived at Bombay on 22 December to a wildly cheering crowd of hundreds of Indians assembled on the quay to greet the two distinguished guests. Bradlaugh and Wedderburn were supplied with a carriage and pair to take them through the crowds to a large bungalow in substantial grounds, which was their residence during the Convention. That evening they were entertained at a reception at the Bombay Royal Yacht Club by two hundred of the senior Conference delegates. There were many agreeable speeches and peals upon peals of cheering. For the 'Member for India' this was a warm welcome to the country for whose future he was so concerned.

Chapter Eighty-four

THE INDIAN NATIONAL CONGRESS HAD BEEN established in 1885 as a political movement with the purpose of increasing harmony between the ruling British and the Indian people. In its early years it was not opposed to British rule and was dedicated to obtaining a greater share in government for educated Indians. It was a middle-class organisation whose members were largely lawyers, teachers, and journalists. Nonetheless it endeavoured to be universal in its appeal, a political umbrella to include socialists as well as conservatives, Muslims as well as Hindus. There were some dissentient voices, mainly from Muslims, but by and large it received broad-based support from Indians as a means of transforming their constitutional prospects.

The 1889 Convention was attended by over 2,000 delegates from all parts of India together with about 3,000 observers. When Bradlaugh arrived on the first day these members all rose to their feet clapping and cheering. Then came the addresses. Bradlaugh was presented with thirty-seven addresses from all parts of the country, from Bombay, Bengal, Calcutta, Lucknow, Nagpur and Poona to name just a small scattered collection. Most of these addresses were printed, some beautifully hand-written, and contained in exquisite caskets of silver, or of ivory, some in rich gold kincob or in highly decorated bags. They were a generous tribute to their English parliamentary advocate. These signed addresses were all written in much the same terms expressing, for example, 'our feelings of gratitude for the zeal, earnestness and devotion which has characterised your philanthropic endeavours to improve British administration in India'. As Bradlaugh wrote to Hypatia, 'Congress is an enormous success, but attending it still tires me considerably. The Indian folk seem inclined almost to worship me.'

Bradlaugh gave the closing speech to the Convention on 29 December. He was introduced by Wedderburn who attempted to summarise the sentiments of all the addresses that Bradlaugh had received: 'You come to us as a stranger in person but not in repute. Your arousal of the people of Great Britain into a sympathetic recognition of India's needs will enshrine your name for all time in the proudest and most imperishable of human homes, the hearts and traditions of a loving and graceful race.' Bradlaugh had listened carefully to the many speeches at the Convention and had discussions with many of the delegates. One of his skills as a speaker was the ability to match the mood and tone of his words to the audience in front of him. He was able to achieve this before an Indian audience in Bombay as he could before secular and political meetings at home.

He began by addressing the audience as 'friends, fellow-subjects, and fellow citizens'. They were his friends because of the special greetings they had given him. They were fellow subjects because they were all loyal to one ruler. And he felt proud to address them as fellow citizens because he hoped that the term would become a reality before his life ended. He identified himself as a visitor from a Parliament within whose walls he was one of the poorest members, describing himself as 'Born of the people, trusted by the people, I hope to die of the people. And I know of no geographical or race limitation to this word "people".' He warned his audience not to expect too much from his advocacy of their cause in England: 'One man is only a waterdrop in the ocean of your life.' He praised Sir William Wedderburn who he hoped to see in the House of Commons speaking with an authority which long residence in India had given him.

He told the Convention that he was pleased to have the title of 'Member for India' which some few had sneered at but others understood the hearty meaning. 'Men whose measure I cannot hope to cope with have held this title; and I am not to hold it simply by great effort on great occasions but by small doings wherever there is injustice to be redressed.' Justice for India was his theme and his advice to his audience was that they seek equality before the law for all – equality of opportunity for all, equality of expression for all – penalty on none, favouritism for none. He ended by declaring: 'In this movement let there be no force, save the force of brain, no secret union – let all be open, frank and before the law. Then if mischief touch you, so far as one man may, and so far as one man's speech can, English liberty shall put itself on the side of yours.' He finished to loud and lengthy cheers as he withdrew from the platform and the 1889 Convention dispersed.

Before leaving for England on 3 January Bradlaugh had many discussions with Indian leaders, princes and presidencies from all over the country. He also met the Freethinkers of India, twenty members of the Bombay and Madras Secular Society. This was an occasion for yet another Address: 'It is impossible for us to forget the immense service you have rendered to humanity in asserting and maintaining the rights of the people to choose their own representatives irrespective of class or creed.' They ended: 'The theological bonds which have bound the brains of thousands of this generation have been snapped asunder by the unwearying effort of such men as yourself to spread the light of reason.'

Bradlaugh arrived back in London at the end of January refreshed by the sea voyage but immediately caught up in a host of activities. One of the first to visit him was George Foote. Entering his library to see Foote, he held out his hand in welcome all the way. Looking at Bradlaugh closely to see how well he was, Foote was both satisfied and dissatisfied. Bradlaugh was undoubtedly improved but there was a sign about him that though his mind was as active as ever his body was devitalised. He told Foote of the voyage, of the success of the Congress, the kindnesses he had received, and showed him some of the Indian gifts he had brought back with him. But he was concerned about his finances. He had received offers of work from several magazine editors, but added, 'One doesn't know how long it will last, it is a precarious business.' Bradlaugh then confided in Foote that he could have made plenty of money in India if he had been less scrupulous. He was offered money by rich Indians who appreciated his fight for their interests and understood his poverty and ill-health. But he was too proud to accept these offerings and, as a precaution, always had an English friend in the room when the wealthy natives called on him. He said to Foote, 'I cannot do that. I'll live like the old Bradlaugh or I'll go under.'

Chapter Eighty-five

THE PRIME TASK FACING BRADLAUGH ON his return from India was to prepare for the Extraordinary Meeting of the National Secular Society at which he was to announce his resignation as President and recommend a successor. This was bound to be a difficult decision for him. He had founded the Society twenty-four years earlier and, except for one brief period, had been President ever since. The Society had proved to be a successful focus for freethought and at its peak in the early 1880s had 120 branches and 10,000 members. Its existence, centrally controlled from London, was a product of Bradlaugh's organisational skill and his authoritarian style.

The Society had supplied Bradlaugh with the best possible platform for the expression and propagation of his ideas. At many of his lectures, and at all of his debates, he had to deal with vigorous opposition that influenced the way he spoke. When he talked to the Society, however, he was before an audience entirely made up of ardent supporters and could address matters of principle knowing they would receive an attentive hearing. Many of his memorable sayings, his most quotable reflections, the purple passages of his oratory, came from his closing speeches at the Annual Congresses of the Society. In 1880 he had predicted: 'The age is not far off when men shall be free and equal, not in the dead level of that equality which can never come, but the age when men rank higher than kings and priests are not.' At the close of the 1888 Congress he had described the purpose of freethought as: 'The enfranchisement of the human mind from the trammels of old legends, which the ignorance of some, the credulity of some, the fraud of some had bound around it, till like the constrictor they cramped and crippled the brain into helplessness.'

Hypatia endeavoured to persuade her father not to relinquish the Presidency. Given his illness, she thought his resignation might be misinterpreted. But Bradlaugh understood he was not well enough to carry on. He had to give priority to his parliamentary work. There was also the matter of his straitened finances. Parliament paid him nothing and the Society paid him nothing. Indeed the Society had been a financial burden, for he had subsidised it from his own resources for many years. The question for him was not whether he should resign but whom he should nominate to succeed him.

When he discussed with Annie his forthcoming resignation it appeared that she was under the impression that he would nominate her despite her well publicised conversion to Theosophy. Bradlaugh explained gently that she could not possibly become President. He and Hypatia, who was present, were astounded at her presumption. Annie had made the mistake of supposing that Bradlaugh's remaining affection for her would override his duty to the Society. This was not his way. His preferred choice to be President was John Robertson, an excellent writer who was proving an effective deputy editor of the *National Reformer*. Hypatia, who was aware of Robertson's loyalty to her father, pressed his claim. But in Bradlaugh's final view Robertson's habitat was the study and the library and not the platform. He had not the organisational skill nor the leadership qualities for the post. The only suitable choice was Foote.

Foote was an eloquent speaker and a brilliant writer. An aggressive atheist, he had devoted his life to the secular movement. His journal *The Freethinker*, vulgar though it might be, was popular. And Foote had earned his spurs: his twelve months imprisonment for blasphemy had given him force and faculty which no one else could match. There had been many difficulties between Bradlaugh and Foote but these were in the past. Bradlaugh realised that Foote was the only candidate who could succeed him effectively and when he told Foote that he would nominate him he coolly gave as his reason, 'There is no one else.'

On the morning of 16 February the Hall of Science swarmed with members. Some of them who had known Bradlaugh for thirty years travelled from all over the country to join those from London who were there in full force. These members had over the years listened to Bradlaugh, some had from time to time opposed him. They had supported him throughout his parliamentary struggle, and were here to welcome him with louder and more persistent cheers than ever. Before the meeting many of them lingered in a minor hall adjoining the main Assembly where the presents that Bradlaugh had brought back from India were on display. Chief amongst these was a richly gilt silver casket containing the Address from the Bombay and Madras Secular Societies. Precisely at 11.15 Bradlaugh, side by side with Annie, walked to the top table. Behind him was Foote and behind him Robertson and Forder, the General Secretary of the Society. As they walked to the table many members of the audience, including some of the strongest of men, held their handkerchiefs to hide their tears.

At the table Bradlaugh too was overcome with feeling. His tears splashed onto the notes he had prepared and for the best part of a minute he allowed those tears to roll. He rose to speak but, trembling with emotion, he had to sit down. He rose a second time but again his reaction was too great. But this was a man who prided himself as having no passion he could not crush like an egg-shell. The third time he rose he managed to crush that shell, and, in a low and quiet voice, was able to address his audience.

He spoke for twelve minutes, explaining his reasons for giving up a task which his health no longer allowed him to continue. He mentioned that some of his kind friends had suggested that he might hold the office nominally. 'But I could not do that. I must be a real President or none. The fault found with me has been that I have been too real in times that are gone.' He asked the meeting to accept his resignation: 'I should like to be your President still, but I could not do the work, and I could not hold the office as a sham.' To much applause he added, 'I lay down the wand of office, which I hope I have held untarnished; I give back the trust you have given me.' The meeting in reluctantly accepting his resignation then proceeded to elect him unanimously as a life member of the Society.

The next business was the election of a new President.

Bradlaugh explained that he had given this matter some thought. 'The duty of the President in a movement like this requires constant watchfulness; it often requires as much courage to do nothing as to do much.' With that he proposed George William Foote [cheers] to be the President until the next Annual Conference. Not everyone in that audience supported Foote. One branch proposed the election of Robertson but he sensibly declined to stand. The resolution that Foote be elected was then carried without opposition. Bradlaugh turned to Foote and said: 'I tender the only emblem of office we have. This hammer, presented to us by the widow of James Watson, was used in days when such freedom as we now enjoy was impossible. Carlile often used it. I give it to you joyfully, Foote, and trust you will hand it to your successor.' When Bradlaugh handed that little wooden hammer to Foote he asked him to now take the chair at the meeting. Foote said, 'No, you must continue in the chair this morning.' For a minute or so, the two men stood facing each other, Bradlaugh seeking to yield the chair to Foote, and Foote insisting that Bradlaugh remain as chairman. Eventually Bradlaugh gave way and resumed the chair. The old bull had given way to the young bull.

When Foote rose to speak he also received prolonged applause. He said he recognised the differences there had been between him and Bradlaugh and therefore appreciated the magnanimity with which he had been proposed. He also understood that he would occasionally need Bradlaugh's help. 'I hardly know how, taking the presidency of an illegal society, one could feel comfortable or even sleep at night unless one had the advice of the best lawyer in England.' So Bradlaugh closed the meeting and the audience dispersed for lunch.

This meeting was the last time Annie Besant appeared on a platform of the NSS. Two weeks later she resigned from the Society.

Chapter Eighty-six

DESPITE HIS LONG RECUPERATIVE SEA VOYAGE Bradlaugh was not restored to full vigour. He looked older than his years and lacked energy. Nonetheless he played as large a part in the new Parliamentary session as he could. The success of his Indian visit prompted him to work even harder on the problems of that country. In the new session he set down forty-five detailed questions for Sir John Gorst to answer; he made a long speech in support of the Maharajah of Kashmir, who had been badly treated by the Indian administration; and he introduced an Indian Councils Bill whose purpose was to improve the constitution of the Governor-General's Council and of the various legislative councils of the princes and presidencies. Although he raised the issue many times, that Bill never reached its second reading because the Leader of the House, W. H. Smith, declined to make room for it.

The political matter that most occupied Bradlaugh in 1890 was the question of the restriction by legislation of the hours of work of adult labourers. The first suggestion of an eight-hour working day had been made twenty years before by Karl Marx in *Das Kapital*. The proposal had simmered since then and in 1889 had been given impetus by a draft Eight Hours Bill published by the Fabians and supported by the Social Democratic Federation. It became a live issue in February 1890 when a Liberal MP, Cunninghame Graham, moved an amendment in the debate on the Address which was designed to restrict the hours of adult labour by international legislation. In a forceful speech Bradlaugh opposed this amendment.

Robert Bontine Cunninghame Graham, to give him his full name, was one of the most unusual members of the 1890

Parliament. He claimed descent from the Earls of Glencairn on one side and from the Earls of Monteith on the other. Despite this aristocratic lineage, his sympathy, he always emphasised, was with the underdog. Asked in Parliament whether he preached 'pure unmitigated socialism' he replied, 'Undoubtedly.' He was flamboyant, mercurial, and often likened to a modern-day Don Quixote. As the first socialist MP he beat Keir Hardie to that title by six years. His predominant political passion was for the eight-hour day which he persistently promoted.

In a long speech Bradlaugh opposed the Cunninghame Graham amendment which was eventually defeated by a large majority. Though Bradlaugh was in favour of shorter working hours, he was concerned about the loss of profits which would result and the destruction of many industries. He said to Cunninghame Graham, 'It is not friendliness to the poor man to propose what you are proposing. His wickedest enemy could not do worse, for you are proposing to render impossible the industries in which many gain their livelihood.' It was in this debate that Bradlaugh defined what he regarded as the purpose of Parliament. It was not, he claimed, Parliament's duty to form public opinion. 'The duty of Parliament is to legislate for the protection of crime, to protect the weak where they need protection against injury to life or limb from the strong, to protect the working man from fraud, but certainly not to interfere between employer and adult employee in the conduct of their business.'

He followed this up with a speech on the eight-hour question in his constituency, affirming his support of trade unions but emphasising that Parliament should have no part to play in determining wages. 'I am not one of those who have ever flattered the people, or striven to win favour by telling them that from the Crown or from Parliament that could be got which could not be got from themselves, by themselves. I would impress upon you this. What the State gives to you, the State takes from you first; it further charges you with the cost of collection, and with the cost of distribution. Better by far that you should save for yourselves and spend for yourselves, than put into the purse of the State your earnings of which only part can at best come back.' The burgesses of Northampton, most of them self-employed, appreciated this sturdy individualism.

The spring brought good news. On 28 April his grandson was born. Hypatia and Arthur did the grandfather the honour of naming the child Charles Bradlaugh Bonner. The *National Reformer* reported that mother and baby were doing well and Bradlaugh might have been referring to himself when he added that his grandson was showing a disposition to make himself heard in the world. Arthur had become a successful printer, producing the *National Reformer* every week and attracting additional work for his business. Hypatia had become her father's mainstay. She organised his domestic life at Circus Road and was the one person he could trust to share his thoughts.

Conscious of his failing health, Bradlaugh was careful to get some relaxation. He visited Loch Long at Easter and again at the beginning of June and once more, for two weeks, in September. He recorded that in his September visit he caught 412 fish with a total weight of 784 lbs. Thoroughly pleased with himself, 'burnt by the sun and wind, but feeling healthier, with most of life's worries far away, though letters and telegrams bring some worry even to this out of the way spot.' Refreshed by these holidays he began lecturing again. Foote, recognising how ill Bradlaugh really was, implored him not to engage in a heavy programme. One day when Bradlaugh was setting off to lecture in Manchester, Foote begged him to cancel the engagement. But Bradlaugh said he could not afford to lose the fee of twenty pounds. 'What is that to your life?' Foote asked and received no more than a grim smile in reply.

In July Bradlaugh was challenged to a debate on the eight-hour movement by the socialist John Burns who attempted to impose such farcical terms, an open air debate with an audience of 200,000, that Bradlaugh declined. Hyndman took up the challenge instead and on 23 July at the St James's Hall, Piccadilly, these two adversaries held their second confrontation. It was a warm evening and the hall was filled with an audience of over 3,000. Hyndman adopted the standard socialist view in favour of an enactment limiting to eight hours the working day for adults in factories, mines and workshops conducted for profit. Bradlaugh wanted hours to be regulated between the employer and the employees, assisted if they wished by trade unions. This was a debate in which the collectivism of Hyndman came face to face with the individualism of Bradlaugh.

The debate between these two six years before had undoubtedly been won by Bradlaugh. But Hyndman had gained experience as a speaker and Bradlaugh was less effective than he had been, especially as he was continually interrupted by a largely socialist audience who were grossly inconsiderate. However there was more to it. Bradlaugh was forced to recognise the growing strength of the socialist movement. He exclaimed at one point in his speech, 'I may have stood still, but I have not changed.' That was a revealing remark. Over more than thirty years Bradlaugh had not modified his views but the world was changing around him. The socialist tide was sweeping in and the mood of the audience that evening clearly showed it.

Bradlaugh's difficult financial situation reached a further crisis in October 1890. He was earning less from lecturing and the shop at 63 Fleet Street was not covering its high cost. Action was necessary. Hypatia suggested he might sell his library but that was one step he would not take. The 10,000 volumes he had lovingly collected were his working tools and he would never part with them. In his straitened circumstances he arranged to let the Fleet Street building from the end of November. The publishing business was transferred to Robert Forder, Secretary of the National Secular Society, and the printing business went to Arthur Bonner. There was a clearance sale of all unsold books and pamphlets. Some debenture holders were willing to write off all or part of their debt for unsold stock but most were not. Bradlaugh had carried heavy debts for years but he now wrote, 'Since my illness I am less capable of bearing pecuniary worry and I am lessening my responsibilities.'

The natural consequence of this business reorganisation was that Annie and Bradlaugh terminate their commercial partnership, their partnership as atheistic radicals having already ended with Annie's conversion to Theosophism. So on 21 December the *National Reformer* gave notice of their joint decision: 'With the closing down of 63 Fleet Street, the partnership between Annie Besant and Charles Bradlaugh under the title of the Freethought Publishing Company, is dissolved by mutual consent. The business will be carried on by Charles Bradlaugh who takes all assets and discharges all liabilities.' There remained affection between these two and one purpose for the dissolution was to free Annie, 'the true good woman', from any liabilities. There was another advantage for Bradlaugh. Dissolution of the partnership meant that on his death the *National Reformer* would go not to Annie but to Hypatia.

Chapter Eighty-seven

10 JANUARY 1891 WAS A BITTERLY COLD day. Walking in the icy fog, Bradlaugh was taken ill and had to retire to bed. At first he thought he could shake off the illness but on 13 January his heart began to trouble him. The next day was critical with severe cardiac spasms. His doctors advised him to cancel all engagements and remain in bed. Some improvement followed and the doctors thought he might make a full recovery. However when Hypatia went to his room on Friday the 16th he looked dreadfully ill. He had suffered severe pain in the night, was paralysed on one side, and had not been able to sleep. The problems with his heart were accompanied by inflammation of the kidneys. Only Hypatia and his two nurses were allowed in the sick room.

One matter troubled Bradlaugh above all others. His name was on the Order Paper for 27 January to move that the Resolution of the House of Commons of 22 June 1880 be expunged. That motion had been defeated in March 1889 and he was anxious to raise the question again. Aware of this deep concern, Hypatia telegraphed John Robertson in Edinburgh asking him to see her urgently and he immediately travelled overnight on the mail train to London. Hypatia's intention was to get another member to move the motion in her father's place. She had Gladstone in mind, hoping that her father's loyalty to him would persuade him to assist. Robertson doubted whether Gladstone would do it and recommended Dr Hunter.

Early on Monday morning, without revealing his plan to Bradlaugh, Robertson went to see Hunter at his chambers in Brick Court. They established that although Bradlaugh's place could not be taken by anyone else, there was a vacant second slot on that day. Hunter readily agreed to use it to move the self-same motion. When Hypatia explained this to her father he was delighted. 'Hunter will do it you say? The very man I would have chosen.' Pondering for a few minutes, he asked again, 'You think I can quite rely on Hunter doing it?' When Hypatia confirmed this, he dictated a letter to Hunter. Though he had no great hope that the motion would succeed he was insistent that the effort be made. Satisfied that Hunter would take on the task, Bradlaugh had his best sleep for a week.

Annie Besant visited Circus Road every day in an attempt to see Bradlaugh, but on each occasion was put off by Hypatia. Her father was exhausted and had asked particularly that Annie not be admitted to his sick room. Hypatia gave a variety of excuses: that her father was asleep, or about to go to sleep, or that the doctors had forbidden visitors. Annie did not regard herself as an ordinary visitor, and suspicious of these excuses, she was not to be denied. On 20 January she wrote to Hypatia pressing her case in imperative terms. The following day, as Hypatia sat at her father's bedside opening his correspondence, that letter obviously embarrassed her.

'What is the matter, my daughter?' Bradlaugh asked.

'Nothing particular,' she replied.

Her father gravely repeated his question.

'It is only that Mrs Besant is vexed that she has not been allowed to see you.'

Sighing, Bradlaugh relented: 'Oh, let her in then.'

When Annie arrived the next day, Hypatia took her into the sick room and left her with her father. She was there for only a few minutes. Bradlaugh spoke scarcely any words. These two, who had been companions for so long, who had gone through so much together, had nothing left to say to each other. Annie did not visit Circus Road again and that was the last time she saw Bradlaugh.

On Friday 23 January a messenger from the House of Commons delivered the Order Paper showing that Hunter had indeed set down the expunging motion that he would move on the 27th. That night Bradlaugh's paralysis worsened and it was evident that he was suffering from an advanced stage of Bright's disease. He hovered between consciousness and unconsciousness, waking from time to time to babble of Loch Long and other rambling recollections. His ability to work, to read, to converse, to speak rationally had gone.

Bradlaugh's colleagues in Parliament knew of his serious illness but were not aware that his death was so near. Many Members wrote to Hypatia assuring her of their support, and that they would be in their place to vote for Hunter's motion. Letters poured in from members of the National Secular Society conveying their hopes for a full recovery. On Sunday, 25 January a few Churches offered prayers for her father. The *Star* newspaper reported Bradlaugh's 'most critical condition' adding that 'Many inquiries were made concerning him in the Lobbies of the House of Commons and sympathy was fully expressed by Members of all shades of opinion.' It concluded, 'How strangely at times public opinion entirely changes on some matter on which it has been greatly agitated.'

By the first post on the day the motion was to be moved, Hypatia received a letter from Hunter explaining that the Leader of the House, W. H. Smith, had sent for him to express firstly how much he appreciated Bradlaugh's services to Parliament, and secondly that it would be painful for him to debate the motion in the present state of Bradlaugh's health. Smith was proposing therefore to find a day later in the session as he thought it would be more convenient for Bradlaugh. Hunter regarded Smith's offer to be a fair one and asked Hypatia to approve by telegram so that he could inform the Leader of the House.

Hypatia was deeply distressed. Receipt of the letter on the morning of the very day fixed for the debate brought despair for her and Arthur. Hypatia had relied on Hunter to move the motion that day and had so reassured her father many times. She could not deceive him. It was that day or never. She immediately dispatched a letter to Hunter. She was agitated but nonetheless worded it carefully for it had to ensure that Hunter would move the motion and yet not reveal that Bradlaugh was close to death. Arthur followed up the letter by seeking out Hunter. He was not easy to find but he located him at midday in the House. By then

Hunter had shown Hypatia's letter to several colleagues who agreed that the motion must go ahead. Hunter then saw Smith who was persuaded to agree that the debate be heard that day. Smith generously went further: he advised that the Government would not oppose the motion.

Chapter Eighty-eight

AT TEN MINUTES PAST FOUR ON Tuesday 27 January Dr Hunter moved: 'That the Resolution of this House of the 22nd of June 1880, that Mr Bradlaugh be not permitted to take the oath or make the affirmation, be expunged from the journals of the House, as being subversive of the rights of the whole body of the electors of this Kingdom.' Hunter made a short sagacious speech, only six minutes long. It was incisive and courteous. He told the House he would avoid a single word that would stir up the memories of past controversies. He directed attention to the facts: the House had abandoned its former position and in 1886 and 1887 had allowed Bradlaugh to take the oath. Moreover in 1888, mainly by the exertions of the junior member for Northampton himself, an Act had been passed which forever put an end to the difficulties that had existed. 'I think I shall have the assent of all parts of the House when I say that there is no Member who exhibits greater courtesy and fairness to his opponents than the honourable Member for Northampton. I think that I shall best consult the wishes of the House by now leaving in its hands the motion which I beg to move.'

The Solicitor-General, Sir Edward Clarke, made a forcible speech against the motion, apparently unaware that W. H. Smith had promised Hunter that the Government would not oppose. The speech, which lasted four times longer than Hunter's, largely repeated the arguments Clarke had given in March 1889. It was not, he said, according to the traditions of the House that a Resolution be expunged and there was no precedent save that of Wilkes, which could readily be distinguished. 'Nothing can do away with the fact that in 1880, after serious challenge and substantial

345

debate, the House came to the resolution now complained of. He pointed out that the resolution was in accord with two Committees of the House and of two decisions of the Courts. He concluded: 'It will answer no useful purpose, nor will it be in furtherance of any principle, or in relief of any individual for disqualification now, to remove it from the journals of the House.'

Gladstone gave his full backing to Hunter's motion. His reason for support was the reason he had consistently held from the beginning, that the decision of the House in 1880 had been in excess of its jurisdiction. 'In an assembly possessed of almost immeasurable powers and with no possibility of appeal, excess of jurisdiction is the greatest fault the House can possibly commit. It is one of the highest functions of this House to limit its own functions and jurisdiction.' There was no doubt that this speech of Gladstone helped to persuade his Liberal colleagues to support the motion.

Another influential speech was that of Sir Stafford Northcote, son of Sir Stafford Northcote (the deceased Earl Iddesleigh) who, as Conservative leader in the Commons, had so persistently opposed Bradlaugh's attempt to take his seat. This young Northcote, because of his father's crucial part, claimed an hereditary interest in the matter. He expressed his support for the motion on the condition that it omitted the final words, 'as being subversive of the rights of the whole body of electors of this Kingdom' which, he said, may have been appropriate in Wilke's case but not in Bradlaugh's. Labouchere immediately saw the opportunity and, regarding himself as the personal representative of Bradlaugh, consented willingly to those words being withdrawn.

The omission of those words made all the difference. It enabled W. H. Smith to keep his promise that the Government would not oppose the motion. With generous comments on Bradlaugh's contribution to Parliament he said, 'There is no longer any necessity for maintaining the resolution on the journals of the house. I shall not resist the motion on the understanding that the last words, impugning the authority and control of the House, are struck out.' Mr De Lisle, a Roman Catholic member, entered his personal protest but it was clear that he was not in tune with the feelings of his fellow Conservatives. 'I have expressed the opinion before that a national assembly which legalises atheism and whitewashes treason cannot long withstand the waves of anarchy which threaten to overwhelm all civilised countries', words which induced much laughter and some mockery. It was left to Sir William Barttelot, himself a Conservative of rigid character, to end the debate by catching the mood of most members: 'By accepting this motion we will have done a generous act to a man who has endeavoured to do his duty.'

The House was not unanimous but there were no dissentients and no division. The Clerk of the House subsequently passed a red line through the Resolution of 1880 in the volumes preserved in the library and in the Journal Office and noted in the margin of the pages that the paragraph had been expunged pursuant to a Resolution of the House. That evening Hunter wrote to Hypatia from the National Liberal Club informing her of the decision of the House. He advised her that he had shown her letter to Smith and it had contributed to the decision. The next day, Smith, formal and generous (he was known to his colleagues as Old Morality) went himself to Circus Road to inform Hypatia of the decision.

Throughout this proceeding Bradlaugh lay unconscious. Letters of congratulation poured in from the House of Commons and the country and only Hypatia could read them. She suffered anguish from not being able to tell her father the good news for she judged it too risky to revive him by conveying a subject so close to his heart. She kept vigil by his bedside throughout 28 and 29 January, alone with her father save for two nurses, and constantly moistening his lips and wiping the damp of death from his brow. Late on the night of the 29th his condition worsened and on Friday 30 January at 6.30 in the morning, as the minute hand of his watch touched the half hour he took his last breath. He had lived for fifty-seven years and four months.

Chapter Eighty-nine

HYPATIA WAS HER FATHER'S SOLE EXECUTRIX and sole beneficiary but the only substantial property he had to leave her was his copyright in the *National Reformer*. He had founded that weekly journal in 1860, had edited it continuously save for three years in the late 1860s, had owned it from 1861 and jointly with Annie Besant from 1877 until six weeks before his death. He had written for it every week and had fought tenaciously for it in the Courts. From its first issue the journal adhered to the purpose set for it in 1860: 'to have the character of a literary, moral, religious, political and scientific periodical'. It therefore had some aspects of a learned journal, with regularly scholarly articles but combined this with appeal to its mainly working-class subscribers and it was priced for the benefit of this readership. It cost 2d a week in 1860 and remained at 2d a week in 1891. The journal was addressed to radical intelligent workers who, like its owner, were free of the illusion that a university education was the only means of gaining a facility for profound thought.

Every week the journal included a diary of Bradlaugh's speaking engagements and those of his associates. Alice and Hypatia, when they were older, supplied it with a summary of news of interest to freethinkers. It was the chronicle of the National Secular Society, regularly reporting its proceedings. It reproduced verbatim many of Bradlaugh's speeches and debates. It pre-printed his writings which later appeared as pamphlets. It included transcripts, more complete than the law reports, of his numerous trials. It was the vehicle for his friends, his colleagues and other radicals, to write articles, opinion columns and reviews. They were free to express their own thoughts for he was a tolerant editor. Bradlaugh ensured, however, that Shelley was the journal's favourite poet and Spinoza its favourite philosopher.

For many years the *National Reformer* carried on its masthead the watchword, 'Atheism, Malthusianism, Republicanism'. These three words summarised the thrust of Bradlaugh's policy. To advocate one of these causes in mid-Victorian England was to be vilified, and to campaign for all three justified the view of many of the people and most of the press that Bradlaugh was an ogre. In his journal he advocated atheism absolutely and without compromise, always remembering that he insisted like a lawyer that the burden of proving the existence of God rested on those who asserted it. For Bradlaugh definitions were everything. 'To me the word "God" conveys no meaning. The Bible God I deny, the Christian God I disbelieve in; but I am not rash enough to say that there is no God as long as you tell me you are unprepared to define God to me.' But atheism was no mere disbelief: 'It is in no wise a cold barren negative; it is on the contrary a hearty affirmation of all truth and involves the positive assertion of action of all humanity.'

Bradlaugh's campaign for Malthusianism began in the *National Reformer* and was the cause of his split from Joseph Barker. The Malthusianism that Bradlaugh embraced was not based on the theory that the growth of population always outruns the growth of production so that poverty is man's ineluctable fate. Malthusianism was a euphemism for birth control, an expression the Victorians were rarely willing to use. Birth control was related to atheism because it was a challenge to religion and the religious concept of sin. For Bradlaugh birth control was a technical means for men to control their own lives, to determine for themselves, rather than let God determine, the size of their families.

Bradlaugh's republicanism was also heavily supported in the pages of his journal and followed from his detestation of hereditary privilege. He believed in a man's personal self-determination, of making his own way in the world, of creating his character by, in Emerson's phrase, 'the cumulative force of a whole life's cultivation'. His republicanism was not revolutionary. As he asserted in his 'Impeachment' pamphlet, the claim to the throne derived from the Acts of Settlement and Union, and Parliament was competent to repeal that legislation. Bradlaugh found no difficulty in expressing allegiance to the Crown but regarded the formation of a republic on the death of Queen Victoria as a constitutional possibility. He saw the Crown as the linchpin of the hereditary system which preserved the State Church and preserved the body of privileged peers which came to exemplify heredity rather than merit as the underlying ethos of the country. Once removed, by legitimate means, the monarchy and then the whole structure of class and heredity would come tumbling down.

In these three causes, so compactly set out at the head of his journal, there was a consistent common thread – the theme of freethought. Bradlaugh believed in the thorough assertion of the right and duty of individual judgment based on reason. Atheism, Malthusianism, Republicanism were founded on reason exercised by the individual for his own behalf. He used the sword of freethought to dismember the body of any superstition, to destroy the idols. He understood that freethinking was an individual activity and, in order to allow it, the fetters had to be removed from man's mind.

The two fetters he spent his life fighting were faith and force. The priest represented faith and the monarchy represented force. His greatest fight and his greatest triumph was against the oath, which he recognised as a conspiracy between faith and force in which each supported the other in a self-sustaining system. It was Iconoclast's task to defeat that system by legitimate means, a task he began with his Affirmation Bill which established for all time that neither by his religion, nor by his lack of it, should a man be disqualified to serve in Parliament, accept public office, present evidence, or serve in any other official capacity.

The *National Reformer*, page by page, week by week, propagated these ideas in a learned, tolerant way. It was a serious journal keeping the promise of its first issue 'not to be a flashy flippant newspaper'. It was always hard hitting; but never vulgar, coarse or discourteous. It gave no quarter to its opponents and never succumbed to compromise. Hypatia described the journal as her father's voice, his sword and his shield, and in this sense it was his embodiment. There would, in years to come, be many monuments to Bradlaugh, but the greatest monument would remain the one he created with thorough effort week by week over the years, the many volumes of his *National Reformer*.

Chapter Ninety

THE DAY AFTER HER FATHER'S DEATH Hypatia published the notice of his funeral. It was to be at the Brookwood Cemetery, near Woking, at 2.30 p.m. on Tuesday 3 February. She emphasised that, in accordance with her father's wishes, there was to be no ceremonial, no speeches, and those attending were asked not to wear mourning. In Hamlet's words Bradlaugh wanted none of 'the trappings and the suits of woe'. These wishes had been conveyed in Bradlaugh's will which had also directed 'that my body shall be buried as cheaply as possible'. Hypatia was faithful to this direction, arranging for him to be buried in one of the London Necropolis Company's earth-to-earth coffins made from papier-mâché and designed to decompose. On the lid was a brass plate with the inscription: 'CHARLES BRADLAUGH. Died January 30th 1891. Aged 57'.

On Monday night the coffin with the body in it rested in the mortuary of the London Necropolis Company by Waterloo Station and was transferred to Brookwood the next morning. Hypatia ordered a special train to leave Waterloo for Brookwood at 1.30 p.m. Long before that time the roads converging on the station were blocked by crowds intent on attending the funeral. More than 3,000 sought to travel by train and the London and South Western Railway hastily added two extra trains, all three being crowded to capacity. In the first train Hypatia and Arthur had their own compartment with Elizabeth Norman and Emma Bradlaugh, sisters of Bradlaugh. Labouchere, who had written a charming letter of condolence to Hypatia, arranged a saloon carriage for MPs. Including Labouchere and Dr Hunter there were seventeen in that carriage. One of them was David Lloyd George, twenty-eight years old, who had been in Parliament a year and was fast gaining a reputation as a Radical Liberal. John Morley arrived late, just managing to step aboard, a subtle expression perhaps of his ambiguous regard for Bradlaugh.

Those travelling by train were joined by another thousand who made their way to Brookwood directly. This concourse of over 4,000 came from all parts of Britain. The cities in which Bradlaugh had repeatedly lectured, Manchester, Liverpool, Birmingham, Leeds, Bradford, Sheffield, Newcastle, Plymouth, Bristol and Nottingham were all represented. Branches of the National Secular Society and of Radical Liberal clubs all sent members. There was a contingent of miners from the North of England, there to testify to their appreciation of Bradlaugh's work on the Truck Act. This was a congregation of all classes, rich and poor, though the majority were hardworking men who were willing to travel hundreds of miles to pay their tribute. The army turned out in substantial numbers, including Bradlaugh's old regiment, the 7th Dragoon Guards, in their splendid uniforms. It seemed that every Indian student in London attended, with their dusky faces and red turbans, wishing to demonstrate their respect for the man who had advocated their cause in Parliament. Among these Hindoos was Mohandas Ghandi, twenty-two years old, and a law student at the Inner Temple. Highly visible were a large number from Northampton wearing their rosettes of mauve, white and green. That aggressive atheist the ninth Marquess of Queensbury was there, a man whose view of the parliamentary oath had always been that it was an exercise 'in Christian tomfoolery'. George Jacob Holyoake, now seventy-four, and who had presided at Bradlaugh's first lecture forty years before, was in attendance. A recent friend of Bradlaugh's, Walter Sickert the young artist, was there with his wife Ellen Cobden Sickert.

It had been Hypatia's task to choose the six pallbearers, and the test she applied was loyalty to her father. She selected four men from Northampton, Richard Roe, James Benford, John York and James Smith who had all supported Bradlaugh faithfully since 1868. The fifth pall bearer was William Digby, the London agent of the Indian National Congress, who had proved a dependable ally. The sixth was a choice between George Foote and John Robertson and without hesitation Hypatia had chosen Robertson. These two had a bond of friendship forged when they both lived at 19 Avenue Road and Robertson, unlike Foote, had been consistently devoted to her father. Foote was deeply offended for as President of the National Secular Society he expected to be a pall bearer and when he arrived at the Brookwood mortuary to assume this position was bewildered and annoyed to find it claimed by Robertson.

Annie Besant appeared at the funeral dressed completely in black with a heavy veil. She resolutely ignored the request that there be no trappings and suits of woe. She was conspicuous as the only one attending in mourning clothes. But she was used to being conspicuous, that was how she lived. She had never been seen in a veil before, but Bradlaugh had never died before, and this was the last occasion she could publicly express her grief at the passing of the man who had described her as 'the true good woman who has so stood side by side with me'.

On that grey February day, bereft of sunshine, the pallbearers carried the coffin, with Hypatia's laurel wreath on top, from the mortuary to the prepared grave in unconsecrated ground. Hypatia took the place of chief mourner but George Foote, still confused at not being a pall bearer, attempted to walk directly behind the coffin as if he were its official escort. Annie would have none of this. She came forward and elbowed Foote out of the way, with more force than was necessary, exclaiming 'How dare you come between the daughter and the dead father?' Hypatia hardly cared. She was absorbed in her overwhelming sorrow.

Bradlaugh's grave was next to that of his daughter Alice and near to the graves of his wife Susannah and his grandson Kenneth. Close by was the grave of Thomas Allsop, mentor of Bradlaugh's early years. The mound of earth at the graveside was hidden by a mass of more than fifty wreaths. The last wreath to be added was from the Northampton deputation and consisted of an arrangement of mauve violets, white lilies and green maidenhair fern. The message on it was four simple words: 'Brave, Honest, Incorruptible, Thorough'.

Amid the stillness of that afternoon and watched by the vast crowd, the coffin was slowly lowered into the grave. The calmness was in profound contrast to the stormy life that Bradlaugh had led. There was silence for this man whose sonorous, stentorian voice had resounded throughout the halls, the lecture platforms, the political assemblies of Britain. Hypatia stood at the edge of the grave as the coffin was lowered. She did not bow her head but stood upright, glancing with dignity at the immense throng gathered to honour her father. There were some in that crowd who thought they saw in her face at that moment the features of her father, his firmness, his fortitude.

The family stayed at the graveside a short while and then slowly made their way back to Brookwood Station, allowing others to take their turn to view the coffin. The crowd, guided by Marshals from the National Secular Society, filed one by one past the grave, many weeping, all with their private thoughts of Bradlaugh. One of his supporters from Northampton overcome by the premature ending of a valued life cried out, 'Oh! Charlie, this is no place for you yet.' Many threw their rosettes into the grave until the coffin was covered by a sea of Northampton colours. An hour later, when the crowd was gone and light was fading, four men from Northampton came back to the grave to take one last look. There they found the gravediggers shovelling the mound of earth back into the grave. These Northampton men took the spades from the gravediggers and did the work themselves. They were unwilling to part with Bradlaugh and this was their only way of saying goodbye.

Note on the Four Portraits of Bradlaugh by Walter Sickert

IN 1890 WALTER RICHARD SICKERT, THEN thirty years old, was one of the most interesting artists of his generation. He had been an apprentice of James McNeill Whistler, and a protégé of Edgar Degas, but was difficult to pigeonhole. Sometimes he was described as an impressionist, because of his esteem for the French School, sometimes as a realist, because of his depiction of the seamy side of life, and sometimes as a tonalist because of his close attention to light and shade. Until 1890 he had painted mainly landscapes and scenes from the music halls and was now eager to break into portraiture. He had been married since 1885 to Ellen Cobden, twelve years his senior and the eldest daughter of Richard Cobden the great advocate of free trade and at one time a power in the Liberal party. Cobden had left his daughter in comfortable circumstances and she was subsidising her husband's work. Sickert was anxious to earn his own money and portraiture was the obvious route. A portrait painter could earn substantial sums and one well-regarded picture led to other commissions. Sickert had experimented with a few portraits of family and friends but his first portrait of a public figure was that of Charles Bradlaugh.

Ellen had many contacts with leading Liberals and it was through this network that Sickert came to know Bradlaugh. The two got on well and Sickert was invited to Circus Road to sketch Bradlaugh whilst he was at work. Sickert sat in a corner of the room watching and sketching while the older man worked at his desk, spoke to his visitors, wrote his letters and consulted his books.

A preliminary sketch in chalk and pencil [PLATE 2] led to an oil painting of Bradlaugh's head and shoulders [PLATE 3]. In this painting Bradlaugh is seen at his desk in three-quarter profile. It is a dark picture save for strong light playing on his face and on glimpses of his white shirt. The portrait was generally recognised as a vivid likeness and was exhibited at the 1890 Spring Exhibition of the New English Art Club (of which Sickert was a member). As a result of this exhibition, the National Liberal Club in 1891 raised a subscription to purchase the picture to hang on its walls. It has been there ever since.

This first major endeavour in portraiture brought Sickert further commissions. He was invited to contribute a weekly pen and ink portrait to a new journal, the *Whirlwind*, a lively newspaper, somewhat eccentric like Sickert himself. In the first issue, on 28 June 1890, Sickert presented a drawing of Bradlaugh [PLATE 4] which was widely admired. In announcing this first Whirlwind portrait the journal added a brief comment on Bradlaugh which, like the portrait, captured his essence: 'We consider ourselves especially fortunate in being able to present our readers with the portrait of Bradlaugh as our first cartoon. By his unflinching opposition to the socialist hierarchy and his lucid exposition of their fallacies, he has established an indisputable claim to be considered the leader of the Individualist party in this country.'

These three pictures made Sickert the acknowledged expert on the portraiture of the junior member for Northampton. When in 1891, soon after Bradlaugh's death, a wealthy Manchester freethinker, who preferred to remain anonymous, commissioned a new portrait of Bradlaugh to donate to the Manchester branch of the National Secular Society, Sickert was the natural choice as artist. The portrait was a remarkable challenge for the young painter, for it was a posthumous full-length portrait of Bradlaugh at a crucial moment of his life, the occasion of his first speech at the Bar of the House of Commons in 1880. No doubt the significance of the event appealed to Sickert's histrionic temperament. He painted the portrait using a photograph of Bradlaugh as he was in 1880 taken by Mr

Vanderwylde. This was the first time Sickert had painted from a photograph and not every critic appreciated this artistic innovation. In addition to the photograph Sickert used a model dressed in the actual suit of clothes worn by Bradlaugh which was borrowed for the purpose.

The completed portrait [PLATE 1: FRONTISPIECE], oil on canvas, was 7½ feet by 4½ feet, the largest picture Sickert ever painted. Entitled: 'Charles Bradlaugh at the Bar of the House of Commons', it shows Bradlaugh standing alone in a dignified pose with his left hand holding the octagonal Bar which the Serjeant-at-Arms had drawn across the entrance to the Chamber. The legend on the massive frame came from one of Bradlaugh's speeches at the Bar: 'The grave alone shall make me yield.' The painting is dark, illustrating a solemn moment, but with light coming from apertures in the wooden panels at the back. The pose shows Bradlaugh listening, rather than speaking, and the stillness of the scene adds to the sense of aloneness conveyed by the picture.

Sickert worked diligently to ensure the painting was ready for unveiling by George Foote in Manchester on the evening of 26 September 1891, the anniversary of Bradlaugh's birth. The ceremony was held in the Rushmore Street Hall, the property of the Manchester freethinkers. The hall could hold 600 people and was full that evening. John Robertson took the chair and Hypatia was on the platform with leading Manchester freethinkers together with Sickert and Foote. The portrait was hung high above the platform on the back wall.

Foote unveiled the portrait to a burst of cheering and gave a short eloquent address, explaining that the picture represented Bradlaugh on a great historical occasion. This was a man, he said, who had the courage to be a minority voice but who by force of logic and persuasion could turn minorities into majorities. He was an example to the time-serving politician who first asked what people wanted and then discovered that his principles were in accordance with those desires. He ended: 'It was something to have taken his hand and looked into those great, strong, fearless, and yet kind eyes. This picture will ensure that Bradlaugh will have a life beyond the dust of death.'

Sickert spoke briefly, expressing his profound interest in recording for posterity this great man on a great occasion. Hypatia, in a voice broken with emotion, returned her thanks to Sickert as her father's only surviving child. She recalled seeing her father standing there alone at the Bar on one of the four occasions when he had so to present himself. She expressed her satisfaction with the dignity of the work. Sickert, she said, had the opportunity of seeing her father in ways no other artist had. He was an admirer of her father who in turn had a high opinion of Sickert. She recommended the picture to the care of the National Secular Society in Manchester. The Manchester branch possessed the portrait until 1911 when they donated it to the Manchester City Art Gallery where it remains.

Permission to reproduce these four portraits of Bradlaugh has been kindly granted by the Design and Artists Copyright Society on behalf of the Walter Sickert estate. Copies of the portraits were kindly supplied by the Manchester City Art Gallery, the Trustees of the National Liberal Club, the National Portrait Gallery and the Bishopsgate Institute.

Bibliography

A Books And Pamphlets About Charles Bradlaugh

Headingly, Adolphe S., *The Biography of Charles Bradlaugh* (London, 1880).

Parry, Edward, *Charles Bradlaugh and the Parliamentary Struggle* (London, 1885).

Mackay, Charles R., *Life of Charles Bradlaugh, M.P.* (London, 1888).

Strandring, George, *Biography of Charles Bradlaugh, M.P.* (London, 1888).

Holyoake, G. J., *Life and Career of Charles Bradlaugh, M.P.* (Buffalo, N.Y., USA, 1891).

Foote, G.W., *Reminiscences of Charles Bradlaugh* (London, 1891).

Bonner, Hypatia Bradlaugh and Robertson, J.M., *Charles Bradlaugh: A Record of His Life and Work, with an Account of His Parliamentary Struggle, Politics and Teachings*. In two volumes (London, 1895).

Hubbard, Elbert, *Bradlaugh: Little Journeys to the Homes of Great Reformers* (New York, USA, 1907).

Robertson, J. M., *Charles Bradlaugh* (London, 1920).

Cohen, Chapman, *Bradlaugh and Ingersoll* (London, 1933).

Gilmour, J. P. (Ed.), *Champion of Liberty: Charles Bradlaugh* (London, 1933).

Gilmour, J. P. (Ed.) *Bradlaugh and Today, Speeches at Centenary Celebrations* (London, 1933).

Arnstein, Walter L., *The Bradlaugh Case: A Study in Late Victorian Opinion and Politics* (Oxford, 1965).

Tribe, David, *President Charles Bradlaugh, M.P.* (London, 1971).

B   The Writings of Charles Bradlaugh

Bradlaugh was a prolific author and from his first pamphlet, 'A Few Words on the Christian Creed' of 1850 to the book on *Labor and Law* on which he was engaged at the time of his death, he published more than 140 works, most of them pamphlets. The most important of these writings are included in the following books.

Saville, John, *A Selection of the Political Pamphlets of Charles Bradlaugh with a Preface and Bibliographical Notes.* (New York, 1970).

Bradlaugh, Charles, *Labor and Law, with two portraits and a Memoir by J. M. Robertson.* (Reprinted by Clifton, New Jersey 1972).

Bradlaugh, Charles, *Humanity's Gain from Unbelief, and other selections from the works of Charles Bradlaugh, with a prefatory note by his daughter Hypatia Bradlaugh Bonner*, The Thinkers Library (London 1929).

The most important of Bradlaugh's speeches are reprinted in:

Bradlaugh, Charles, *Speeches*, Freethought Publishing Company (London, 1890).

C   Select List of Works Consulted

Anderson, David, *'Scenes' in the Commons* (London, 1884).

Apjohn, Lewis, *Life of John Bright* (London, 1889).

Askwith, Lord, *Lord James of Hereford* (London, 1930).

Ball, William Platt, *Mrs Besant's Socialism* (London, 1886).

Barker, Joseph, *The Life of Joseph Barker Written by Himself* (London, 1880).

Bax, Ernest Belfort, *Reminiscences and Reflexions of a Mid and Late Victorian* (London,1918).

Baylen, Joseph O., and Gossman, Norbert J. (eds.), *Biographical Dictionary of Modern British Radicals, Volume 3* (1870 - 1914) (London, 1988).

Benn, A. W., *The History of English Radicalism in the Nineteenth Century.* Two volumes (London,1962).

Bennett, Olivia, *Annie Besant* (London, 1998).

Benny, J., *Bradlaugh and Hyndman, An Account of the Debate on Socialism Between these Two at St. James's Hall on 17 April 1884.* (London,1884).

Berman, David, *A History of Atheism in Britain: From Hobbes to Russell* (London,1988).

Besant, Annie, *Biographical Sketches,* (London, 1885).

Besant, Annie, *Why I Became a Theosophist* (London, 1889).

Besant, Annie, *An Autobiography* (London, 1895).

Besant, Arthur Digby, *The Besant Pedigree* (London, 1930).

Bryce, James, *Studies in Contemporary Biography* (London, 1903).

Bridon, Crane, *English Political Thought in the Nineteenth Century* (London, 1933).

Budd, Susan, *Varieties of Unbelief: Atheists and Agnostics in English Society, 1850 - 1960* (London,1977).

Canning, John (ed.), *100 Great Nineteenth Century Lives* (London, 1983).

Carlile, Richard, *Every Woman's Book* (London, 1826).

Chandrasekhar, S., *'A Dirty Filthy Book', The Writings of Charles Knowlton and Annie Besant on Reproductive Physiology and Birth Control and an Account of the Bradlaugh–Besant Trial* (University of California Press, (1981).

Churchill, Winston S., *Lord Randolph Churchill* (London, 1905).

Coleridge, Ernest Hartley, *Life and Correspondence of John Duke, Lord Coleridge, L. C. J.* (London, 1904).

Collet, Collet Dobson, *History of the Taxes on Knowledge* (London, 1833).

Conway, Moncure Daniel, *Autobiography. Two Volumes* (Cambridge, 1904).

Courtney, Janet Elizabeth, *Freethinkers of the Nineteenth Century* (London, 1920).

D'arcy, Fergus A., *Charles Bradlaugh and the World of Popular Radicalism,1833 - 1891,* Thesis Accepted for the Degree of PhD, University of Hull (1978).

Dinnage, Rosemary, *Annie Besant* (London,1986).

Dobell, Bertram, *The Laureate of Pessimism, A Sketch of the Life and Character of James Thomson ('B.V.')* (London, 1910).

Drummond Wolff, Sir Henry, *Rambling Recollections*, Two Volumes (London, 1908).

Ensor, R. C. K., *England 1870 - 1914* (Oxford, 1936).

Erskine May, Sir Thomas, *A Treatise on the Law, Privileges and Usages of Parliament.* 11th Edition, edited by T. Lonsdale Webster and William Edward Grey (London, 1906).

Feuchtwanger, E. J., *Gladstone* (London, 1989).

Foote, G. W., *Blasphemy No Crime* (London, 1882).

Foote, G. W., *Randolph Churchill: The Woodstock Bantam* (London, 1885).

Foote, G. W., *Prisoner for Blasphemy* (London, 1856).

Foote, G. W., *Mrs Besant's Theosophy* (London, 1889).

Foster, R. F., *Lord Randolph Churchill, A Political Life* (Oxford, 1981).

Fowler, L. N., *Phrenological Delineation of Charles Bradlaugh with Biographical Details.* (Phrenological Magazine,1882).

Fox, Alice Wilson, *The Earl of Halsbury (1823 -1921)* (London, 1929).

Fremantle, Anne, *This Little Band of Prophets: The British Fabians* (London, 1960).

Fryer, Peter, *The Birth Controllers* (London, 1965).

Gorst, Harold E., *The Fourth Party* (London, 1906).

Hamilton, Lord George, *Parliamentary Reminiscences and Reflections, 1868 to 1885* (London, 1917).

Herrick, Jim, *Vision and Realism: A Hundred Years of 'The Freethinker'* (G. W. Foote, London, 1982).

Hilton, G. W., *The Truck System, Including a History of the British Truck Acts 1465 -1960* (Cambridge, 1960).

Himes, Norman E., *Medical History of Contraception* (New York, USA, 1963).

Hindoo, from A Hindoo Point of View, *Mr Bradlaugh and the House of Commons* (London, 1884).

Holyoake, George Jacob, *Sixty Years of an Agitator's Life, Two Volumes* (London, 1900).

Hoppen, K. Theodore, *The Mid-Victorian Generation (1846 -1886)* (Oxford, 1998).

Hostettler, John, *Lord Halsbury* (London, 1998)

Hunter, Archie, *A Life of Sir John Eldon Gorst: Disraeli's Awkward Disciple* (London, 2001).

Hyndman, Henry, *The Record of an Adventurous Life* (London, 1911).

Hyndman, Henry, *Further Reminiscences* (London, 1912).

Irving, William, *Charles Bradlaugh, as a Politician, Social Reformer and Thinker* (London, 1887).

Jackson, T. A., *Trials of British Freedom* (London, 1940).

Jennings, G. H., *Anecdotal History of the British Parliament* (London, 1892).

Knight, Robert, *The Indian National Congress: Its Aims and Justifications* (Calcutta, 1898).

Leonard, Tom, *Places of the Mind: The Life and Work of James Thomson ('B. V.')* (London, 1993).

Leslie, Shane, *Henry Edward Manning: His Life and Labours* (London, 1921)

Lucy, Henry W., *A Diary of Two Parliaments, Volume II: The Gladstone Parliament (1880-1885)* (London, 1886).

McCabe, Joseph, *Life and Letters of George Jacob Holyoake, Two Volumes* (London, 1908).

McCabe, Joseph, *A rationalist encyclopedia; a book of reference on religion, philosophy, ethics and science* (London, 1950).

Maccoby, S., *English Radicalism (1853 -1886)* (London, 1938).

MacDonagh, Michael, *Parliament: Its Romance Its Comedy Its Pathos* (London, 1902).

Manvell, Roger, *The Trial of Annie Besant and Charles Bradlaugh* (London, 1976).

Matthew, H. G. C., *The Gladstone Diaries* (Oxford, 1994).

Mawer W., *The Latest Constitutional Struggle: A Register of Events from 2 April 1880* (London, 1883).

Maxwell, Sir Herbert, *Life and Times of the Right Honourable William Henry Smith M.P.* (London, 1893).

Morley, John, *The Life of William Ewart Gladstone, Volume 2* (London, 1905).

Nash,David, *Blasphemy in Modern Britain, 1789 to the Present* (Aldershot, 1999).

Nash, David and Taylor, Anthony, *Republicanism in Victorian Society* (Stroud, 2000).

Nethercot, A. H., *The First Five Lives of Annie Besant* (Chicago, 1960).

O'Connor T. P., *Gladstone's House of Commons* (London, 1885).

O'Connor, T. P., *Memories of an Old Parliamentarian, Volume 1* (London, 1929).

Oxford and Asquith, The Earl of, *Fifty Years of Parliament, Volume 1 (1868-1918)* (London, 1926).

Page, Martin, *Britain's Unknown Genius: The Life Work of J. M. Robertson* (London, 1984).

Pearson, Hesketh, *Labby (The Life and Character of Henry Labouchere)* (London, 1936).

Robertson, J. M., *A History of Freethought in the Nineteenth Century. Two Volumes.* (London, 1929).

Royle, Edward, *Victorian Infidels* (Manchester, 1974).

Royle, Edward (ed.), *The Infidel Tradition: From Paine to Bradlaugh* (London, 1976).

Royle, Edward, *Radicals, Secularists and Republicans, Popular Freethought in Britain, 1866 -1915* (Manchester, 1980).

Royle, Edward, *Freethought: The Religion of Irreligion. In: Nineteenth Century English Religious Traditions – Retrospect and Prospect* (ed. D. G. Paz) (London, 1995).

Salt, H. S., *The Life of James Thomson ('B. V.')* (London, 1889).

Smith, Warren Sylvester, *The London Heretics (1870 -1914)* (London, 1967).

Snell, Henry, *Men Movements and Myself* (London, 1936).

Stacpoole, William Henry, *The Utility of Parliamentary Oaths* (London,1880).

Stansky, Peter, *Gladstone: A Progress in Politics* (New York and London, 1979).

Strachey, Lytton, *Essay on Cardinal Manning, in Eminent Victorians* (London, 1918).

Sturgis, Matthew, *Walter Sickert: A Life* (London, 2005).

Taylor, Anne, *Annie Besant: A Biography* (Oxford, 1992).

Temple, Sir Richard (Bt.), *Life in Parliament* (London, 1893).

Temple, Sir Richard (Bt.), *Letters and Character Sketches from the House of Commons* (London, 1912).

Thorold, Algar Labouchere, *The Life of Henry Labouchere* (London, 1913).

Tribe, David, *100 Years of Freethought* (London, 1967).

Tsuzuki, C., *H. M. Hyndman and British Socialism* (London, 1967).

Tsuzuki, C., *The Life of Eleanor Marx, 1855 -1898, A Socialist Tragedy* (Oxford, 1967).

Tyler, James Endell, *Oaths: Their Origin Nature and History* (London, 1834).

Varley, Heny, *Address to the Electors of Northampton* (London, 1881).

Walker, Imogen B., *James Thomson ('B.V.'): A Critical Study* (Ithaca, N.Y., 1950).

Webb, Sidney and Cox, Harold, *The Eight Hours Day* (London, 1891).

Wedderburn, Sir William, *Allan Octavian Hume, 'Father of the Indian National Congress'* (London, 1913).

Wells, G. A. (ed.), *J. M. Robertson (1856 -1933)* (London, 1987).

West, Geoffrey, *Mrs Annie Besant* (London, 1927).

Wharton, Chas. H. M., *Mr Bradlaugh and the Oath* (Manchester, 1882).

Wheeler, J. M., *A Biographical Dictionary of Freethinkers of all Ages and Nations* (London, 1889).

White, A. P., *The Story of Northampton* (Northampton, 1914).

Whyte, Frederic, *The Life of W. T. Stead, Volume 1* (London, 1925).

Wiener, Joel H., *Radicalism and Freethought in Nineteenth Century Britain: The Life of Richard Carlile* (London, 1983).

Williams, Gertrude M., *The Passionate Pilgrim: A Life of Annie Besant* (London, 1932).

Woodward, E. L., *The Age of Reform (1815 -1870)* (Oxford, 1938).
Wright, Thomas, *The Romance of the Shoe* (London, 1922).
Young, Kenneth, *Arthur James Balfour (1848 -1930)* (London, 1963).

Acknowledgements

ANYONE WHO EMBARKS ON A STUDY of the life of Charles Bradlaugh must be deeply indebted to the Bradlaugh Bonner family for making available their collection of Bradlaugh papers, personal and political, for open consultation. These papers, assembled in eighteen large volumes and twelve accompanying boxes, are an essential source of original material and constitute a special collection of the Bishopsgate Institute in London. I am pleased to express my gratitude to Basil Bradlaugh Bonner, great grandson of Charles, for donating these papers and for allowing me to see a private memorandum remaining in the possession of the family. This Bradlaugh collection has been expertly arranged, largely in chronological order, by Professor Edward Royle of the University of York who is the leading authority on secularism, republicanism and radicalism as it was in Victorian England. I have benefited significantly from discussion with Professor Royle and from his books which are listed among the works I have consulted.

Much of the research on which my story of Bradlaugh is based has resulted from many pleasant hours spent in libraries. The Librarian of the Bishopsgate Institute was most indulgent in allowing me long and frequent access to the Bradlaugh collection and to other of their materials. My local library, the Bodleian in Oxford, has been invaluable and I thank especially the staff of the Lower Reserve Room for the efficiency with which they met my many requests. Similar thanks are due to the staff of the British Library, both in the Euston Road and at Colindale. The Library of the South Place Ethical Society has a valuable collection of relevant books and journals and I am grateful to the Librarian for ready access to these. Most useful in this collection has been the Society's complete set of volumes of the *National Reformer* from its establishment in 1860 until it ceased publication in 1893.

I am grateful to the archivist of the special collections at the Library of the University of Bristol for making available their interesting assembly of Bradlaugh material. The Rush Rhees Library of the University of Rochester, New York State, has a Thomas Allsop collection and my thanks go to the Assistant Director for supplying copies of letters to Allsop from Charles Bradlaugh and Annie Besant. The Public Library at Northampton has a substantial number of Bradlaugh documents, many of them relating to parliamentary elections, and the Librarian kindly allowed me to peruse these. I am also indebted to the archivist at the House of Lords Record Office for the opportunity to study many relevant papers held there. Particularly useful were documents from the papers of Speaker Henry Brand and of the Clerk of the House of Commons, Sir Erskine May. The Curator of the Palace of Westminster generously supplied copies of images of Charles Bradlaugh from their collection.

My final thanks are due to the Serjeant-at-Arms of the House of Commons. The Chamber of the House has been thoroughly renovated since Bradlaugh's time but its essential features remain the same. The Serjeant-at-Arms kindly withdrew the octagonal Bar from its holder so that it extended across the Chamber entrance. There I was able to place my hand on that Bar and survey the Chamber, albeit when it was empty, from the same vantage point where Bradlaugh stood alone to deliver his four most memorable speeches to the House.

Index

NOTE: Page numbers for each index entry are given in numerical order which corresponds (mostly) to chronological order. The following abbreviations are used:

AB for Annie Besant; CB for Charles Bradlaugh; NR for National Reformer; NSS for National Secular Society.